Dachshunds

FOR

DUMMIES®

by Eve Adamson

IDG Books Worldwide, Inc.
An International Data Group Company

Foster City, CA ◆ Chicago, IL ◆ Indianapolis, IN ◆ New York, NY

Dachshunds For Dummies®

Published by
IDG Books Worldwide, Inc.
An International Data Group Company
919 E. Hillsdale Blvd.
Suite 300
Foster City, CA 94404
www.idgbooks.com (IDG Books Worldwide Web site)
www.dummies.com (Dummies Press Web site)

Library of Congress Control Number: 00-110872

ISBN: 0-7645-5289-9

Printed in the United States of America

10 9 8 7 6 5 4 3 2 1

1B/RR/QR/QR/IN

Distributed in the United States by IDG Books Worldwide, Inc.

Distributed by CDG Books Canada Inc. for Canada; by Transworld Publishers Limited in the United Kingdom; by IDG Norge Books for Norway; by IDG Sweden Books for Sweden; by IDG Books Australia Publishing Corporation Pty. Ltd. for Australia and New Zealand; by TransQuest Publishers Pte Ltd. for Singapore, Malaysia, Thailand, Indonesia, and Hong Kong; by Gotop Information Inc. for Taiwan; by ICG Muse, Inc. for Japan; by Intersoft for South Africa; by Eyrolles for France; by International Thomson Publishing for Germany, Austria and Switzerland; by Distribuidora Cuspide for Argentina; by LR International for Brazil; by Galileo Libros for Chile; by Ediciones ZETA S.C.R. Ltda. for Peru; by WS Computer Publishing Corporation, Inc., for the Philippines; by Contemporanea de Ediciones for Venezuela; by Express Computer Distributors for the Caribbean and West Indies; by Micronesia Media Distributor, Inc. for Micronesia; by Chips Computadoras S.A. de C.V. for Mexico; by Editorial Norma de Panama S.A. for Panama; by American Bookshops for Finland.

For general information on IDG Books Worldwide's books in the U.S., please call our Consumer Customer Service department at 800-762-2974. For reseller information, including discounts and premium sales, please call our Reseller Customer Service department at 800-434-3422.

For information on where to purchase IDG Books Worldwide's books outside the U.S., please contact our International Sales department at 317-572-3993 or fax 317-572-4002.

For consumer information on foreign language translations, please contact our Customer Service department at 1-800-434-3422, fax 317-572-4002, or e-mail rights@idgbooks.com.

For information on licensing foreign or domestic rights, please phone +1-650-653-7098.

For sales inquiries and special prices for bulk quantities, please contact our Order Services department at 800-434-4322 or write to the address above.

For information on using IDG Books Worldwide's books in the classroom or for ordering examination copies, please contact our Educational Sales department at 800-434-2086 or fax 317-572-4005.

For press review copies, author interviews, or other publicity information, please contact our Public Relations department at 650-653-7000 or fax 650-653-7500.

For authorization to photocopy items for corporate, personal, or educational use, please contact Copyright Clearance Center, 222 Rosewood Drive, Danvers, MA 01923, or fax 978-750-4470.

is a registered trademark under exclusive license to IDG Books Worldwide, Inc., from International Data Group, Inc.

About the Author

Eve Adamson has been a Dachshund fan since childhood and a regular writer for *Dog Fancy* magazine, specializing in breed profiles, for the past five years. Eve also writes for many other dog and pet magazines, including *Dogs USA, Puppies USA*, and the "Dachshunds" and "Training and Behavior" issues of the *Popular Dogs* series. She received her MFA from the University of Florida and is a member of the Dog Writer's Association of America. Eve coauthored (with Joel Walton) *Labrador Retrievers For Dummies* and has written many other books. She lives in Iowa City with her two sons and her dog, Sally.

ABOUT IDG BOOKS WORLDWIDE

Welcome to the world of IDG Books Worldwide.

IDG Books Worldwide, Inc., is a subsidiary of International Data Group, the world's largest publisher of computer-related information and the leading global provider of information services on information technology. IDG was founded more than 30 years ago by Patrick J. McGovern and now employs more than 9,000 people worldwide. IDG publishes more than 290 computer publications in over 75 countries. More than 90 million people read one or more IDG publications each month.

Launched in 1990, IDG Books Worldwide is today the #1 publisher of best-selling computer books in the United States. We are proud to have received eight awards from the Computer Press Association in recognition of editorial excellence and three from Computer Currents' First Annual Readers' Choice Awards. Our best-selling ...*For Dummies*® series has more than 50 million copies in print with translations in 31 languages. IDG Books Worldwide, through a joint venture with IDG's Hi-Tech Beijing, became the first U.S. publisher to publish a computer book in the People's Republic of China. In record time, IDG Books Worldwide has become the first choice for millions of readers around the world who want to learn how to better manage their businesses.

Our mission is simple: Every one of our books is designed to bring extra value and skill-building instructions to the reader. Our books are written by experts who understand and care about our readers. The knowledge base of our editorial staff comes from years of experience in publishing, education, and journalism — experience we use to produce books to carry us into the new millennium. In short, we care about books, so we attract the best people. We devote special attention to details such as audience, interior design, use of icons, and illustrations. And because we use an efficient process of authoring, editing, and desktop publishing our books electronically, we can spend more time ensuring superior content and less time on the technicalities of making books.

You can count on our commitment to deliver high-quality books at competitive prices on topics you want to read about. At IDG Books Worldwide, we continue in the IDG tradition of delivering quality for more than 30 years. You'll find no better book on a subject than one from IDG Books Worldwide.

John Kilcullen
Chairman and CEO
IDG Books Worldwide, Inc.

VIII
WINNER
*Eighth Annual
Computer Press
Awards ≥1992*

IX
WINNER
*Ninth Annual
Computer Press
Awards ≥1993*

X
WINNER
*Tenth Annual
Computer Press
Awards ≥1994*

XI
WINNER
*Eleventh Annual
Computer Press
Awards ≥1995*

IDG is the world's leading IT media, research and exposition company. Founded in 1964, IDG had 1997 revenues of $2.05 billion and has more than 9,000 employees worldwide. IDG offers the widest range of media options that reach IT buyers in 75 countries representing 95% of worldwide IT spending. IDG's diverse product and services portfolio spans six key areas including print publishing, online publishing, expositions and conferences, market research, education and training, and global marketing services. More than 90 million people read one or more of IDG's 290 magazines and newspapers, including IDG's leading global brands — Computerworld, PC World, Network World, Macworld and the Channel World family of publications. IDG Books Worldwide is one of the fastest-growing computer book publishers in the world, with more than 700 titles in 36 languages. The "...For Dummies®" series alone has more than 50 million copies in print. IDG offers online users the largest network of technology-specific Web sites around the world through IDG.net (http://www.idg.net), which comprises more than 225 targeted Web sites in 55 countries worldwide. International Data Corporation (IDC) is the world's largest provider of information technology data, analysis and consulting, with research centers in over 41 countries and more than 400 research analysts worldwide. IDG World Expo is a leading producer of more than 168 globally branded conferences and expositions in 35 countries including E3 (Electronic Entertainment Expo), Macworld Expo, ComNet, Windows World Expo, ICE (Internet Commerce Expo), Agenda, DEMO, and Spotlight. IDG's training subsidiary, ExecuTrain, is the world's largest computer training company, with more than 230 locations worldwide and 785 training courses. IDG Marketing Services helps industry-leading IT companies build international brand recognition by developing global integrated marketing programs via IDG's print, online and exposition products worldwide. Further information about the company can be found at www.idg.com.
1/26/00

Author's Acknowledgments

Many people assisted in helping to bring this book to fruition. First and foremost, thanks to Adrian Milton, for providing knowledge, enthusiasm, information, wonderful pictures, and for tech-editing the manuscript. Damian must be proud! Thanks to Darryl E. McDonald, DVM, MS, Diplomate ACVS of the Dallas Veterinary Surgical Center in Dallas, Texas, for his expertise on Dachshund orthopedics. Thanks to the Dachshund Club of America for lending expertise via their excellent illustrated breed standard, informative Web site (www.dachshund-dca.org), their *Canine Intervertebral Disk Disease* booklet (available on the Web site) prepared for the DCA by Patricia J. Luttgen, DVM, MS, Diplomate, American College of Veterinary Internal Medicine, Specialty of Neurology, in Denver, Colorado, and via the friendly and helpful efforts of Andra O'Connell, Ann Gordon, and Jan Oswald. Thanks to Bob Brennert up in Canada, who, along with his wonderful Wiener Dogs Web site (www.wienerdogs.org), was also a great source of information and support, and continues to inform Dachshund lovers all over the world about the progress of this book. And thanks, of course, to all those smooths, longhairs, and wirehairs out there, mighty, mini, and in-betweeny, for inspiring such great love and devotion in their two-legged human servants.

Publisher's Acknowledgments

We're proud of this book; please register your comments through our IDG Books Worldwide Online Registration Form located at www.dummies.com.

Some of the people who helped bring this book to market include the following:

Acquisitions, Editorial, and Media Development

Senior Project Editor: Tim Gallan

Acquisitions Editor: Scott Prentzas

Copy Editor: Sandy Blackthorn

Technical Editor: Adrian Milton

Editorial Manager: Pam Mourouzis

Editorial Assistant: Carol Strickland

Cover Photos: Carol Irvine

Production

Project Coordinator: Dale White

Layout and Graphics: Amy Adrian, Heather Pope, Julie Trippetti, Jeremey Unger, Erin Zeltner

Proofreaders: Andy Hollandbeck, Susan Moritz, Nancy Price, York Production Services, Inc.

Indexer: York Production Services, Inc.

Illustrator: Barbara Frake

General and Administrative

IDG Books Worldwide, Inc.: John Kilcullen, CEO; Bill Barry, President and COO; John Ball, Executive VP, Operations & Administration; John Harris, CFO

IDG Books Consumer Reference Group

Business: Kathleen A. Welton, Vice President and Publisher; Kevin Thornton, Acquisitions Manager

Cooking/Gardening: Jennifer Feldman, Associate Vice President and Publisher

Education/Reference: Diane Graves Steele, Vice President and Publisher; Greg Tubach, Publishing Director

Lifestyles: Kathleen Nebenhaus, Vice President and Publisher; Tracy Boggier, Managing Editor

Pets: Dominique De Vito, Associate Vice President and Publisher; Tracy Boggier, Managing Editor

Travel: Michael Spring, Vice President and Publisher; Suzanne Jannetta, Editorial Director; Brice Gosnell, Managing Editor

IDG Books Consumer Editorial Services: Kathleen Nebenhaus, Vice President and Publisher; Kristin A. Cocks, Editorial Director; Cindy Kitchel, Editorial Director

IDG Books Consumer Production: Debbie Stailey, Production Director

IDG Books Packaging: Marc J. Mikulich, Vice President, Brand Strategy and Research

◆

The publisher would like to give special thanks to Patrick J. McGovern, without whom this book would not have been possible.

◆

Contents at a Glance

Cartoons at a Glance

By Rich Tennant

page 193

page 69

page 231

page 5

page 117

Cartoon Information:
Fax: 978-546-7747
E-Mail: richtennant@the5thwave.com
World Wide Web: www.the5thwave.com

Table of Contents

Introduction

· ·

Dachshunds: What's not to love? They're cute, cuddly, smart, and friendly, and they're shaped like hot dogs, which is why I occasionally call them wiener dogs throughout the book. They come in all kinds of different colors and patterns, and you'll even find them in two different sizes. If you like small- to medium-size dogs, you'll love Dachshunds.

This book is your primer on Dachshund care. I describe what Dachshunds are, not only in terms of the breed standard but also in terms of personality and temperament, so that you can decide if a Dachshund is the right dog for you. And I show you how to take care of your Dachshund from the day you bring him home. I cover housetraining, feeding, pest prevention, vet care, obedience training, and much more. If you have a Dachshund or are considering buying one, this book has all the information you need.

How to Use This Book

The great thing about *...For Dummies* books is that they are references rather than tutorials. I've organized this book into self-contained chapters that you can read in pretty much any order you wish. So skip around if that's what you want to do. Of course, the progression of chapters in the book is logically arranged just in case you want to read the book from cover to cover.

So you can pick a topic out of the Table of Contents and start reading, or you can flip to the first page of Chapter 1 and read till you get to the end. Either way, I'm sure you'll enjoy the experience.

What I Assume about You

You don't have to know diddly-squat about Dachshunds to use this book. If you know nothing about dog care, this book has plenty of information for you to start a rewarding relationship with a Dachshund.

And if you're a seasoned dog-care veteran, I bet you'll find this book plenty useful. It's filled with tips, tricks, and advice for life with Dachshunds, including a good bit of technical information keeping your Dachshund healthy in all stages of its life.

How This Book Is Organized

This have five parts, each containing related chapters. Here's what I cover in each part:

Part I: Preparing for Life with a Dachshund

I start out by defining the Dachshund and I describe the different varieties of Dachshunds that you're likely to encounter. I then provide advice on where to find the Dachshund that may become your new friend, and I include a discussion on the pros and cons of working with rescue shelters.

Part II: Introductions: Starting Out on the Right Foot

You find out how to prepare your home, yourself, and your family for the fun-filled life with a Dachshund. I tell you what things to buy, and I explain what to expect when you bring your wiener-shaped friend home for the first time.

Part III: The Obedient Dachshund

After describing the Dachshund personality and helping you understand your role as a trainer, I show you how to housetrain your Dachshund. Then I provide helpful advice on how to teach your Dachsie all of the behaviors that any good dog should know. I conclude this part with coverage of dog shows and competitions.

Part IV: The Healthy Dachshund

You find out what it takes to keep you Dachshund happy and healthy. I also describe in detail the back problems that many Dachshunds develop and show you some preventative measures. I then discuss the health needs of older dogs.

Part V: The Part of Tens

Every ...*For Dummies* book ends with top-ten lists and this one is no exception. I give you ten great Dachshund books and Web sites, as well as ten Dachshund clubs and organizations.

Icons Used in This Book

Look for these icons next to tidbits of useful information:

Here you'll find dog-related tips and common-sense hints to make life with your Dachshund easier and more enjoyable.

I place this icon next to information that will help you prevent mistakes or warn you against doing things that may potentially cause a problem.

When you see this icon, expect to find interesting tidbits, lore, and information about Dachshunds and dogs in general.

You'll see this icon when I'm describing technical terms.

I use this icon when I want you to . . . um . . . remember a general concept.

Where to Go from Here

If you already know a lot about dog care, feel free to skip around and check out whatever Dachshund-related topics catch your fancy. The detailed Table of Contents and Index should help you out. If you don't really know much about Dachshunds, be sure to read the first part of this book to get the lowdown.

Part I
Preparing for Life with a Dachshund

The 5th Wave   By Rich Tennant

"OK, I'LL LET HIM PLAY AS LONG AS YOU STOP SAYING, 'YOU CAN'T TAKE AN OLD DOG'S NEW TRICKS'."

In this part . . .

I start out by telling you what the heck a Dachshund actually is (as defined by the breed standard), and then I describe the different kinds of Dachshunds you're likely to encounter. I then provide advice on where to find the Dachshund that may become your new friend, and I include a discussion on the pros and cons of working with rescue shelters.

Chapter 1

Dachshund Dilemma: Are You Made for Each Other?

*E*verybody loves a Wiener dog. Those funny bodies, those short little legs, those floppy ears, those pleading eyes, and those *antics*. Dachshunds are clowns. They can keep a room in stitches, and they can coax even the most stolid disciplinarian into slipping them just one more dog cookie. Who can resist a pet like that?

Apparently, not many. As of 1999 (the most current statistics available at the time of this printing), Dachshunds were the fourth most-popular dog breed in terms of numbers of registrations with the American Kennel Club (AKC) — climbing on those short little legs from the number seven spot in 1997 and the number five spot in 1998. And you're tempted, aren't you? Dachshunds aren't big dogs, so they don't take up much room. Lots of people have them, so they can't be too much trouble, can they? And they're so darned *cute*.

Of course, you know that a cute face and a good sense of humor aren't reasons in and of themselves to take on the 15-year-or-so responsibility of a dog. Too many people don't give pet ownership in general and Dachshund ownership in particular a lot of thought. But you're not like them because you've already begun research by getting this book. Good for you. So before you even begin your quest for the Dachshund of your dreams, read this chapter to look closely at the responsibilities of Dachshund servitude (because, as you'll soon see, they own you, not the other way around). And what if you've already got a Dachsie pup curled in your lap? Better late than never: You're still at the right chapter.

The Pros and Cons of Dog Ownership

Dog ownership is easy to romanticize: You and your dog, together forever. You see yourself taking leisurely walks through the park with your dog by your side; relaxing with a good book and his warm body on your lap; having a loyal companion and friend and playmate for the kids; and having friends comment on how well-behaved, well-trained, and intelligent your dog is.

Well, guess what? Life with a dog isn't always like that. From sleepless nights with a new puppy to expensive prescription medication to treat any of a number of health problems in your aging pet, having a dog as a family member is a lot like having a child. It takes a lot of work and a lot of time. It takes a physical, emotional, and financial commitment. Sometimes it ends in heartbreak, even when your dog lives to a ripe old age, because humans usually outlive dogs and no one wants to say good-bye to a best friend.

But on the flip side, living with a Dachshund *will* fill your life with fun, and you'll soon find yourself the object of your Dachshund's colossal affection. You just need to be realistic and decide whether you're ready to take on the responsibility. This section helps you put your feelings in perspective.

The pros

Here are some major benefits to owning a dog:

- ✔ Dogs love you unconditionally.
- ✔ Studies show that having a pet lowers blood pressure and helps to manage stress.
- ✔ Fulfilling your dog's exercise needs may help you to keep yourself in shape.
- ✔ Dogs are great companions and listeners.
- ✔ Dogs can help teach children to respect and be kind to animals.
- ✔ Many dogs (including Dachshunds) are good at warning you if someone is outside the house, welcome or not.
- ✔ If you bring home a rescued dog, you can feel good about having saved a life. And your dog will show his gratitude every day.

The cons

A hard fact of life is that the drawbacks to owning a dog can sometimes outweigh the benefits:

- ✔ Dogs need lots of attention and affection. They want to be with you, not tied to a chain in the backyard.

- ✔ Dogs aren't people and must be taught how to live with people. Without proper and consistent teaching and socialization efforts, your dog may end up an annoyance to you, your family, or your neighbors. He may even inflict damage on your possessions, other people, or himself.

- ✔ Dogs must be housebroken, and until they are, your carpet or other household surfaces may suffer. (And housetraining a Dachshund is no picnic.)

- ✔ Dogs cost a lot of money. Expect to spend over $1,000 in the first year to give your new puppy the proper care and supplies.

- ✔ Dogs need your time. They require walking, feeding, training, grooming, and attention *every single day* to stay healthy and happy.

- ✔ Dogs aren't a commitment to be taken lightly. Many, including Dachshunds, live 15 years or more.

- ✔ Your dog will probably grow old and die before you do. You have to deal with decisions about your dog's health care and quality of life and, eventually, your own grief.

- ✔ Your dog requires regular preventive veterinary care, and if he becomes ill or injured, you're also responsible for his care and treatment. These medical costs can be high.

- ✔ Dogs tie you down. You can't just fly off on a spontaneous vacation for a long weekend or decide not to come home after work without arranging for your dog's care.

- ✔ Dogs don't speak English. You have to learn to communicate with your dog in a way he understands.

How's that for a reality check? Think long and hard about the commitment you're about to make.

Dachshunds are more stubborn than some breeds, so training efforts can sometimes be frustrating for the beginner. Don't give up. When in doubt, talk to your vet, hire a trainer, and practice, practice, practice every day. Eventually, you'll be speaking the same language, and your Dachshund will understand what you want. She really does live to please you, even if it sometimes seems like you live to please her.

DACHSIE TALK

A word about the AKC

The American Kennel Club (AKC) is a nonprofit organization, established in 1884, that is devoted to the advancement of purebred dogs. The AKC maintains a record of all registered dogs; publishes ideal standards for each recognized breed; sponsors a variety of dog events, including dog shows, obedience and field trials, agility, and the Canine Good Citizen program; and publishes educational information.

Dachshunds: Not Just Any Dog

It's one thing to prepare for a dog. It's another thing to prepare for a Dachshund. Dachshunds have all the basic needs of a dog but also have a few of their own special quirks and considerations. If you have your heart set on a Dachsie, and who wouldn't have seeing a cutie like the one shown in Figure 1-1, you must be ready to handle a few extras:

- ✔ Dachshunds have faulty backs that can become injured when handled incorrectly, sometimes for no apparent reason. Going up and down stairs can be hard on Dachshund backs and can even result in severe disk problems. Get ready to carry your Dachshund up and down the stairs.

- ✔ Dachshunds love to jump, but jumping is similarly hard on a Dachshund's back. You need to keep an eye on your Dachsie to keep him from jumping off high places like beds, high chairs and couches, porches, and so on. Some people install ramps in their homes for their Dachshunds. (For more on making your home Dachshund-friendly, see Chapter 6.)

- ✔ Dachshunds live to eat, and obesity puts a further strain on a Dachshund's back — not to mention his heart and entire body. Cute and pleading as he may be, you must be prepared to keep your Dachshund's eating under control. No, your Dachshund shouldn't eat that extra quarter-pounder with cheese, let alone too many extra dog treats.

- ✔ Dachshunds bark. It's part of their *modus operandi*. They were bred to hunt badgers or other small game underground. Once the game is cornered, a Dachshund barks to alert his human. Although you can train any dog not to bark excessively, Dachshunds bark pretty frequently. Get used to it or get a different dog.

- ✔ Dachshunds are manipulative. They are cute, and they know it. They are clever, too. They can get you to do just about anything unless you have preset rules and you stick to your guns. Those Dachshund wiles may be endearing, but your dog has to know that rules are rules and that what you say goes. If you're a big marshmallow when it comes to consistency and enforcing the rules, you can't very well get angry at your dog for making his own rules.

What would your Dachsie's rules be? Here's a good guess:

I can do whatever I want to do, whenever I want to do it.

If I touch it, lick it, chew it, shred it, smell it, or see it, it's mine.

Humans live to serve me.

So unless those rules sound reasonable to you, prepare to accept your role as pack leader.

Figure 1-1: This longhaired Dachsie, while cute and clever, loves to bark, jump, and manipulate.

Photo courtesy of Gail Painter.

So that's why the dog's looking for food in the diaper pail

Dachshunds (and all dogs) have fewer taste buds than humans, so the taste of food isn't as intense for them as it is for us. For this reason, dogs are more likely to eat just about anything, taste not withstanding.

The name game

The name *Dachshund* is obviously German, and although lots of people say *dash-hound*, the word is correctly pronounced *daks-hoondt*. Yet, in Germany, the Dachshund isn't called a Dachshund at all. It is a Teckel or Dackel. (Back in the 19th century, the Dachshund was sometimes even called the Royal Teutonic Dog.)

The name *Dachshund* has actually been somewhat misunderstood. *Dachs* means *badger* in German, but *hund* doesn't, contrary to what you might think, mean *hound*. It simply means *dog*. Although Dachshunds are, to this day, classified in the Hound group according to the American Kennel Club, they can arguably fit just as well with the Terriers. *Terrier* means *earth dog*, and going underground is what Dachshunds do best (well, one of the many things they do best). Dachshunds do hunt by scent and have keen noses like their Hound brothers and sisters, but if you're on the other side of the door, that bark sounds an awful lot like a Terrier.

In any case, categories don't really matter. What matters is knowing that your dog will display characteristics of the Hound and the Terrier. And you can call him anything you like.

Are You Ready to Be Owned by a Dachsie?

I hear ya: "Yes, yes, I'm ready! Sure, Dachshunds have minds of their own, but I can handle one. How tough could it be with a dog that short?"

Ah, but Napoleon was short, too. Take the following little quiz to make sure that you're truly prepared and ready to be owned by a Dachshund:

1. Dachshunds believe they should

    A. Guard the house.

    B. Rule the house.

2. A Dachshund loves to please you

    A. No matter what.

    B. When you're holding a doggy treat.

3. Dachshund training sessions should be

    A. Fastidiously structured.

    B. Cleverly disguised as playtime.

4. When your Dachshund really, really, really, really wants that (third) oat-meal cookie, you should

    A. Just give it to him.

    B. Close your eyes tightly, take a deep breath, try not to think about that cute little cocked head, and just say no.

5. Dachshunds are obedient

    A. Once you've trained them.

    B. When the spirit moves them.

6. When it comes to crowds, Dachshunds

    A. Are a little shy and would rather blend.

    B. Love to be the center of attention and will do just about anything for applause.

7. When it comes to the power of destruction, a Dachshund

    A. Doesn't do too much damage after the initial teething stages.

    B. Can rival a Labrador Retriever in his ability to dismantle a sofa.

8. Dachshunds often keep their noses to the ground because

    A. They are surveying their environment through scent.

    B. They are hoping beyond hope that they'll run across a piece of food.

9. If you don't allow your Dachshund on the furniture, he will

    A. Never get on the furniture.

    B. Quickly learn to get off the furniture when he hears you coming.

10. To a Dachshund, a fence is

    A. A safe enclosure.

    B. Something to dig under.

11. To a Dachshund, the outside world is

    A. An intimidating place.

    B. His personal playground.

12. A Dachshund likes to perch in high places in the room because

    A. She doesn't want to get stepped on.

    B. She likes to survey her kingdom.

13. Dachshunds bark

    A. Only when a true threat is approaching.

    B. When anyone approaches anything — or just for fun.

Body of a hot dog; eye of a tiger

Dachshunds are big fans of people (although not necessarily strangers), well-behaved children, other Dachshunds, and often, other dogs. A Dachshund may even befriend the family cat. Everything else, however, is quite literally fair game. Neighborhood cats, rabbits, squirrels, birds, field mice, hamsters, and anything else small and fast look like prey to your Dachshund. And being bred to hunt, he *will* pursue.

14. To a Dachshund, any animal under ten pounds is

   A. Not worth noticing.

   B. Prey! Hamsters beware!

15. Dachshunds love

   A. People.

   B. Kids.

   C. Other Dachshunds.

   D. Other dogs.

   E. The occasional cat.

   F. All of the above.

Count up all your responses. If you answered mostly As, you may not be ready for a Dachshund. Your ideas of what a dog should be and do may be better fulfilled with another breed. On the other hand, to grasp that special Dachshund mode of thinking, give this book a once-through and then try the quiz again. Converts abound.

If you answered mostly Bs, you're already talkin' Dachsie. You already know, or can guess at, what life will be like with a Dachshund in the house. Challenging? Yes. Fun? Oh, yes. Easy? Oh, no. But, as long as you know what you're getting into and are ready to trade in the easy parts for some great fun, you may be just the kind of companion a Dachshund needs.

And, of course, although the answer to Number 15 is F (all of the above), *you* will be top on your Dachshund's list.

A Dachshund's Special Needs

Dachshunds have special care needs related to preserving the integrity of their spinal cord. (For a more detailed discussion of disk disease in Dachshunds, see Chapter 17). Briefly, Dachshunds are *chondrodystrophic*. The root *chondro* means cartilage and *dystroph* means disorder. Back disks are made of cartilage, and chondrodystrophic disks have a thinner covering and are more brittle than normal, making them more prone to rupturing and disk disease. The coverings around the disks that cushion the vertebrae in a Dachshund's back are thinner and more brittle than in other breeds, so disks can rupture more easily. One hard jump off a high bed, a fall from a porch, or even a sudden twisting movement to catch a ball gone astray can be all it takes to rupture a disk. The result can range from severe pain to paralysis, temporary or permanent.

Of course, not every Dachshund is doomed to suffer this debilitating and painful condition, and I hope you won't be dissuaded from bringing a Dachshund into your life out of fear. But caution is warranted. Avoiding long or steep flights of stairs and jumps off high places, as well as any activities like vigorous tug-of-war games that can twist the spine, is an important precautionary measure. So is keeping your dog slim.

Exercise is another important preventive measure. Daily walks and lots of activity are important to keep a Dachshund's muscles strong and stable so they can best support the spine. Just be sure that the activities are the kinds a Dachshund excels in — brisk walks and hikes, organized field-trial or earth-dog competitions (see Chapter 15), or just lots of brisk play in the park.

Just like a human with a weak back, Dachshunds need to exercise properly, eat a healthy diet, and avoid certain movements to minimize the possibility of injury. Chances are, your Dachshund will never have a problem.

"So just how common is this disk problem?"

According to the Dachshund Club of America, Inc., in its must-have publication *Canine Intervertebral Disk Disease* (available from the DCA for free — see Chapter 20 for contact information), approximately one in four Dachshunds will experience a disk problem. Most incidents occur between the ages of 3 and 7 years, with age 4 being the most common age of occurrence.

What's Your PQ (Patience Quotient)?

You may already have received the impression that living with a Dachshund requires a degree of patience. Let me emphasize this one: *Patience*.

Do you have the patience required not to lose your cool when your Dachshund steals your pot roast right off your plate? Or eats the last half of your book before you get to the exciting conclusion? Or has an accident in the house *again*? That's not to say you can't get irritated — or even downright angry — at your Dachshund. But yelling, screaming, flailing your arms around, or, dog-forbid, hitting will do more harm than good every single time.

Every time your Dachshund makes a mistake — accidentally or on purpose — you have an opportunity to teach her something, especially when you catch her in the act. But this teaching has to be performed calmly and rationally. Teaching a Dachshund is a lot like teaching a child. Losing your temper will only scare and confuse your charge. Keeping your cool will prove that you are the pack leader and the one with all the power.

Think long and hard about whether you have a short fuse or a long one before bringing home a Dachshund. And then, who knows? You may end up with a perfect little angel and the whole discussion will be moot. Better to be prepared, however, because most Dachshunds are about half-angel, and half-, well . . . you know.

Dachshund Dollars: The Financial Commitment

Before you purchase any dog, whether Dachshund or Great Dane, be aware that you're making a financial commitment as well as emotional and time commitments. Sure, you don't *have* to take your pet to the vet. But without regular veterinary visits, puppies have a much higher chance of becoming sick and dying from a serious disease like *parvovirus* or *distemper*, and throughout their lives, adult and senior dogs need regular check-ups, vaccinations, and tests to maintain health and catch health problems in the early stages. In addition, your vet can help you with wormings, flea control, and heartworm prevention, and your vet can also give you advice on general issues of care, behavior, and training. Worth every penny.

Canine *parvovirus* is a quickly spreading, highly contagious viral disease that comes in two forms: enteric (diarrheal) and myocardial (affecting the heart). Young puppies are particularly vulnerable, and the disease is often fatal. *Distemper* is also a virus that spreads quickly and is highly contagious. In advanced stages, distemper affects the brain and can cause permanent neurological damage and, often, death. Distemper is the principal cause of disease and death in unvaccinated dogs.

In addition to a lifetime of regular veterinary care and vaccinations, especially in the first year (for more on the first vet visit and which vaccinations your puppy really needs, see Chapter 16), you also need to spend some of your hard-earned cash on supplies. Dogs need food — probably your most significant expense, all told — as well as feeding supplies, collars and leashes, dens (a crate or kennel), chew toys, and a number of other necessities and luxuries (see Chapter 8 for a major discussion on Dachshund accessories).

While researching an article for the 1999–2000 issue of *Puppies USA* magazine, I compiled a breakdown of expenses involved in the first year of owning a puppy. That breakdown is shown in Table 1-1. Although expenses can vary dramatically from region to region, I list in the table approximate costs somewhere in the middle of the extremes and assume that you bought your puppy from a good breeder for an average price of $400.

Table 1-1	First-Year Expenses for Puppy Owners
Item	*Cost*
The dog	$400.00
Veterinary:	
First office visit	$25.00
Four vaccinations at $22.50 each	$90.00
Rabies shot	$15.00
Bordatella	$15.00
Leptospirosis	$15.00
Spay/neuter operation	$125.00
Registration	$15.00
Total vet cost	**$300.00**
Prevention:	
Heartworm prevention at $3.50/month	$42.00
Flea control spot-on at $8.00/month	$96.00
Total prevention cost	**$138.00**

(continued)

Table 1-1 *(continued)*

Item	Cost
Obedience classes:	
Puppy class (6–8 sessions)	$50.00
Basic obedience (6–8 sessions)	$50.00
Total obedience classes cost	**$100.00**
Services:	
Pet sitter for one-week vacation at $15.00/day	$105.00
Professional grooming (for longhairs and wirehairs), six times/year at $25.00/session	$150.00
Total services cost	**$255.00**
Pet supplies:	
Food	$400.00
Leash	$10.00
Retractable Leash	$15.00
Collar or harness	$8.00
Food and water bowls	$10.00
Dog bed (although Dachsie will probably prefer to sleep with you)	$40.00
Crate	$60.00
Shampoo, two bottles	$20.00
Toothbrush/paste	$5.00
Nail clippers	$10.00
Brush	$5.00
Comb	$6.00
ID tags	$4.00
Pet gate	$40.00
Toys (chew toy, squeaky toy, ball, and plush toy)	$50.00

Item	Cost
Treats, one box/month	$30.00
Chewing/teething treats (rawhides, hooves, etc.), one/month	$50.00
Poop scoop	$10.00
Breed book	$15.00
Training book	$15.00
Pet odor remover, 1 gallon	$20.00
Total pet supplies cost	**$573.00**
GRAND TOTAL	**$2,016.00**

Not cheap, as you can see in Table 1-1, and this grand total assumes that your pup is healthy. If your puppy suffers from serious health problems, you can add quite a bit to the grand total. Are you ready for this?

Sure, you can cut corners here and there, but if you have to cut so many corners that you compromise the health and welfare of your dog — or if you aren't willing to spend money on your pet because he's "just a dog" — perhaps you should reconsider bringing a dog into your life right now. Dogs deserve proper care and a comfortable existence just like you do.

The Size of Love: Standards versus Minis

A Dachshund Decision you need to consider is what size will work best for you. Dachshunds come in two sizes — Standard and Miniature — according to the standard published by the American Kennel Club and the Canadian Kennel Club. Although the AKC doesn't officially consider the two sizes as separate classifications, the sizes are divided by weight for the purpose of competition. Miniatures are 11 pounds and under at 12 months of age and older, and Standards are over 11 pounds, usually falling between 16 and 32 pounds.

Unofficially, many people call those Dachshunds between 11 and 16 pounds "Tweenies," since they are in between the two preferred Dachshund sizes. "Tweenies" may not be preferable in the show ring, but they are just as good as the larger Standards and the Miniatures as pets. Some pet owners prefer the medium size. In Europe, Dachshunds officially fall into three sizes: Standard, Miniature, and Rabbit. These sizes are determined not by weight but by chest circumference. Rabbits are what we'd consider the smallest Miniatures.

Vaccinate!

Puppies are immune to many diseases while nursing on mother's milk. As soon as a puppy is weaned and you take him home, however, his immunity quickly disappears and your puppy is vulnerable to a number of serious diseases until he can build up his own immune system. Vaccinate your puppy according to your veterinarian's recommendations to keep him safe during this gap of time.

What size suits your fancy? Maybe you've only seen Standard Dachshund, or you like a sturdier dog. Maybe your heart melts at the sight of a Mini pup, and you can't wait to hold one in the palm of your hand. Maybe you aren't sure.

Either way, Dachshunds are a surprisingly sturdy dog and tend to believe they are much bigger than they look. If you live in an apartment or a house without a fenced yard, a Miniature Dachshund may be best for you. Smaller dogs can fulfill much of their exercise needs inside the house.

If you like the idea of participating in lots of outdoor activities with your Dachshund — things like hiking or long walks, for example — you may want to consider a Standard. I'm not saying Minis can't go on walks. On the contrary, they have a lot of energy and love to exercise. They may not be able to keep up with your fast strides, however. Remember how short their legs are. Minis may need more help with stairs and ledges because every jump is bigger for them than for a Standard, and they are just as prone to disk disease.

The size matter is largely a personal one. Some people just like smaller dogs or larger dogs — although Standards can hardly be considered large, even at their biggest and most roly-poly. Whatever size you choose, a Dachshund is a Dachshund — challenging and fun, full of mischief, and brimming with love for you (yes, even when she tips over that trash can). A Dachshund wants only your care, loving authority, and devoted attention in return.

Chapter 2

Dachshunds Defined

. . . .

In This Chapter

▶ Why Dachshunds look like they do

▶ The difference between a croup, a hock, a stifle, and a pastern

▶ The American Kennel Club's breed standard

▶ Whether your Dachshund should fit the standard

. . . .

*Y*ou know one when you see one. You can easily describe one. But can you actually define what a Dachshund is? If you read this chapter, you'll be able to do just that.

The *definition* of a breed can mean several things. For example, it can mean the *breed standard*, which is (and this is a mouthful) a description of the nonexistent, ideal specimen of a particular breed, against which actual dogs of that breed are measured for the purposes of improving the breed through breeding programs and judging the conformation of dogs in dog shows. On the other hand, the definition of a breed can also mean, simply, the enumeration of the qualities that make a breed unique. I cover both definitions in this chapter.

Hey, Who Stretched Out My Dog?

If you ask anyone on the street to describe a Dachshund, chances are you'll get some version of "those long dogs," "those wiener-shaped dogs," or "those short, stretched-out dogs." Most people know Dachshunds have unusually short legs and unusually long bodies (see Figure 2-1). But why on Earth would anyone try to "make" a dog like that?

Dachshund-shaped dogs are nothing new. Some historians claim that the Dachshund shape was in evidence 4,000 years ago in ancient Egypt. But the Dachshunds we know and love today were developed primarily for one purpose: to hunt.

Figure 2-1:
Short legs
and a long
body:
That's a
dachshund.

Photo courtesy of Ronald Globus.

The right stuff for the hunt

Although they share many features (and lots of ancestors) with the Basset Hound, Dachshunds are certainly unique. Lighter, smaller, finer-boned, and quicker than their Basset cousins (although some sources say that, originally, the Dachshund was the larger of the two breeds), Dachshunds can fit into places a Basset can't, and they can usually move more quickly and with greater agility.

Dachshunds also have a keen scenting ability, facilitated by their low stance and long ears, but the Dachshund personality is even more highly prized. Their energy, eagerness, and Terrier-like feistiness in the pursuit of small game have historically distinguished Dachshunds as excellent hunting companions.

How breeds are "made"

All purebred dogs are made, to some extent. A tiny Chihuahua and a giant Tibetan Mastiff are both variations on the same theme, created by humans through selective breeding to serve a specific purpose. Dachshunds, too, were designed to serve a specific purpose: to follow a badger, or other burrowing game, into its tunnel and either flush it out or bark to alert the accompanying human of its whereabouts. Breeders developed Miniature Dachshunds during the 1800s specifically for hunting purposes. Their tiny bodies could fit into even smaller holes in pursuit of small game.

Why Dachshunds have long bodies

The Dachshund's long body is unusual but useful for its original purpose. Dachshunds had to be large enough to contend with badgers and other game that could sometimes put up a fierce counterattack. On the other hand, the Dachshund had to be low to the ground and compact, able to follow the badger into its burrow without getting stuck. The Dachshund's long, slender body was the perfect solution. Adding length gave the dog more power and weight while maintaining the low height.

At first, the Dachshund's long body may seem more of an impediment to agile movement, but Dachshunds are surprisingly lithe and light-footed. Their spines are flexible (although they don't respond well to sudden movements, hard jolts, or twists — see Chapter 1). And although Dachshunds are a fairly deep-chested breed, their bodies are perfect for wriggling. If you've got a Dachshund at home, you've probably already seen this wriggling as your Dachshund slyly makes his way to the foot of your bed underneath the covers.

Unlike human spines, dog spines aren't attached to the ribcage, which allows the Dachshund's long body to be flexible and adaptable to a variety of movements and positions.

Why Dachshunds have short legs

The other distinguishing feature of the Dachshund is the short legs. It seems obvious that Dachshunds have short legs to best fit into badger dens and burrows of other small game. But Dachshunds have been used for all sorts of hunting, not just burrowing, and the characteristically short legs serve the Dachshund well in several ways:

✔ Short legs allow a Dachshund to move quickly through dense brush and into spaces that, even though above ground, would be a tight fit for a taller dog. In fact, Dachshunds have even been used to flush out wild boar because once the boar is on the loose the Dachshund can hide, protected, under the dense underbrush.

✔ Underground, the Dachshund's short legs allow him to maneuver well in a burrow. If the game being pursued turns to attack, short legs allow the dog to back up.

✔ The Dachshund's compact legs serve as powerful excavators. Dachshunds can dig out anything and dig into or out of anywhere.

✔ A Dachshund's short legs keep the dog closer to the ground in order to enhance his ability to catch and follow a scent.

Dachshund Anatomy 101

Although the Dachshund's unusual form makes it an ideal hunting dog, and many are still used for this purpose, the Dachshund's more common role today is one of companion, friend, and resident court jester. But the Dachshund's unusual shape is worth understanding even if you don't plan to hunt a day in your life. Knowing your Dachsie's anatomy will help you understand his individual health needs as well as prevent or prepare for potential problems.

Talking dog anatomy means using lots of terms that many folks may not be familiar with. So Figure 2-2 shows a Dachshund with all his parts labeled. And following is a mini Dachs-tionary that defines the anatomical terms shown in the figure. (***Hint, hint:*** This Dachs-tionary comes in mighty handy when you're reading the section "The Perfect Dachsie.")

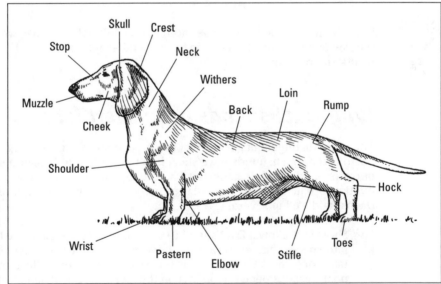

Figure 2-2:
The Dachsie's anatomy, in full glory.

- ✔ **Cheek:** The fleshy area behind the corners of a Dachshund's mouth.
- ✔ **Muzzle:** The part of a dog's head in front of the eyes, including the nose and jaws.
- ✔ **Stop:** The place where the muzzle meets the skull.
- ✔ **Skull:** The head bone, of course.
- ✔ **Crest:** The back of the skull where it begins its descent.

✔ **Neck:** The area attaching the head to the shoulders and upper chest.

✔ **Withers:** The highest point of the shoulder blades, used to measure a Dachshund's height.

✔ **Back:** The top of the dog, from withers to tail.

✔ **Loin:** The section of the dog between the ribs and hipbones.

✔ **Rump:** The area above the hipbones, in front of the base of the tail.

✔ **Hock:** The joint on the rear legs between the second thigh and the *metatarsus* (the area between the heel and toes, or *rear pastern*), corresponding to the human heel. In a Dachshund, this joint sticks out from behind.

✔ **Toes:** The digits at the ends of the paws.

✔ **Stifle:** The dog's knee, the first leg joint between the thigh and what's called the second thigh.

✔ **Elbow:** The joint between the front arm and forearm.

✔ **Forearm:** The lower part of the front leg, between the elbow and wrist. In Dachshunds, the forearm should be relatively straight but comfortably shaped around the chest.

✔ **Dewclaw:** A functionless fifth toe, often — but not necessarily — removed.

✔ **Pastern:** The area of the foot between the wrist and the toes.

✔ **Wrist:** The joint between the forearm and the toes.

✔ **Shoulder:** The top end of the front legs, connecting the legs to the body.

Now that you've got some basic anatomical vocabulary down, read on for the American Kennel Club's version of the Dachshund breed standard. Get ready for more dog terminology you may never have heard before. But never fear. I'll translate all 'shop talk' into plain language in the following section.

The Perfect Dachsie

The American Kennel Club publishes a standard for the Dachshund that was developed by the Dachshund Club of America, Inc. (DCA), and that standard defines and describes — in great detail — the *ideal* Dachshund. Of course, what's ideal for one person may not be ideal for all people. But the breed standard has a specific purpose. It's designed to guide breeders in their pursuits so that they don't bring puppies into the world with faults (some with serious consequences and others, mostly cosmetic), and the standard can further the good health and good looks of the Dachshund breed.

In addition, the standard serves as a guide for dog-show judges, who are judging, in essence, the work of those same breeders. Judges in dog shows measure each Dachshund they see against an imaginary perfect Dachshund, and the dogs coming closest to that ideal do the best in competition.

So what does the breed standard mean for you, the pet owner? Some aspects of the breed standard detail important qualities for a Dachshund. For instance, the breed standard says that a Dachshund should appear "neither crippled, awkward, nor cramped in his capacity for movement" and that his temperament should be "clever, lively, and courageous. . . ." However, if your Dachshund's eyes aren't perfectly "almond-shaped and dark-rimmed," if your smooth Dachshund's coat is a little too thick, or if your Standard Dachshund is the biggest one you've ever seen, he can still be the most perfect pet you've ever had — provided that you do your share of the work teaching him the rules. Although he may not win points in a dog show, if you aren't a breeder and aren't trying to win championships for your breeding stock, who cares?

That said, some people do like to know that their dog is as close to perfect as possible. And, since it never hurts to understand the ideal for your breed, this section goes over the AKC breed standard for the Dachshund. It's sensible and largely based around qualities that ensure good health and the betterment of the breed (the goals of any good breeder).

Don't be too critical of your beloved pet if she doesn't fit the breed standard very well. Lots of love, attention, and care — coupled with proper management and training — are the things that make a good pet, *not* the perfect coat texture or profile.

The AKC's official breed standard

This standard was approved April 7, 1992, and became effective on May 27, 1992.

- ✔ **General Appearance:** Low to ground, long in body and short of leg with robust muscular development, the skin is elastic and pliable without excessive wrinkling. Appearing neither crippled, awkward, nor cramped in his capacity for movement, the Dachshund is well balanced with bold and confident head carriage and intelligent, alert facial expression. His hunting spirit, good nose, loud tongue, and distinctive build make him well suited for below-ground work and for beating the bush. His keen nose gives him an advantage over most other breeds for trailing. *Note:* Inasmuch as the Dachshund is a hunting dog, scars from honorable wounds shall not be considered a fault.

- ✔ **Size, Proportion, Substance:** Bred and shown in two sizes, standard and miniature, miniatures are not a separate classification but compete in a class division for "11 pounds and under at 12 months of age and older." Weight of the standard size is usually between 16 and 32 pounds.

✔ **Head:** Viewed from above or from the side, the head tapers uniformly to the tip of the nose. The eyes are of medium size, almond-shaped, and dark-rimmed, with an energetic, pleasant expression; not piercing; and very dark in color. The bridge bones over the eyes are strongly prominent. Wall eyes, except in the case of dappled dogs, are a serious fault. The ears are set near the top of the head, not too far forward, of moderate length, rounded, not narrow, pointed, or folded. Their carriage, when animated, is with the forward edge just touching the cheek so that the ears frame the face. The skull is slightly arched, neither too broad nor too narrow, and slopes gradually with little perceptible stop into the finely-formed, slightly arched muzzle. Black is the preferred color of the nose. Lips are tightly stretched, well covering the lower jaw. Nostrils well open. Jaws opening wide and hinged well back of the eyes, with strongly developed bones and teeth.

✔ **Teeth:** Powerful canine teeth; teeth fit closely together in a *scissors bite*. An *even bite* is a minor fault. Any other deviation is a serious fault.

Different breeds have different bites. In other words, their upper and lower jaws and teeth meet in different ways. In many breeds, including Dachshunds, a *scissors bite* is the preferred bite. In this bite, the outside of the lower teeth touches the inner side of the upper teeth when the dog's mouth is closed. In an *even bite*, also called a *level bite*, the top and bottom teeth meet with no overlapping.

✔ **Neck:** Long, muscular, clean-cut, without *dewlap*, slightly arched in the nape, flowing gracefully into the shoulders.

The *dewlap* is the name for loose, pendulous skin that hangs down from a dog's throat and neck. Dachshunds shouldn't have one.

✔ **Trunk:** The trunk is long and fully muscled. When viewed in profile, the back lies in the straightest possible line between the withers and the short very slightly arched loin. A body that hangs loosely between the shoulders is a serious fault.

✔ **Abdomen:** Slightly drawn up.

✔ **Forequarters:** For effective underground work, the front must be strong, deep, long, and cleanly muscled.

✔ **Forequarters in detail, Chest:** The breastbone is strongly prominent in front so that on either side a depression or dimple appears. When viewed from the front, the thorax appears oval and extends downward to the mid-point of the forearm. The enclosing structure of the well-sprung ribs appears full and oval to allow, by its ample capacity, complete development of heart and lungs. The *keel* merges gradually into the line of the abdomen and extends well beyond the front legs. Viewed in profile, the lowest point of the breast line is covered by the front leg.

The *keel* is the outline of the lower chest (in profile), stretching from the top of the breastbone to the bottom of the ribs.

✔ **Forequarters in detail, Shoulder Blades:** Long, broad, well laid-back and firmly placed upon the fully developed thorax, closely fitted at the withers, furnished with hard yet pliable muscles.

✔ **Forequarters in detail, Upper Arm:** Ideally the same length as the shoulder blade and at right angles to the latter, strong of bone and hard of muscle, lying close to the ribs, with elbows close to the body, yet capable of free movement.

✔ **Forequarters in detail, Forearm:** Short; supplied with hard yet pliable muscles on the front and outside, with tightly stretched tendons on the inside at the back, slightly curved inwards. The joints between the fore-arms and the feet (wrists) are closer together than the shoulder joints, so that the front does not appear absolutely straight. *Knuckling over is a disqualifying fault.*

Knuckling over refers to a faulty wrist joint that flexes forward when a dog stands. Knuckling over is a serious fault in Dachshunds. It weakens what should be strong front legs and disqualifies any Dachshund from the show ring.

✔ **Forequarters in detail, Feet:** Front paws are full, tight, compact, with well-arched toes and tough, thick pads. They may be equally inclined a trifle outward. There are five toes, four in use, close together with a pro-nounced arch and strong, short nails. Front dewclaws may be removed.

✔ **Hindquarters:** Strong and cleanly muscled. The pelvis, the thigh, the second thigh, and the metatarsus are ideally the same length and form a series of right angles. From the rear, the thighs are strong and powerful. The legs turn neither in nor out.

✔ **Hindquarters in detail, Metatarsus:** Short and strong, perpendicular to the second thigh bone. When viewed from behind, they are upright and parallel.

✔ **Hindquarters in detail, Feet-Hind Paws:** Smaller than the front paws with four compactly closed and arched toes with tough, thick pads. The entire foot points straight ahead and is balanced equally on the ball and not merely on the toes. Rear dewclaws should be removed.

✔ **Hindquarters in detail, Croup:** Long, rounded and full, sinking slightly toward the tail.

The *croup* is the entire pelvic girdle region.

✔ **Hindquarters in detail, Tail:** Set in continuation of the spine, extending without kinks, twists, or pronounced curvature, and not carried too gaily.

✔ **Gait:** Fluid and smooth. Forelegs reach well forward, without much lift, in unison with the driving action of hind legs. The correct shoulder assembly and well-fitted elbows allow the long, free stride in front. Viewed from the front, the legs do not move in exact parallel planes, but incline slightly inward to compensate for shortness of leg and width of chest. Hind legs drive on a line with the forelegs, with hocks (metatarsus) turning neither in nor out. The propulsion of the hind leg depends on the dog's ability to carry the hind leg to complete extension. Viewed in profile, the forward reach of the hind leg equals the rear extension. The thrust of correct movement is seen when the rear pads are clearly exposed during rear extension. Feet must travel parallel to the line of motion with no tendency to swing out, cross over, or interfere with each other. Short, choppy movement, rolling or high-stepping gait, close or overly wide coming or going are incorrect.

The Dachshund must have agility, freedom of movement, and endurance to do the work for which he was developed.

✔ **Temperament:** The Dachshund is clever, lively, and courageous to the point of rashness, persevering in above- and below-ground work, with all the senses well developed. Any display of shyness is a serious fault.

Special characteristics of the three coat varieties

The Dachshund is bred with three varieties of coat: (1) Smooth, (2) Wirehaired, and (3) Longhaired and is shown in two sizes, standard and miniature. All three varieties and both sizes must conform to the characteristics already specified. The following features are applicable for each variety.

Smooth Dachshunds

Coat: Short, smooth, and shining. Should be neither too long nor too thick. Ears not leathery.

Tail: Gradually tapered to a point, well, but not too-richly haired. Long sleek bristles on the underside are considered a patch of strong-growing hair, not a fault. A *brush tail* is a fault, as is also, a partly or wholly hairless tail.

A *brush tail* is a tail that's bushy and heavy with hair. Dachshunds shouldn't have one.

Color of hair: Although base color is immaterial, certain patterns and basic colors predominate. One-colored Dachshunds include red (with or without a shading of interspersed dark hairs or sable) and cream. A small amount of white on the chest is acceptable, but not desirable.

Nose and nails: Black.

Two-colored Dachshunds

This variety includes black, chocolate, *wild boar,* gray (blue) and fawn (*Isabella*), each with tan markings over the eyes, on the sides of the jaw and underlip, on the inner edge of the ear, front, breast, inside and behind the front legs, on the paws and around the anus, and from there to about one-third to one-half of the length of the tail on the underside. Undue prominence or extreme lightness of tan markings is undesirable. A small amount of white on the chest is acceptable but not desirable.

Dachshund colors, such as red or black are easy to picture, but other colors are less well known. *Wild boar* is most common on wirehaired Dachshunds but can also occur on smooths. It refers to a black or dark outer coat over a lighter-colored undercoat. *Isabella* is a fancy word for a fawn color. Some two-color Dachshunds are fawn with tan markings, called *Isabella and tan.*

The nose and nails for two-colored dachshunds is as follows: in the case of black dogs, black; for chocolate and all other colors, dark brown, but self-colored is acceptable.

Dappled Dachshunds

The "single" dapple pattern is expressed as lighter-colored areas contrasting with the darker base color, which may be any acceptable color. Neither the light nor the dark color should predominate. Nose and nails are the same as for one- and two-colored Dachshunds. Partial or wholly blue (wall) eyes are as acceptable as dark eyes. A large area of white on the chest of a dapple is permissible. A *"double" dapple* is one in which varying amounts of white coloring occur over the body in addition to the dapple pattern.

Nose and nails: As for one- and two-color Dachshunds; partial or wholly self-colored is permissible. Brindle is a pattern (as opposed to a color) in which black or dark stripes occur over the entire body, although in some specimens, the pattern may be visible only in the tan points.

Wirehaired Dachshunds

Coat: With the exception of jaw, eyebrows, and ears, the whole body is covered with a uniform tight, short, thick, rough, hard, outer coat but with finer, somewhat softer, shorter hairs (undercoat) everywhere distributed between the coarser hairs. The absence of an undercoat is a fault. The distinctive facial furnishings include a beard and eyebrows. On the ears, the hair is shorter than on the body, almost smooth. The general arrangement of the hair is such that the wirehaired Dachshund, when viewed from a distance, resembles the smooth. Any sort of soft hair in the outer coat, wherever found on the body, especially on the top of the head, is a fault. The same is true of long, curly, or wavy hair, or hair that sticks out irregularly in all directions.

A debriefing on dappled Dachshunds

Some Dachshunds sport patterns in addition to their color schemes. *Dappled* Dachshunds are marked with random patches of lighter colors over a darker color. The markings occur in no distinguishable pattern, and the patches are sometimes ragged. *Double-dappled* Dachshunds are dappled Dachshunds with an additional sprinkling of pure white patches. *Brindled* Dachshunds are marked with darker stripes over a lighter background. *Piebald* Dachshunds are white with large spots of any color.

Tail: Robust, thickly haired, gradually tapering to a point. A *flag tail* is a fault.

A *flag tail* is a relatively long tail carried high with feathering on it. Dachshunds shouldn't have one.

Color of hair: While the most common colors are wild boar, black and tan, and various shades of red, all colors are admissible. A small amount of white on the chest, although acceptable, is not desirable.

Nose and nails: Same as for the smooth variety.

Longhaired Dachshunds

Coat: The sleek, glistening, often slightly wavy hair is longer under the neck and on the forechest, the underside of the body, the ears, and behind the legs. The coat gives the dog an elegant appearance. Short hair on the ear is not desirable. Too profuse a coat which masks type, equally long hair over the whole body, a curly coat, or a pronounced parting on the back are faults.

Tail: Carried gracefully in prolongation of the spine; the hair attains its greatest length here and forms a veritable flag.

Color of hair: Same as for the smooth Dachshund.

Nose and nails: Same as for the smooth.

That Doesn't Sound Like My Wiener Dog!

The AKC's official breed standard info is drawn out and sometimes tricky to understand. If you read it, you may become thoroughly confused. Or the standard may make perfect sense to you. (Note that if you're in the latter group, you can feel free to skip Chapter 3, which translates the breed standard into laydog's terms, although you may want to check out the international Dachshund standard info in that chapter.)

The bottom line about the breed standard is that it's a description of the *perfect* Dachshund — the Dachshund by which show champions are measured; the Dachshund against which stud dogs are compared; and the Dachshund picture that show-dog judges keep in their heads when ranking the best Dachshunds in the country.

But when it comes to *your* pet, that beloved little bundle of puppy burrowing under your covers, perfection is in the eye of the beholder. Your Dachshund may be way too big, hold his tail too high, have flat feet or blue eyes or a white patch on his chest, or have any number of so-called faults or undesirable traits. So what? You can love him just the same.

The most important thing to worry about with a Dachshund is temperament and health. Buying a Dachshund from a breeder can be a good move because good breeders breed for that classic friendly, funny, brave Dachshund temperament and for dogs that are sound and free of health problems. For the average pet owner, those are the priorities. The average pet owner is proud when his or her Dachsie looks "like a champion," but the breed standard is simply interesting side reading to him or her. (Of course, if you plan to breed, then the breed standard needs to be more than just side reading. Think twice. Think three times. Think *ten* times. And don't skip the discussion in Chapter 15 about sterilization and why you may want to reconsider breeding your Dachshund.)

Chapter 3

The Long and Short of It: Dachshund Variety

*I*t's time to refine your thinking: What about the actual Dachshund you plan to bring into *your* home and make a part of *your* family? You've got some choices ahead of you, and you need to think about some issues and weigh some options before you can choose the Dachsie that best suits your life. Not all Dachshunds are the same in size, coat, and color, and although some differences don't make any, well, difference, others can make all the difference in the world.

Size Matters (Or Does It?)

When it comes to Dachshunds, size does matter — at least for some things. By North American standards, Dachshunds come in two sizes: Standard and Miniature, as shown in Figure 3-1. By European standards, Dachshunds come in three sizes: Standard, Miniature, and Rabbit (the smallest size, approximately equivalent to a Miniature Dachshunds by North American standards). Many Dachshund breeders and fanciers believe that North American Dachsies should also come in three sizes, and Dachshunds that fall right in between the Miniature and preferred Standard weights are unofficially called *tweenies* by some.

Figure 3-1:
A Standard
and
Miniature
Dachshund

But weight or chest circumference aside (North Americans size Dachshunds by weight, while Europeans size Dachshunds by chest circumference), what difference does size make? Plenty. Standards and Minis were bred differently, and their personalities and needs, although similar, aren't interchangeable. Also, one size may fit your lifestyle better than another.

This section runs down the differences between micro- and macro-Wiener dogs. But before you dive into the details, take a minute to answer the following questions to get a feel for which Dachshund size may best suit you:

1. When you imagine yourself bonding with your new Dachshund puppy, what qualities do you picture yourself treasuring most?

    A. Energy, playfulness, and the Romp Factor.

    B. The clowning, the hilarity of the big watchdog in a little package, and, of course, the Cute-as-a-Button Factor.

    C. The combination of independent thinker and devoted companion.

2. The quality you're least looking forward to dealing with in your new Dachshund is

    A. Shedding — you can't stand the thought of dog hair everywhere.

    B. Barking — shrill noises really get to you.

    C. Housetraining — yuck. There's nothing worse than cleaning up a dog mess.

3. The other members of your family include

    A. Kids under 5.

    B. One other adult.

    C. Another dog and/or a cat.

4. You live

    A. On a farm.

    B. In an apartment.

    C. In a house with a fenced backyard.

5. Your activity level is

    A. Pretty high. You like to go on walks, and you like to keep moving. You wonder, "Can Dachshunds catch a Frisbee?"

    B. Pretty low. You are housebound or can't move too quickly, for whatever reason. Or maybe you just don't like to move more than you have to!

    C. About average. You plan to walk your dog every day, but you're no athlete.

6. Your house has

    A. Lots of high places — high couches, steep stairs, high beds, and such.

    B. Lots of low and level places — futon beds and couches, for example, but no stairs.

    C. Some high places and some low places, but the high places and steep stairs can be modified if necessary with ramps, or the dog can probably be easily averted from jumping or climbing.

7. You worry most about

    A. The costs associated with your Dachshund. You're willing to do what it takes, but you wonder, "How much is this going to run me, anyway?" (Check out Chapter 8.)

    B. Accidentally injuring your Dachshund. "They look so delicate."

    C. Training your Dachshund. You've heard they're pretty darned stubborn.

8. Above all, you're looking for

    A. A playmate that can really play. "No wimpy, sissy dogs for me!"

    B. A precious little lap dog to dote on and spoil.

    C. A companion to be with you throughout your days and nights, sharing your life as much as possible.

OK. Tally up how many As, Bs, and Cs you have. If you have mostly As, a Standard is probably the dog for you. Mostly Bs? Consider a Miniature. If your tally is heavy on the Cs, it probably doesn't matter. Either size will work for you 'cause you're just glad to have a Dachshund, period.

But each of the preceding questions also brings up some specific issues, so you need to look closely at each size, one at a time. Pay particular attention to the section on the size that interests you the most. If size truly doesn't matter to you, read all three of the following sections so you're best prepared for the dog you end up with.

In general, whether you prefer a Standard or a Mini is largely a matter of personal preference, but if you aren't sure, visit several breeders and meet lots of Dachsies. One size or the other will probably capture your heart.

If your main concern is to have a dog with the classic Dachshund personality — an independent and devoted Dachsie, a clown, a chow hound, a dog that's full of mischief and love — then it really doesn't matter which size you choose. All sizes reflect the classic Dachshund personality.

The Standard Dachshund

Standards are bigger and more boisterous than Miniatures, and they can probably last longer, run farther, and play harder than Minis, too. That's not to say that Minis aren't little balls of Dachshund dynamite. They were "created" to be hunting dogs, just like Standards. But the larger size of the Standard (although keep in mind that even Standards aren't all that big compared to, say, a Labrador Retriever) may be better suited for a very active lifestyle.

You need to consider a few things with a Standard. Because they're bigger, you'll notice more dog hair on the furniture than you will with a Mini, although having a Standard Dachshund around is nothing like having a large dog when it comes to shedding, and a daily brush-through helps a lot. Standards are typically great with other dogs and with kids, although all children should learn how to treat a dog and should be instructed in the proper way to pick up a Dachshund in order to avoid causing a back injury.

Standards need more room to exercise than Minis. Standards do best with a daily walk or two and some time to romp in a fenced backyard — and I mean fenced *well*, preferably buried at least 6 inches underground. *Earth dog* is not a misnomer when it comes to Dachsies. They love to dig and dig and dig, and the bigger, stronger Standards are most efficient at burrowing their way out of a yard you thought was secure (although many a Mini excels at digging, too).

Some Dachsie owners find that they need to bury their fence a foot or more into the ground to prevent escapes. Others pour concrete under the fence or line the yard with cement blocks. Even then, the persistent digger will find a way to escape. And with their keen scenting ability, Dachshunds tend to pursue small game with a single-mindedness that can put them at risk. Your Dachshund-on-the-loose will be much too interested in that squirrel across the street to notice the car speeding down the street. Avoid tragedy and make sure that the fence is Dachsie-proof. (For more on Dachsie-proofing your home, see Chapter 6.) Also, make sure that your Dachshund wears ID tags at all times. If he does escape, ID tags will help you locate him.

If you're going for a star with lots of champions in his pedigree, don't expect to get by cheap. Standards cost more to feed than Minis because they're larger, but still, a 30-pound dog doesn't eat too much.

The Miniature Dachshund

All Dachshunds are clowns, but there's something particularly hilarious about the antics of the Mini Dachshund. Of course, that may depend on your preference. Small-dog aficionados are particularly charmed by the Mini's attitude, obstinacy, independence, and over-confident, rapid-fire barks. And, of course, if you love small dogs, a Mini Dachshund really is as cute as a button.

Love cats? Miniature Dachshunds make great cat companions as long as you introduce the two carefully and give each pet its space until they accept each other. Some people with successful cat-Dachshund households claim that it helps if the Dachshund puppy is second on the scene. If the cat has the home-field advantage, the Dachshund puppy is more likely to afford his new feline housemate the respect she deserves.

Not everyone is fond of Minis, however. Although their personalities are essentially the same as Standards, a few differences exist. First and foremost is their tendency to be more vocal. Minis bark, and their bark can be shrill (particularly, the longhaired Minis). If you've had Toy dogs in the past, you know that many of them like to bark. Perhaps they compensate in volume for what they lack in size. Perhaps they want to make sure that you see them. Whatever the reason, if you really, really hate barking, you may be better off with a Standard, although all Dachshunds like to bark.

Kids and Dachshunds

Kids and Dachshunds are made for each other — especially when the Dachshund is the more durable Standard size. Encourage your children to take an active part in the care, socialization, and training of your Dachshund. Draw up a feeding schedule and let the kids measure out or prepare the dog food. Make walks a family affair. Look for local puppy- or dog-training courses for kids. If your child is a natural, he or she can even compete as a junior handler in a dog show. (Contact your local dog club or the AKC for info on how to become a junior handler. Chapter 20 contains the AKC's contact info.)

If you have young children, you're probably better off with a Standard. Children under 5 (some breeders even say under age 7 or 8) usually aren't able to understand how to properly treat a dog, and a very small dog can easily be injured if it's dropped, fallen on, or pushed by a toddler or baby. Likewise, Minis like to be the center of attention and don't take kindly to poking, prodding, and pulling. Small dogs can injure a small child if they lose patience and decide to snap at those curious fingers (or that inquisitive face). Standards may or may not be more patient, but because they're bigger, children may not seem as threatening or be as likely to injure.

The Miniature Dachshund's size makes it particularly suited to life in an apartment or a small house. When paper-trained, a Mini Dachshund doesn't necessarily even need to go outside at all, which is a particular advantage for people who are housebound or who live somewhere that makes forays outdoors inconvenient (such as in a high rise). Minis get plenty of exercise dashing around the house, so you don't need to feel guilty if you can't quite muster a daily walk.

A big thing to consider if you have a Mini is the layout of your home. If you have a lot of stairs, be prepared to cart your Mini up and down. Too much stair walking, especially if the risers are steep, can be dangerous for your Mini's back. Stairs are no picnic for a Standard Dachsie, either, but the back strain is less severe for a larger dog. You should also try to keep your Mini from jumping down off tall beds, chairs, and couches.

Miniature Dachshund *puppies* are quite, quite small, and although they can act pretty feisty, they're much more fragile than a standard-sized puppy. If you've got a Mini puppy around, watch where you step, watch where you sit, and always put the puppy firmly onto the ground after holding her. Letting her jump out of your arms can result in a back injury or even a broken leg. It has happened.

If cost is a concern, Minis cost less to feed, and vet bills may be lower because the Mini's small size requires less medication.

Although Minis can act an awful lot like privileged little lap dogs, they can also act an awful lot like a Terrier three times their size. For the most part, a Dachsie is a Dachsie, but if you prefer tiny, then you probably won't be able to resist the first little teacup-sized Miniature Dachshund puppy you meet.

Tweenies?

You may want to consider what some breeders and fanciers are calling *tweenies* — especially if you like a smaller dog but are intimidated by the very small size of a Mini. Tweenies are often cheaper, too, because their size makes them less suited for success in the show ring. As pets, they're perfect because no one in your family will care whether they're in the ideal weight range for a Standard or a Mini.

Pick a Coat, Any Coat

Dachshunds come in three coat varieties: smooth, longhaired, and wirehaired, as shown in Figure 3-2. Coat type makes a difference. Each type has different grooming needs and also makes for subtle differences in the Dachsie's personality. You may have a first reaction to which coat you like best, but read this section to make sure that you're prepared for the necessary grooming responsibility. Also, you want to make sure that your personality won't clash with the Dachsie personality of the coat type you think you love.

Figure 3-2:
The many
coats of the
Dachshund.

The smooth

The smooth Dachshund is the quintessential Dachshund. Say *Dachshund*, and the smooth is what most people picture. The sleek, shiny coat best shows off the Dachshund's form, and grooming takes little effort — just an occasional brush, nail clipping, and teeth scrubbing, and you're done.

When it comes to personality, the smooth is similarly representative. Breeders like to describe the smooth as the most consistent personality type, and many agree that the smooth is the most Dachshund-like. Incomparable to any other breed, the smooth *is* the Dachshund incarnate.

Smooths are perfect for people who don't have the time or patience for grooming, who love the stereotypical Dachshund look, or who simply prefer a sleek, short coat. Smooths shed but don't noticeably drop their coats to grow in new ones like the longhairs do. Daily grooming sessions may seem like overkill on your smooth, but you should keep those teeth clean. And a daily brushing minimizes shedding, keeps the coat shiny, keeps the skin healthy, and accustoms your Dachshund to handling — perhaps the most significant argument for this daily ritual.

Here's a trick to add some serious sheen to your smooth Dachshund's coat: After brushing, rub a drop or two of baby oil in your palms and then smooth the oil over your Dachshund's coat. *Gorgeous.*

The longhaired

If you like to groom, or you don't mind it and think it's worth the time to have a dog with a lovely, silky, flowing coat, a longhaired Dachshund may be the dog for you. Longhairs are, indeed, beautiful, and a longhaired Dachshund puppy is one of the cutest things around. But keeping a longhaired Dachshund requires a significant grooming commitment. That gorgeous coat will soon become a mess of tangles and mats if left unattended. And if your dog likes to romp outside, his coat will pick up leaves, sticks, burrs, and, yes, ticks.

A daily brushing takes longer on a longhair than on a smooth. You may feel that you're constantly picking out tangles, but keeping up the task is essential. A matted coat can result in skin problems, a more difficult time with parasite control, and a dog with an unkempt and sorry appearance. If you aren't prepared for the commitment, please don't invest in a longhair.

Which came first?

Some historical accounts claim that the smooth Dachshund was the original version, with the longhaired developing later and the wirehaired developing later still. Other accounts put the development of the smooth, longhaired, and wirehaired at about the same time, and still others differ as to whether the longhaired or wirehaired developed next. In any case, all three coats are well established now and have large gene pools, making interbreeding between coat types unnecessary and undesirable.

Some Dachshund owners find that their daily grooming session is a joy. Longhairs are notoriously sweet, gentle creatures who love to spend time with you and may revel in the attention they get from you as you brush, comb, and tend to their personal beauty routine. Grooming sessions are a great opportunity for you to bond with your Dachshund, and you'll feel good about keeping your dog looking so lovely.

The longhaired Dachshund personality is unique, too. Longhairs were probably developed by blending the Dachshund with the Cocker Spaniel, and the longhaired Dachsie has something of the Spaniel about him. Crazy for the hunt, the longhair has the endurance of a Spaniel in the field, but he's also crazy for your attention and loves to cuddle. Longhairs like nothing better than to have you stroke that long, luxurious coat, and you may sometimes wonder if they have Velcro under all that hair because they practically stick to you.

The longhaired Dachshund's hair isn't naturally the same length all over. The longest hair grows on the Dachshund's underside — on the throat and chest — as well as on the ears and behind the legs. You should groom longhairs to accentuate the areas where the hair is long, smooth, silky, and flowing. However, the longhair should never look messy, and the coat should lie smooth and flat instead of appearing curly or in any way inelegant.

The wirehaired

If you like Terriers, you'll love the wirehaired Dachshund. Obviously influenced by Terrier stock, the wirehair takes the Terrier characteristics of the Dachshund to the max. Although all Dachsies make great earth dogs, who better to maneuver through the bracken than a dog with a wiry coat that is impervious to wind, rain, burrs, and brush? Add to that the wirehair's feisty spirit and a bark that can cow any small creature into submission, and you've got a great hunter — not to mention a pet that will keep you laughing.

Wirehairs shed the least but require a fairly extensive grooming regimen several times a year. Their coats must be *stripped,* a process in which the loose, dead undercoat is plucked out to make room for new growth. Some people like to do this process themselves, but others would rather pay a groomer.

Wirehairs have a distinctive look. They're typically groomed to keep their eyebrows and beard long. The rest of the coat stays short. Wirehairs also have a distinctive personality. You want to see energy? Obstinacy? Hilarity? Wirehairs have it all. They are little extremists, always on the go, always vocalizing their opinions, and always ready for a game of catch or a romp around the yard. They are plenty cuddly, too, so don't be surprised to find your wirehair under the covers at your feet when you retire for the night.

Those Terrier genes

Many different Terriers probably contributed to the dog we know today as the wirehaired Dachshund. Get to know a few Scottish Terriers, Skye Terriers, Cairn Terriers, Dandie Dinmont Terriers, and Wirehaired Fox Terriers, and you may start to feel like you've become acquainted with your dog's cousins.

A Dachshund Rainbow: Your Color and Pattern Options

Color and pattern are subjects of some controversy among Dachshund people, but they probably matter the least in terms of choosing a pet. You like red? Black and tan? Cream? Double dapple? Fine. If you find a dog in the color you like, great. Color and pattern don't influence personality, so the choice is purely aesthetic.

Some breeders like to breed for certain colors and patterns, however, and color genetics is an interesting subject, although beyond the scope of this book. Suffice it to say that Dachshunds can come in just about any color typical of dogs and can also come in several different patterns. Wirehairs tend to come in fewer colors, one of the more common being a color called *wild boar*, which means that the shorter undercoat is lighter and that the longer outer coat is black.

Color genetics is a subject well known to good Dachshund breeders but not of much concern for the pet owner. Color genetics concerns itself with the *genes*, or parts of the chromosomes, that affect what color and pattern a dog will be. Each gene has several versions, called *alleles*, and each allele can be dominant or recessive. The dominant allele determines which color and pattern show up on the dog — in other words, its *phenotype*. The particular combination of dominant and recessive alleles determines the dog's *genotype*, or gene profile. In case you, like, wanted to know.

Color and pattern are two different things. For the sake of clarity, check out the following sections for a description of the colors and patterns that most typically occur in Dachshunds. Any color can occur in any pattern, but some are more typical than others. For example, the red and cream shades are typically solid; and black, chocolate, and Isabella (a silvery gray) usually come with tan points on the eyebrows, chin, feet, and tail (and sometimes in other places).

Although a silvery Isabella and tan Dachshund or a double-dappled Dachshund may attract more attention around the neighborhood than your typical black and tan Dachsie, keep in mind that color and pattern make no difference when it comes to personality. Actually, I need to qualify that statement: Some breeders may get a little carried away experimenting with colors and patterns. If a breeder breeds for colors and patterns with little regard for health and temperament, a dog's personality can be influenced for the worse. Look for a breeder who's knowledgeable about color genetics but puts health and temperament first and foremost as a breeding priority. Then check out your color and pattern options. And remember: Beauty is as beauty does. That plain old red Dachshund might make the best friend you've ever known, and be the most beautiful dog in the world in your eyes.

The Dachsie color wheel

Dachshunds come in many different colors and color combinations. The more typical colors are usually more successful in the show ring. Here's the color scoop:

- ✔ **Red (in various shades).** Some shades of red look pretty much like brown, but Dachshund people still call these dogs red.

- ✔ **Wheaten.** This is really just a very light red.

- ✔ **Cream.** Cream Dachshunds can range from gold to almost white.

- ✔ **Wild boar.** This is a double color common on wirehaired Dachshunds. The shorter, softer undercoat is lighter in color, and the longer, dense, wiry outer coat is black.

- ✔ **Sable.** This is a rare inheritable color reserved for longhairs. Similar to the wild boar coat in the wirehairs, the sable coat is marked like a black and tan coat, but up close you can see that under the black base coat is a layer of red. In some dogs, the tan points on the face are so exaggerated that they appear to form a mask around the eyes or a widow's peak on the forehead.

    Sometimes a Dachshund puppy appears to be sable in color, but all evidence of the sable coloration disappears by the time the puppy is a year old, at which point the color is clearly a solid red. These puppies aren't really sable and shouldn't be registered as such. If your puppy looks like a sable, delay registration until he grows up, to be sure that you list the color correctly.

- ✔ **Black and tan.** This common color combination is found on many dogs, from Rottweilers and Dobermans to Chihuahuas. The Dachshund is black with tan points.

- ✔ **Chocolate and tan.** This combo is just like black and tan, but the base color on the Dachshund is a chocolate-brown color.

- ✔ **Fawn and tan.** The base color on these dogs is a yellowy-brown, which is lighter and redder than in the chocolates. The points are tan.

- ✔ **Isabella and tan.** Isabella is a silvery gray color, like the color of the Weimeraner breed (those dogs popularized by photographer William Wegman, whose own dogs frequently appear on Sesame Street). Isabella is the base color; the points are tan. Some people call Isabella "blue," or describe it as bluish-gray.

A marked difference: The patterns

In addition to having different colors, Dachshunds can have different patterns, or markings. From solid to double-dappled, Dachshund markings have no influence on a dog's personality, only her appearance. Pick what you like or don't worry about it at all. The subtleties are really only relevant to breeders and dog-show judges. Here are the patterns:

- ✔ **Solid.** A solid color is really an absence of markings instead of a marking itself. Solid means the whole dog is one color. The most common solid color is red, followed by wheaten, and cream.

- ✔ **Solid with points.** Black, chocolate, fawn, and Isabella (silver-gray, sometimes described as blue-gray) dogs commonly have tan points on their eyebrows, chin, feet, and tail.

- ✔ **Dappled.** Dappling, also called merling, is a pattern in which random, ragged patches of a lighter color (not white) occur over a darker color. Any color can have dappling on it, and the dappled patches are typically a lighter shade of the base color.

- ✔ **Double-dappled.** A double-dappled Dachshund (can you say *that* ten times really fast?) is a dappled Dachshund that also has random patches of white.

Dapples come in many colors. Black and tan-dappled Dachsies are dappled with gray. Reds are dappled with lighter red. Chocolates are dappled with cream. Isabella and tan-dappled Dachsies are dappled with a lighter silver-gray. The double-dappled dog has white patches in addition to the colored dappling. In the extreme, these dogs are called *piebald* and have very large patches of white, which is usually considered undesirable.

- ✔ **Brindled.** Brindling is a striped pattern. The stripes are typically thin and somewhat ragged, not clear and sharp like a tiger's.

- ✔ **Piebald.** Typically, the presence of white on a Dachshund is discouraged, and in a piebald pattern, the dog exhibits large patches of white. Some breeders don't like this pattern because they suspect that it could be the result of introducing Beagles into the line. Piebald Dachshunds are disqualified in competition in every country except the United States. But although a piebald Dachshund can compete in the show ring in the United States, not everyone is happy about it.

The problem with piebald and double-dappled

The piebald pattern on Dachshunds is a disqualification from the show ring in all countries except the United States. In the States, many breeders discourage its perpetuation because it is associated with certain health problems. Many piebald and/or double-dappled Dachshunds are stillborn. If not, they may be born blind or deaf or with very small eyes or without any eyes, and they typically have shortened lifespans. Ethical breeders don't purposely attempt to produce a double-dappled or piebald Dachshund.

The Battle of the Sexes

You need to decide whether you want a boy or a girl. In some breeds, gender seems to make a difference. You hear that the boys are sweeter and more affectionate or that the girls are gentler and better with kids — or that either is more standoffish, yippy, aggressive, or independent.

Some breeders describe Dachshunds as *bitch-dominant,* meaning the females are sometimes more independent or seem less needy than the males (something common in many smaller breeds, I've found). But others claim there's no difference. Generally, both sexes are equally sweet, equally stubborn, and equally devoted. Females cost more to spay than males cost to neuter, but this is a one-time expense and probably shouldn't figure into your decision.

It's best to find a healthy, well-bred litter and then see which puppy you feel a connection with. Or better yet, let the puppy pick you, with the breeder's guidance. (The breeder can also help you find a puppy whose temperament best matches your lifestyle.) Boy or girl really doesn't matter. The match between you and the puppy is the most important thing, and either sex may be better suited for you.

Although gender doesn't affect personality, it becomes more of a factor when you bring home two Dachshunds. Unneutered males and unspayed females may not get along with the same sex but may get along perfectly with a dog of the opposite sex. Of course, that means you risk the chance of becoming a breeder without meaning to. But *you're* going to neuter or spay your dog or dogs anyway, aren't you? Don't delay.

The Big Priority

The bottom line? All the cosmetic considerations don't really matter all that much. *Health and temperament, health and temperament, health and temperament.* Make it your mantra as you visit breeders and meet puppies and their parents. The best puppies have two healthy parents — better yet, four healthy grandparents besides. They are raised in a home with people by a breeder who makes an effort to socialize them. They are given proper medical care from the beginning of their lives and are bred to exhibit the classic Dachshund personality: fun, funny, feisty, fearless, and fantastic. Need I say more?

Chapter 4

Where to Find Your Dachshund

Ready to go Dachshund hunting? Because Dachshunds are popular, they're easy to find. The trick is that well-bred, healthy dogs with great temperaments aren't the only ones out there. Unfortunately, disreputable breeders often churn out dogs for profits. Just seeing an adorable Mini Dachshund in a pet store window doesn't mean your search is over. You have some more work to do, and this stuff's important. It's time to track down the right Dachshund for you.

Fortunately, in addition to the many disreputable and unethical sources for dogs, great Dachshund breeders also abound. A good Dachshund breeder is absolutely crazy for his or her beloved breed and is working in whatever way possible to ensure that Dachshunds get better and better — in health, looks, and temperament. How do you know the good breeder from the not-so-good breeder? Well, that's what this chapter is about. (Chapter 5 covers how to get your poochie from other reputable sources.)

Forming a Solid Bond with Your Dachsie Breeder

Finding a good breeder is like finding gold in them-thar hills. Not only do you benefit right now, but you and your Dachshund benefit for the rest of your lives — if you play your cards right, invest in your breeder, and proceed wisely. Once you find a good Dachshund breeder, forge a partnership. Good breeders are happy to provide you with all the information you need, and most are excited to continue the relationship. If a problem comes up, the breeder can guide you. If the dog gets sick or develops a problem, the breeder can tell you what course of action to take.

Breeders love, more than anything, to be able to keep abreast of how your dog is doing. Holiday cards, an occasional call, and a visit to a dog show are all ways you can cement your relationship with your breeder, which enables you to maintain and nurture this valuable source of information.

Most great breeders have been in the Dachshund business a long, long time. They know things most Dachshund owners don't know, as well as things most Dachshund owners don't need to know. But what if your dog is getting too fat or is suddenly yelping in pain when you touch her or becomes inexplicably irritable and snappy or stops eating? You can call your vet, and in most cases, you should call your vet first. But a breeder may be able to shed additional light on the situation. Call the breeder next.

This advice doesn't mean, of course, that you should harass your breeder. Breeders have lives — usually pretty busy ones, at that. Because responsible dog breeding is not a profit-making venture, most breeders are in it purely for the love of Dachshunds, and so they have to hold regular jobs, too. They also often have families, take their dogs to dog shows on weekends, and generally have a tough time getting a full night's rest when they have a litter of puppies in the house! They don't have time to talk to you on the phone every day, nursing you through your Dachshund's puppyhood trials and tribulations. That's why doing your research and becoming fully prepared for the responsibility of puppy ownership is so important.

That said, your Dachshund's breeder is also invested in making sure that all of his or her pups have good, healthy, happy, long, satisfying lives, so if your breeder can help, he or she will. The following tips can help you maintain a good relationship with your Dachshund's breeder, ensuring that you, the breeder, and, most importantly, your Dachshund receive the maximum benefit of your commitment and the breeder's experience:

- ✔ Don't call the breeder early in the morning or late at night. Your breeder has a life.

- ✔ When you call, be polite, not demanding. Express your awareness that you're taking up the breeder's time instead of taking the attitude that the breeder is there to serve you.

- ✔ If the problem involves pain, bleeding, broken bones, or drastic changes in habits, appetite, activity level, or behavior, please call your vet first — and fast.

- ✔ Don't assume that the breeder is at fault for a medical problem. An accusatory tone puts anyone on the defensive. Explain what's going on and make sure, *before* you buy, that you have in place a health guarantee that makes arrangements for what will happen in the event of a health problem.

✔ Recognize that your breeder loved your puppy first and helped to bring it into the world. The breeder is more family than business associate.

✔ Good breeders aren't out to make a profit, and that high price only seems high. Your breeder probably just barely covers expenses, and many don't even do that. Plus, most breeders find that higher prices help to screen out impulse purchases and people who aren't really serious about the commitment involved in pet ownership.

✔ Your Dachshund's breeder, if he or she is a good one, truly loves Dachshunds and has devoted his or her life to the betterment of the breed. Acknowledge and respect the breeder's efforts.

✔ If the breeder in question shows any signs of being in it only for the money, not being straightforward, or being in any way dishonest, run the other way and don't look back (and don't even look at the puppies!). It isn't worth your time to try to develop a good relationship.

Some breeders aren't worth your time, no matter how cute the puppies. If a breeder tells you one thing on the phone but you find something else when you visit, if the terms of a sale change when the breeder learns more about you (perhaps the dogs suddenly become more expensive when the breeder sees your sports car, or the one you want suddenly isn't available but a smaller, sicker one is conveniently on sale), or if you get any kind of bad feeling about the situation, trust your intuition and move on. No matter how cute and/or cheap the puppies are, dealing with a disreputable or irresponsible breeder isn't worth the price.

Finding the right breeder

So how do you find these gems, these breeders who love Dachshunds and devote their lives to making Dachshunds stronger, healthier, and more beautiful? You do a little research, and you ask for help. Many local and national Dachshund clubs exist and will provide you with referrals to breeders they've found to be good ones. If you have Internet access, your job will be easier. Here are a few information sources to try:

✔ The Dachshund Club of America (DCA). Check out the DCA's Web site, which lists breeder referral contacts by state, at `www.dachshund-dca.org/referral%20folder/state_ref.html`. Or contact breeder referral coordinator Jere Mitternight at 504-835-1025 between 8 a.m. and 6 p.m. Central Time. Jere's e-mail address is `jerem@juno.com`. Also check out `www.dachshund-dca.org/clubs.html` for a list of local branches of the national club. A club in your area may be able to give you the most relevant information.

✔ Check out the Wiener Dog page, created by Bob Brennert, at `www.dachshund.bc.ca/mainpage.html`. This page has an ask-a-breeder section where you can e-mail your questions to experienced Dachshund breeders, and it also has a listing of Dachshund breeders in Canada.

Another great way to find a great breeder is by visiting a dog show or two. Dog shows concentrate breeders all in one place for your browsing convenience. Ask around and see what names you hear over and over. What kennel names have a great reputation? Who is great in your area?

You can also ask breeders any other Dachshund questions, from the price of a healthy pet to the best diet for a Miniature. But beware: You may get bitten by the bug and want to buy a champion and start showing. An obedience or agility match can be great fun, too, because you can see the Dachshunds in action. You may even find that you want to get involved in these activities with your new dog. (For more info on fun activities you can do with your Dachshund, take a look at Chapter 15.)

After you pinpoint breeders you think may work, you're ready for the big interview. Visit *several* kennels (even if you think you've found your dream Dachsie at the very first place you visit). Ask questions. Look at the puppies, the parents, and the surroundings. Watch how the puppies interact and how they behave toward you and the breeder.

Note that the great thing about visiting a dog show is that you can do some preliminary interviewing right there, if you find several possible candidates. You can't see the actual kennel, but you can look at the puppies and sometimes the parents, and you can ask the breeders just about anything. Just whip out your Great Dachsie Breeder Checklist (see the following section) and start checking off boxes.

Here are a few red flags to watch for when visiting a breeder: the puppies shy away from the breeder, the adult dogs other than the mother don't seem approachable or act nervous, the surroundings are very dirty, the breeder avoids certain questions or refuses to let you see the parents of a litter, the breeder is eager to have you take home a puppy younger than 6 or 7 weeks, or the dogs look too thin or sickly.

Using the Great Dachsie Breeder Checklist

Wondering what to ask a breeder to figure out whether he or she is breeding responsibly and producing healthy puppies? You don't have to be a detective. Just bring along my Great Dachsie Breeder Checklist to every kennel and dog show you visit and don't be afraid to ask the breeders you meet every question. You can learn a lot by the answers, and you can also learn a lot by what the breeder doesn't — or won't — tell you, too.

Here you go — the Great Dachsie Breeder Checklist:

✔ **What do I need to know about Dachshunds in general and about your Dachshunds in particular?**

You've probably done lots of research by this point, but you still want to know what the breeder has to tell you about the breed. Listen for a couple of things: Does the breeder seem very knowledgeable about Dachshunds, or does the breeder tell you only very general things you already know? Does the breeder only tell you the good side of the breed, or does he or she let you know about the challenging aspects of Dachshund ownership? Also, the breeder should be able to give you a good idea about the specific dogs and lines of his or her kennel. What are the specific strengths and weaknesses of his or her particular dogs?

✔ **How long have you been breeding Dachshunds?**

Find out how the breeder got started, too. If the breeder has been in it for decades, you've probably found somebody established and very knowledgeable. A breeder new to the game may also be good, have great intentions, and be producing great pups. But lots of people try breeding and give it up, so a breeder who has stood the test of time may be a better bet.

✔ **How often do you breed?**

A breeder in it for 20 years who has only bred a handful of litters won't have 20 years of experience. On the other hand, a breeder in the business for a few years who has already bred 100 litters is probably going for profit, not quality, and chances are, the dogs aren't kept in very good conditions.

✔ **What is your philosophy of dog breeding?**

You can expect as many answers to this one as there are Dachshund breeders, but asking this question gives you a little insight into what the breeder is all about. No breeder is going to say, "Oh, well, you know, I'm just in it for the cold hard cash." But breeders who get all passionate about improving the health of the breed and enhancing the Dachshund's friendly and agreeable temperament — or who say things like "All my dogs would make great pets because, to me, *pet quality* means the highest possible quality" — are probably going to be sources for excellent pets.

✔ **Have any of your dogs suffered from canine intervertebral disk disease? What are the chances my dog will get it?**

If a breeder answers that yes, he or she has had dogs with disk disease, that's no reason to run. In fact, that means the breeder is being honest. Although some breeders have certainly been able to keep their lines largely free of this disease, it's so common in Dachshunds that most breeders who have been in the business for a long period of time have seen it. Look for a breeder who is straightforward about disk disease. Honesty is much more important than waiting for a breeder to tell you, "In 35 years, none of my Dachshunds have ever had back problems." Chances are, if you hear that, you aren't getting the whole truth.

Breeders shouldn't breed Dachshunds that experience canine intervertebral disk disease. Sounds like a clear-cut rule. However, because disk problems don't typically manifest themselves until the average age of 4 years, and because no test is available to determine which dogs will suffer from it, Dachshunds are sometimes bred and then later develop back problems through no fault of the breeder.

✔ **May I call your veterinarian for a reference?**

A breeder who won't give you the number of his or her vet either doesn't want you to know something or doesn't visit the vet very often. Both are bad signs. Better to have a breeder who takes puppies and dogs to the vet often than to have a breeder whose dogs are "so healthy they don't need a vet." All dogs need periodic, regular vet visits, and good breeders make sure they get them. If your breeder is happy to give you his or her vet's contact information, call the vet and ask about the health and temperament of that breeder's dogs. The vet has no personal stake in whether or not the breeder sells a puppy, so assuming that the vet is also a good one, you should get an unbiased view.

✔ **What kind of health guarantee do you offer?**

Good breeders require that you take your puppy to a vet right away, usually within three to seven days of when you bring the puppy home. If the veterinarian finds a serious health problem, the breeder should be willing to refund your money or replace the puppy. Of course, you may not want to give up the puppy, and you may be willing to do whatever it takes to get your puppy through whatever health crisis has arisen. But the breeder should make amends if you so desire. Get it in writing.

✔ **What vaccinations does the puppy have already, and what will I need to do in terms of future health care?**

The breeder should have given the puppy at least one set of standard vaccinations and should give you a schedule of vaccinations to be administered by your vet. If you decide to adopt a dog with special care needs, the breeder should give you any relevant information. Also, be sure to get the name and number of the breeder's vet so that your vet can call the breeder's vet to find out what has been done so you don't have it done twice. Overvaccinating isn't good for your puppy.

✔ **I plan to keep this puppy forever. If something comes up, however, that makes it impossible for me to keep the puppy at any time in the future, will you take it back?**

Not all breeders will do so, but many will because they care just as much that their puppies find and remain in a good home as you care about finding the right puppy. That doesn't mean you'll get a refund ten years later, and you shouldn't expect it. But breeders who truly love their Dachsies will want them back rather than have them end up in a shelter or rescue program. Of course, you do plan to keep the puppy forever, don't you? A commitment on your part is as necessary as a good health guarantee, and the breeder will be looking for signs that you'll be a responsible and committed puppy owner.

✔ **When can I take the puppy home?**

Most breeders won't let you take a puppy home until it's at least 8 weeks old. Six weeks is simply too young, especially for a small dog. The ideal time to adopt your puppy is between 10 and 12 weeks of age. Between the 9th and 12th week, puppies learn to interact with their littermates, building a healthy foundation for future interaction with other dogs and possibly even facilitating future socialization efforts on your part. Even if the breeder says you can take your puppy home at 6 weeks (and I'd be a bit wary of a breeder who would suggest this), you may want to wait until it's 10 to 12 weeks. In addition to the benefits of sticking by their littermates, puppies get important immune benefits from nursing longer. Reserve your puppy, put down a deposit, and wait it out.

✔ **What sizes are your dogs?**

Because Miniature Dachshunds are popular, some breeders try to pass off *tweenies*, or small Standards, as Miniatures. Technically, a Miniature Dachshund is a dog that weighs 11 pounds or less at 1 year of age. Since you're probably buying a puppy, you can't know absolutely for certain that your dog will grow up to be a true Miniature. However, experienced breeders can usually tell whether a puppy is going to be a true Miniature. The average Standard puppy is about 8.5 ounces at birth, although some can be as big as 13 ounces. A Miniature puppy is much smaller. The best way to tell that your puppy will be a true Miniature is to see *both* parents. Ask to have them weighed in front of you. If both are true Minis, chances are good that your puppy will be, too, especially if the puppy's pedigree has lots of champions. Lots of champions in your puppy's pedigree means the line is probably breeding true, and your puppy will be more likely to look like its parents.

Dachshund prices can vary by geographical region, as well as by how closely a Dachshund pup fits the breed standard. Expect to pay between $400 to $800 for a well-bred pet.

✔ **May I see some of your other dogs?**

A breeder should be proud to show you his or her dogs. Look for good health and friendly temperament. The dogs should be approachable and easygoing. The breeder should be able to take any of the adult dogs out on a lead, and you should be able to go up to it and pet it without the dog displaying any growling, shying away, or nipping. These are serious signs of temperament problems in healthy adult dogs. One important exception: There's a part of the breed standard that says the Dachshund should be bold to the point of brashness. This characteristic makes the new mothers pretty protective, so if the mother of the litter you like doesn't seem to want you to get within a six-foot radius of her precious babies, don't be alarmed. That's just nature in action.

Don't think that you'll be doing all the interviewing. A good breeder will screen you just as carefully as you screen him or her. Expect to be asked where you plan to keep your dog, why you want a dog, and if you can afford a dog. And get ready for a lecture on the responsibilities of pet ownership. The buyer who has done research and is open to instruction, and who truly seems to bond with a puppy, will look like a good prospect to the breeder.

Last of all, keep your eyes open for signs that things are as they should be:

- ✔ Kennels should be clean. A few puppy piles are perfectly natural. The breeder can't chase the dogs around all day, scooping up every pile as soon as it lands on the ground. Many breeders' homes are sometimes a little worn, too. Lots of puppies means lots of wear and tear. But things should be generally clean, you shouldn't smell any rank odors, and you should have the impression that the environment is cleaned and disinfected on a regular basis.

- ✔ If the breeder seems to have more dogs than he or she can handle and socialize, or if the dogs are kept outside in lots of little cages and don't seem to have the opportunity to run around free or go in the house, or if you get the impression the dogs rarely see humans, move on.

- ✔ The dogs should seem happy, friendly, and fond of the breeder. Also, they're Dachshunds, so they should bark.

- ✔ You should have a good feeling about the breeder. Trust your intuition. If you just don't feel right about something, even if you can't put it into words, go with your feelings and keep looking. Unfortunately, not everyone is trustworthy or honest. If, on the other hand, you feel very comfortable with the breeder and believe he or she is honest and working in the best interest of the dogs, you're probably right. Gut feelings don't often lie, but pay attention to all the signs so your intuition can work for you.

There's no dog like a show dog

Think you're buying a show dog? Technically, if a breeder sells you a show dog, that only means your dog is guaranteed not to have any disqualifying faults, and Dachshunds don't have many disqualifying faults. The dog should have a scissors bite, and its front legs shouldn't knuckle over. The body shouldn't hang loosely in the middle, and the dog shouldn't be shy. That's about it. If you ask to see the dog's pedigree, and there's one champion four generations back, but the breeder is charging more than other breeders in the area, look elsewhere.

Getting the Real Scoop on Contracts

Any lawyer would cringe if you said you bought an $800 dog without a contract, but not all breeders use contracts. Breeders get a sense about buyers, and vice versa, and if everyone feels good about the purchase of a pet, both you and the breeder may feel a contract is an unnecessary formality. For a show dog extraordinaire or a puppy of champion parentage that you plan to breed, sure, a contract makes sense. But do you really need one for a little puppy-dog pet?

You bet. Okay, I've bought expensive things without a contract — even leased a house without one. (Don't tell my lawyer.) And maybe you don't want to bother with the legal mumbo jumbo. But a contract can really prove invaluable if something goes wrong. What if your puppy has parvovirus and dies six days after you bring it home? What if you go to the breeder and demand your money back, and you get a big fat "Too bad!" What if your dog turns out to be deaf, but you don't find out for a couple of months? What if you bring your dog home, only to find out it has a dangerous temperament and inflicts serious injury on your child? If you screen your breeder carefully and go with your instincts, chances are, none of these things will happen. But they could. Better to be protected.

Both you and the breeder are protected by a contract. The contract should state, in very specific terms, what happens if something goes wrong and what kinds of things are whose responsibility. For instance, the contract could state that if your dog is injured while in your care, the breeder isn't responsible. Or, if the dog gets sick with something it contracted while with the breeder or suffers from some serious genetic problem, the breeder is responsible. The contract should also mention

- That if something goes wrong, the responsible party should have a certain specified amount of time to correct the problem. This setup prevents either you or the breeder from rushing off to sue the moment something happens to someone's dissatisfaction.

- What laws will apply. If you and the breeder live in different states, the contract should say what state has jurisdiction should a conflict arise.

- What constitutes correction of the problem. Will you get your money back, or will you get a replacement puppy, or will the choice be up to you? If you want to keep the dog and pay to have a genetic problem corrected or an illness treated, will the breeder help you with the costs?

In general, contracts aren't a sign that you don't trust someone, and no good breeder should be offended if you ask for one. Most probably already have a contract they always use. Contracts are simply a way to protect you and the breeder. Sure, contracts can be broken, but if they are legal and well written, you have recourse if you suffer a loss.

Picking a Pup: How to Choose Your Pick of the Litter

Once the terms of the deal are set, all you have left to do is pick a puppy. But how do you know which one to pick? They're all so cute (see Figure 4-1). Is one as good as the next?

Yes and no. All the puppies up for sale in a well-bred litter will probably make great pets. In some cases, however, the temperament and tendencies of a particular puppy may turn out to be best suited to you. Who knows the litter best? The breeder, of course.

Tempted by that shy or incredibly sleepy puppy — the one that's smaller than all the rest? You may be able to nurse it back to health, but excessive fatigue, lack of energy, or unusual shyness may all be signs that your puppy isn't thriving. You may be asking for heartbreak. Let the breeder handle that puppy and choose a healthy one instead.

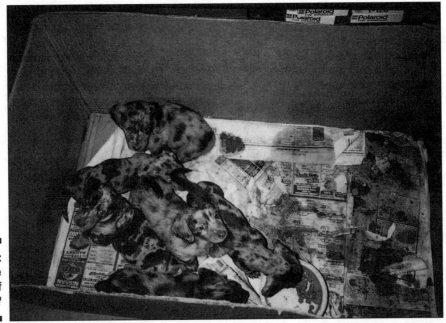

Figure 4-1: Which one is the pick of the litter?

Photo courtesy of Sonja Rusche.

Signs of a healthy pup

Wondering how to spot a healthy Dachshund puppy? Look for a healthy coat with no bald patches; bright, shiny eyes that don't run; clean, white, sharp puppy teeth; clean ears that are free of parasites; a clean rear end with no encrusted feces; free and easy movement with no limping; and a healthy display of energy and curiosity.

The breeder can be an invaluable resource in helping you pick the puppy that will best match you and your situation. Good breeders get to know their puppies as they care for them, socialize them, and teach them the ropes of life in a human world. The breeder will know which ones tend to be more boisterous, which are quieter, which love to fetch, which seem fond of cats, and which seem to adore kids. Let your breeder help you pick.

Of course, sometimes you'll see one particular puppy, and you'll know that he's the one. Or perhaps the puppy will choose you. You can't argue with chemistry. If you bond with a particular pup, and he's healthy and well bred, and if the breeder agrees that the match would be a good one, go for it. You've found your friend.

Chapter 5

Rescue Me!

In Chapter 4, I talk a lot about breeders, and good breeders are great. But as you probably already know, buying a Dachshund puppy from a breeder isn't your only option. Many Dachshunds are waiting in breed rescue programs, in animal shelters, and with families who can't keep them any longer. Many of these dogs are wonderful, devoted, well-trained family members who got the short end of the dog bone for one reason or another and no longer have a place to go. This chapter points you in their direction.

On the other hand, some dogs are in rescue programs or shelters because their owners thought they were more trouble than they were worth. These dogs may or may not be reformable, but even if they are, are you up to the task? This chapter helps you find out.

Adopting a Dachsie Makes You a Friend for Life

Adopting a rescued or animal-shelter Dachshund can be one of the most rewarding things you ever do. People who've adopted such dogs often claim that their dogs seem eternally and exuberantly grateful throughout their entire lives. Do the dogs know what you've done for them? Maybe not in so many words, but a dog who has lost her home and then finds one with you will probably be as devoted a dog as you will find.

A rescue program's reason for being

According to the DCA's rescue program, Dachshund rescue is active around the country and was established

"... to aid Dachshund owners in the recovery of their animals when lost, strayed or stolen; to keep Dachshunds out of the hands of laboratories, animal dealers, puppy mills and similar enterprises, and to attempt to keep dachshunds out of pounds and animal shelters. Sadly, Rescue is most used to place the hundreds of Dachshunds that have been abandoned each year and find homes that will provide the love and care these dogs deserve."

Help out the rescue program if you can, and if you can't, at least don't make the problem worse by abandoning a dog you've promised to keep.

Of course, not every rescued or shelter dog comes pretrained, presocialized, and ready to accept you without question. Some were abused. Some weren't well trained or socialized in the first place. Some may be sick or have a health problem of some kind. Some were badly bred in the first place. Some, unfortunately, won't ever make good pets because they have too many strikes against them.

But it doesn't hurt to look, and chances are the Dachshund you find in the animal shelter or with a rescue group will make a great pet. Even if you know you want a Dachshund puppy from a great breeder, you may consider visiting an animal shelter and/or calling your local Dachshund rescue organization. (Call the AKC or the DCA for the names of rescue groups in your area; Appendix B has the contact information.) There are distinct advantages to adopting an older dog (most rescued or shelter Dachshunds aren't new puppies, although there are exceptions). Older dogs may already be housetrained, which is one major hurdle you can avoid. They may already love kids, and they may even know a trick or two. These dogs want nothing more than a loving home. Maybe you can provide one.

Looking at the Pros and Cons of Adopting a Dachsie

Before you run right out and sign the papers to adopt a rescued or shelter Dachshund, put some serious thought into it. There are pros and cons to adopting a Dachshund, and you need to weigh them against your own situation and inclinations before making a commitment. The very last thing a rescued or shelter Dachshund needs is to think he has a new home and then to end up back in rescue or in the shelter again. Adopting any dog means being very committed to keeping that dog until the end of his life. Someone has already broken that commitment to the dog at least once, which is why the Dachshund is waiting for a home. Don't do it to the poor dog again.

Table 5-1 lists the pros and cons involved in adopting a rescued or shelter Dachshund. Look over the list again and again. Give the matter serious thought. Listen to your heart and to your head. You may feel awfully sorry for that Dachshund, but if what you really, really want is a puppy from a breeder, everyone will be better off if you get your new dog there.

Table 5-1	The Pros and Cons of an Adopted Dachsie
The Pros	**The Cons**
He may already be housetrained.	She may never have been housetrained, and older dogs make a bigger mess.
She may already be accustomed to family life, love kids, and understand your routine.	He may never have been socialized and may be frightened of — even aggressive toward — children or strangers.
He may be eternally devoted to you for taking him in.	She may have suffered so much in the past that she's not capable of bonding with you.
She may already be trained to obey basic commands.	He may be more difficult to train, and you may need to hire a professional trainer or canine behavioral consultant.
He may come with lots of good habits already in place.	She may come with lots of bad habits already in place.
She costs less than a dog from a breeder.	He may not be as well bred as a Dachshund from a breeder, and he may suffer from health, conformation, or temperament problems.
He may be the best pet you could ever dream of.	Your experience with her may be a nightmare of massive vet bills and training traumas.

You may think that Table 5-1 leaves a lot up in the air. How do you know which way your dog will be? Housetrained or not? Well socialized or not? Kid lover or not? Healthy or not? Will your Dachsie be a lifelong companion like the one in Figure 5-1.

Fortunately, rescue organizations and many animal shelters carefully screen the Dachshunds they're attempting to place, so they can usually tell you what they've observed about the Dachshund's behavior and temperament, as well as his health status. Take advantage of the people who know and ask a lot of questions. They also want to know that they're placing the dog with someone who won't bring him right back in a couple of days.

Figure 5-1:
Will your adopted Dachsie be a kid lover like this one?

Photo courtesy of Gail Painter.

Although some people are reluctant to adopt a rescued or shelter Dachshund because they don't want to "take on somebody else's problem," many Dachshunds are relinquished to rescue groups and animal shelters due to problems that had nothing to do with them. Common causes for abandonment are divorce, a death in the family, a move to a place that doesn't allow dogs, or an owner who simply can't handle the responsibility. Many of these dogs are friendly, sweet, and well behaved, and they need only a loving home to make their lives — and your life — complete.

Using Dachshund Rescue Organizations

Animal shelters sometimes have Dachshunds, but your best bet is to contact a local or regional Dachshund rescue organization. These organizations are manned by people who work long hours, usually for no pay, purely for the love of Dachshunds — to find a good home for every Dachshund they believe would make a good pet. But the job is stressful and often frustrating. It can also be supremely rewarding, however, when a dog finally finds the perfect place to live.

If you contact a Dachshund rescue organization, please be considerate. These people usually work out of their homes, so find out what time zone they're in and don't call early in the morning or late at night. Many rescue people have a phone message that allows you to leave your number, but they'll call you back collect. Don't be offended. Remember, they aren't getting paid, and if they had to pay for every returned phone call, their phone bills would get pretty hefty. Give them a break and accept the collect call.

Once you hook up with a Dachshund rescue, you'll probably find a fantastic network of Dachshund lovers eager to help you help the displaced Dachshunds of the world. And The cause can be compelling. You may find yourself deciding to be a Dachshund foster home or otherwise involved in Dachshund rescue. There are worse ways to spend your free time.

Find rescue coordinators by state through the DCA's Web site. Check out `http://dachshund-dca.org/Rescue%20folder/RescuebyState.html` or call the AKC in New York at (212) 696-8200, or check their Web site for the most updated information on Dachshund rescue. The AKC's Dachshund page can be found at `www.akc.org/breeds/recbreeds/dach.cfm` and their list of national breed club rescue networks is at `http://www.akc.org/breeds/rescue.cfm`.

Some rescued Dachshunds have been abused or neglected and may need some patient, kind, positive retraining and behavior modification. If you're determined not to give up on your rescued Dachshund (and I hope you are), be prepared to exercise supreme patience and exhibit lots of affection. Also consider hiring a canine behavioral consultant, an animal behaviorist, and/or a private trainer. These professionals have experience with dogs that have been mistreated and can provide you with a variety of approaches to your dog's particular problems. Worth every penny.

You can find additional information on the Internet by looking at the following Web sites and contacting the correct people listed via e-mail:

- ✔ The Love A Dox Rescue Page includes a geographical Dachshund Rescue/Referral Contact list to better help you in your search for a Dachshund in need. Find it on the Web at `www.thedachshundnetwork.com/loveadox.htm`.

- ✔ E-mail Karen Henry at the Dallas Fort-Worth Dachshund Rescue Foundation, Inc., `KLHenry@ix.netcom.com`, to request an adoption application. Or contact a club representative by phone at 972-516-4329 if you live in Texas. A representative will discuss your request with you, and, if appropriate, the rep will mail you an application. For more information, check out the foundation's Web site at `http://lonestar.texas.net/~standi/rescue.html`.

✔ Search for Dachshunds in need of a home in your area, find information about adopting a Dachshund, volunteer to provide a foster home for Dachshunds in your area, and get lots of good information on Dachshunds at the Dachshund Rescue Web Page, at `www.drwp.net/index.html`.

✔ You can also view or add your site to the Dachshund Rescue Web Ring. For information or to enter the Web Ring, surf to `www.geocities.com/ Colosseum/Loge/9606/dachrescue.html`.

Working with Animal Shelters

If you don't have a Dachshund breed rescue program in your town, you probably have an animal shelter. Animal shelters sometimes get Dachshunds, and they may take your name and contact you if they do receive one. Shelter workers, like rescue workers, are overworked and underpaid, though, so don't be surprised if they don't call you. Your best bet is to visit often and keep looking. If nothing else, frequent shelter visits will probably convince you to have your Dachshund spayed or neutered.

Some animal shelters are the spectacular culmination of the efforts of many people who are seriously committed to helping place the dogs they receive and educating the public. Others are barely scraping by on tiny budgets and have a hard time handling the load of animals they receive.

Whatever the case in your area, be aware that adopting a shelter dog often involves a lot of paperwork. You can't usually just walk in and get one. Many shelters check out your living situation by calling your landlord to ensure that he or she allows dogs, for example. Don't be offended by the questions and endless forms. The shelter only wants to feel confident that you won't bring the dog right back in a few weeks or months.

No dogs for college kids

If you're a college student, you may be frustrated to find out that your local animal shelter won't let you adopt a dog under any circumstances. Is that fair? You just know you'd be a fantastic dog owner. Actually, although many college students would make great and committed dog owners, students are notorious for abandoning their animals when they graduate.

So many shelters have been burdened by a huge influx of pets come graduation time year after year that this policy is simply in place to safeguard the well-being of pets. Don't be offended. Be glad the shelter is working in the overall best interest of its animals. You can always adopt a pet after you're settled.

Also, an understaffed shelter may not have the time to screen individual dogs for temperament and health. Buyer beware, in other words. You may get a great dog, and you may get a short-legged, long-bodied bundle of trouble. Best to do your research, trust your intuition, and be prepared for a lot of work, rehabilitation, and retraining. Then, if you get a great pet, you'll be happily surprised.

Adopting a shelter dog is a wonderful — even noble — thing to do. So many dogs desperately need good homes, and most of them won't ever find one. And the dog isn't the only one who benefits. So many people with shelter dogs are devoted to the point of fanaticism to their rescued pets.

Adopting a shelter dog is a serious commitment, so please don't take it lightly. Just because a dog doesn't cost $500 doesn't mean it isn't just as deserving of love, good medical care, and your time. Be ready for a nervous, scared, confused pet that needs a lot of patience, attention, and consistent, kind, positive training. Work with your new friend, and you may just discover that you've got a diamond in the rough.

How Much Is That Dachsie in the Window?

I don't generally recommend buying a Dachshund from a pet store for a few reasons:

- ✔ You can't usually see the puppy's parents.
- ✔ You can't visit the breeder's breeding facility.
- ✔ You can't ask the breeder questions.
- ✔ Most pet store employees don't know as much about individual dog breeds as a breeder.
- ✔ The price is usually higher.

The problem with not being able to see the parents, the breeding facility, or even the breeder is that you can't get a sense as to whether those adorable, tiny little Dachshunds have been socialized at all, raised in healthy conditions, or bred to minimize health problems like disk disease. That Dachsie in the window might turn out to be a wonderful pet, and you may not be able to resist those pleading eyes or that joyous tail wag, but your odds for securing a pet with good health and temperament are better if you buy from a breeder.

A Dachshund for life

Wherever you get your Dachshund, once you've got it, it's yours. Dachshunds live a long time — often 12 to 16 years — and you should plan to keep your new friend through thick and thin, for better or for worse, unless it's absolutely impossible to do so. Dachshunds (and all dogs, for that matter) are living, breathing, sentient beings who form a relationship with you, depend on a regular routine, and look to you for guidance, care, and affection. Although they may be considered *chattel* by legal definition, they are more than property. They feel pain, loss, and neglect if they're hurt, abandoned, or abused. If you take on the responsibility of a dog, take it on for life. Don't let your friend down. And if you absolutely must give up your dog, at least see that it finds a new home where it can receive proper care and love.

However, if you find you simply cannot resist that Dachshund puppy at the pet store (you are only human, after all) and are willing to pay more money for a dog that comes with less background information, at least take a few very important precautions. You won't be able to tell everything from looking — not even a vet can do that. Health problems like disk disease may not become evident for several years (and of course, even well bred Dachshunds sometimes succumb to disk disease). But you can spot some signs that the puppy has been raised in less than ideal conditions:

- ✔ **Get background information.** Your pet store puppy probably won't have parents on the premises, but the store should have a written record of the shots and wormings the puppy has already had. Don't expect to learn much about your puppy's temperament from the pet store, however. The puppy probably hasn't been in the pet store very long, and pet store employees usually aren't trained to determine things like temperament.

- ✔ **Give the puppy a once-over.** Is the coat clean and shiny? Are the puppy's eyes, ears, nose, and rectum clean? Does the puppy act happy and energetic? Red flags include small bald spots, "hot spots" (red, itchy places), dry scaly patches, runny or crusty eyes or nose, dirty ears, a dirty rectum, and tired, slow, low-energy behavior. The puppy could be napping, of course, so come back later in the day to see if the puppy perks up and shows interest in you.

- ✔ **Get the guarantee in writing.** Most pet stores will guarantee their puppies for a certain amount of time, but that time period is often pretty short (a day or two, a week or two). Take the puppy to a vet immediately after purchase with the (written) understanding that, should the vet determine the puppy is in ill health, you may bring it back for a full refund. If you know and accept exactly where the pet store's responsibility begins and ends in terms of a health guarantee, then you won't run into misunderstandings later.

✔ **Make a commitment.** That pet store puppy, like any other puppy, may suffer from health problems later on. That pet store puppy will need lots of socialization, attention, and training. Please make the commitment to care for your Dachshund and give it the care, training, and love it deserves.

Getting Your Vet's Stamp of Approval

Within a few days of bringing home your new Dachshund (preferably within a few hours), take her to your veterinarian. Such a visit is often required to activate a breeder's health guarantee, and many shelters and rescue organizations require it, too. But even if you've adopted a Dachshund for which a vet visit isn't required, that first vet visit is a must.

A vet can alert you to potential problems with your dog, instruct you on proper care, set up a schedule for first-year vaccinations, and even give you training tips and advice on behavior modification. Your vet is an invaluable resource in your dog's care, so take full advantage and visit often. And if your Dachshund has been under the care of another vet before he became yours, get that vet's contact information so your vet can be up to speed on what your Dachshund needs and what has already been done.

If you haven't found a good vet yet, ask your local rescue organization, animal shelter, or even local breeders, who may know which vets are familiar with Dachshunds, for a recommendation. Also talk to friends, especially fellow Dachshund owners, who use their vet for regular check-ups. Although you can always vet-hop if you don't like the one you pick, your best bet, and the best bet for your pet, is to pick someone who receives rave reviews from experienced pet owners and who has a lot of Dachshund experience.

Part II

Introductions: Starting Out on the Right Foot

The 5th Wave   By Rich Tennant

"NAAH- HE'S NOT THAT SMART. THE LAST TIME HE TOOK THE SAT, HE FORGOT TO BRING AN EXTRA PENCIL, CAME UP SHORT IN THE MATH SECTION, AND DROOLED ALL OVER THE TEST BOOKLET."

In this part . . .

You find out how to prepare your home, yourself, and your family for the fun-filled life with a Dachshund. I tell you what things to buy, and I explain what to expect when you bring your wiener-shaped friend home for the first time.

Chapter 6

Dachs-Proofing Your Home

· ·

In This Chapter

▶ Getting the lowdown on how your Dachshund sees the world

▶ Making your home safer for curious puppies, who love to chew and chew and chew

▶ Dealing with stairs and beds and couches and such

· ·

*I*f you've got small children or small siblings, you probably know all about childproofing the house. You cover electrical outlets, put childproof latches on the bottom cabinets, stow all the cleaners and household chemicals out of reach, and put those covers over the doorknobs so the little ones don't open the door and go wandering away.

But how much consideration have you given to puppy-proofing? A new puppy can get into a lot of trouble if the house isn't puppy-proofed, and Dachshunds in particular — who joyfully gnaw through or swallow just about anything they can get their teeth around and who are too short to jump safely from great heights — are particularly in need of a safe, secure, Dachs-proofed household.

How do you Dachs-proof your home? First, you read this chapter. Then you get busy and make a few changes before you let that puppy loose in the house. It only takes a moment for a puppy to get in trouble when you aren't watching, so just as with a baby, better safe than sorry. The extra effort you spend to prepare your home for your newest Dachsie resident is well worth it for everyone.

A Dachs-Eye View

The world looks a lot different to a Dachshund than it does to you. Can you imagine walking around with your eye level less than a foot about the ground? No? Try it. In fact, the best thing to do before you change one single thing about your household in preparation for your new puppy is to get down on your belly and look around each room in your house. (You may want to vacuum first. You'll be sliding around on the floor!)

The danger of choke chains

I don't generally recommend the collars that are often called *choke collars* (one end slips through a loop on the other end so the collar tightens when pulled) because I don't think they're necessary when positive training methods are employed. If you do use them, however, never put one on your puppy while she's unsupervised even for a moment. Reserve choke collars for training sessions only; then remove them. These collars can catch on things, and your puppy can hang herself. Yanking on a choke chain could also damage your Dachshund's delicate spine (not to mention your relationship!).

Find a piece of paper and a pen or pencil; then get on down there. That's it, get right down to the floor. *All* the way down. You're still too tall if you're on your hands and knees. All the way down on your belly.

Now take a good look around: This is a Dachs-eye view of the world.

Now try to think like a Dachshund puppy. Get excited, a little nervous, and very, very curious. From your Dachshund vantage point, what do you see that looks like fun? Ooh, a dangling miniblind cord! Could be perfect for a game of tug of war. Look at that bottle cap under the couch! Feeling the urge to ferret it out and give it a good crunch? What about that nice display of china figurines, almost within reach? Maybe if you jumped. . . .

Make a note of everything you see that could possibly cause trouble for a small dog. Stay down there until you're sure that you've exhausted the possibilities. Read on for some things to look for while you're surveying. Then, after you're done, you may just feel the urge to curl up and take a nap. See any comfy pillows? A Dachshund-friendly house should have at least a few.

Demolition Dog

So you think your sweet little dog couldn't make *too* much of a mess? You'd be surprised. Do you really love your collection of antique teacups or crystal vases? Then either display them well above the level any Dachshund can reach or put them away for a while. Puppies are exuberant and curious, and they haven't yet learned what areas are off limits to them (see Figure 6-1). It's not the puppy's fault if he jumps onto that end table to see just what's up there and breaks something valuable. Imagine that you have a toddler in the house and pack away the fragile stuff accordingly.

The Dachshund philosophy

How does a Dachshund view the world? Much like a toddler. You may have seen versions of this list before, referring to Dachshunds or, in a slightly different form (but not too different!), to small children. This is how a Dachsie thinks:

🖛 If I like it, it's mine.

🖛 If I think I might like it, it's mine.

🖛 If it's in my mouth, it's mine.

🖛 If it was ever in my mouth, it's mine.

🖛 If I can take it from you, it's mine.

🖛 If you take it from me, it's still mine.

🖛 If I had it a little while ago, it's mine.

🖛 If it's mine, it must never appear to be yours in any way.

🖛 If I'm chewing something, all the pieces are mine.

🖛 If it looks just like mine, it's mine.

🖛 If I saw it first, it's mine.

🖛 If you are playing with something and you put it down, it automatically becomes mine.

🖛 Everything I've ever laid eyes or teeth upon is mine . . . including you!

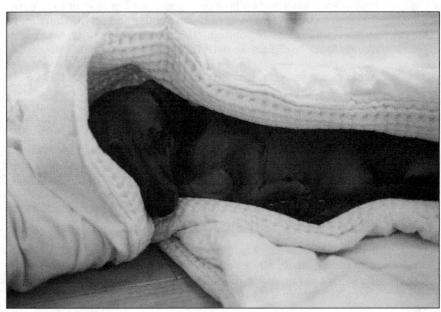

Figure 6-1: Dachshunds love to get into things, and that includes making a bed out of your favorite blanket.

Photo courtesy of Melody Levine.

Also, although a Dachshund is small, he has a pretty big mouth, and I don't just mean he barks a lot. He can also chew to the point of major destruction. *Really*. No two ways about it, Dachshunds love to chew. In fact, they not only love it, but they also consider it their dog-given right. Your Dachshund will consider anything that looks chewable to be his own personal property. So you thought that slipper was yours? Think again. As far as your new puppy is concerned, if he sees it and decides he wants to chew it, it's his.

The world is their chew toy

The best way to combat the loss of some of your more valuable pairs of shoes, not to mention your furniture, is to have a good supply of acceptable chew toys on hand. Stow them everywhere so one is always within reach. Look for sturdy chew toys without small parts that could come off or become dislodged. If you're consistent about enforcing the house rules, your new puppy will soon learn what is okay to chew and what isn't. Then, eventually, he'll learn enough self-control to stop himself from chewing that juicy-looking, brand-new tennis shoe.

Some Dachshunds chew more than others, but if yours takes a fancy to that brocaded, fringed sofa pillow or the left rear leg of your dining room chair, you'll soon learn the power of those Dachshund teeth. Yours may well decide to gnaw on the legs of your couch, shred your area rug, eat your shoes, or decide to try to dig a hole right through the baseboards in your kitchen.

Avoid giving your Dachshund cat toys, even if you've got a Mini. Dachshunds are more enthusiastic chewers than cats and they have larger mouths and stronger jaws. Cat toys often have small pieces like bells, feathers, or felt that a Dachshund can easily swallow or choke on.

The best way to discourage this sort of destruction in the early stages is to offer a firm "No" when your Dachshund is in the process of chewing or clawing; then immediately redirect him to an acceptable but similar activity. For example, if your Dachsie is chewing your shoe, say "No!" and then take away the shoe, replacing it with a chew toy in his mouth. If he chews the chew toy, heap on the praise.

If you've got a piece of furniture or other object that your Dachshund just won't leave alone, buy a bottle of Bitter Apple spray and follow the directions. This spray makes the object taste horrible, and your Dachshund will probably learn quickly to leave it alone.

If you have a digger, you may want to consider purchasing a few carpet squares or remnants that are reserved for your Dachshund. He can dig and scratch on them to his heart's content. If he scratches and digs on your carpet or wall, move him immediately to his carpet — even help move his paws in a digging motion over it. If he gets it, praise him for all you're worth. He'll get the idea eventually.

Choking hazards

Babies aren't the only small creatures that can choke on small, hard objects. Take a good look around your home for small objects on the floor or within reach that would fit in your Dachshund's mouth. Things like bottle caps, rubber bands and string or thread (which are particularly hazardous because they can cause internal damage), loose screws, twist ties, small blocks or balls (such as cat toys), and even small wads of paper trash. All these things can be hazardous to your puppy. Small, hard objects can lodge in a dog's throat and block the air passages. String-like objects can actually kill your puppy by getting caught in his intestines.

If your puppy does choke on something, let him try to dislodge it himself. If your dog isn't breathing, whether unconscious or not, try to hook the object out with your finger, if he'll let you. Just don't force the object in farther. If that procedure doesn't work, you can try a movement similar to the Heimlich maneuver:

1. **Place your Dachshund up on all fours and then lift his front end slightly off the ground.**

2. **Put your fist (on a Standard) or thumb (on a Mini) on his upper abdomen just below his rib cage and then thrust upward.**

   Don't be too rough. You don't want to injure him. And keep doing this procedure a few times to try to get the object out.

3. **Do one of the following:**

   If you can dislodge the object, once your dog can breathe, take him straight to the vet. He may have internal injuries.

   If you can't dislodge the object, rush your pet to the nearest vet or emergency pet care facility. If you can, take someone with you who can keep trying the modified Heimlich maneuver to dislodge the object en route.

If all this choking talk sounds scary to you, it is. The best thing to do is keep all choking hazards out of reach, especially if your puppy tends to try to chew on everything in sight. Some puppies are more inclined to chew than others, but chewing is definitely a Dachshund trait.

When you're looking for potential choking hazards, don't forget to look for strangling hazards, too. More cats than dogs are probably strangled in blind cords, but it can happen. Keep blind cords out of reach — especially if you have children. Keep *all* the little ones safe: human, canine, and feline. Small dogs can also get caught up in drapery sashes or miniblinds. Also remove any hook-like objects that are within reach but off the floor because they may possibly catch on your puppy's collar or leash.

Poisons

Want another thing to worry about with a chew-happy puppy? Poisons. Even if you keep the drain cleaner and the bleach out of reach, plenty of other household items and substances can poison your puppy, from Tylenol or aspirin tablets to rotten food in your trashcan. Here are some common household poisons that you should keep well out of reach from your puppy:

- ✔ **Cleaners of all types.** Some are more toxic than others, but who wants to wait and see which ones may be okay?

- ✔ **All human and pet medication.** You never know, so better to be safe. Some human medications, like Tylenol, can be highly toxic to small animals.

- ✔ **Pesticides of any type.** Even your pet's flea control product can be toxic if gobbled up. Don't let your puppy play with or chew any insect traps or bait, like rat, mouse, or roach traps.

- ✔ **Chocolate.** Some dogs experience a severe allergy-like reaction to chocolate (especially dark chocolate), and even small amounts can be fatal.

- ✔ **Some houseplants.** They're poisonous to varying degrees. Keep your plants above Dachshund level.

- ✔ **Some miscellaneous items.** Does it smell strongly? Keep it out of reach — especially things like mothballs, potpourri oil or other essential oils, coffee grounds, fabric softener sheets, dishwashing detergent, batteries, cigarettes, alcohol, even homemade play dough.

While doing poison control, don't forget the yard. Keep your puppy off the lawn if you've recently sprayed it with insecticides or fertilizer. Keep all lawn and garden chemicals out of reach (not to mention sharp objects). Keep your puppy out of the garage, too. Gasoline, oil, and antifreeze can kill your puppy. Also, the following common outdoor plants are poisonous to dogs:

- ✔ Azalea
- ✔ Oleander
- ✔ Castor bean
- ✔ Sago palm
- ✔ Yew plant

One tablespoon of antifreeze can kill a 20-pound dog, and antifreeze smells and tastes yummy to dogs. So Dachs-proof your garage and driveway in the winter by keeping antifreeze out of reach. Even leaking or spilled puddles on the driveway can mean death to your dog. (Note that you can now buy antifreeze that's advertised as safer for pets, but that doesn't mean you shouldn't still do everything you can to keep your pet away from it.)

If you know or suspect that your dog has been poisoned, call the National Animal Poison Control Center (NAPCC), a 24-hour emergency veterinary poison hotline. The NAPCC is a nonprofit group with no state or federal funding. The charge is $45 and includes as many follow-ups as required to get the problem resolved. Call 1-888-426-4435. Post these numbers on your refrigerator with your other emergency numbers. When you need the number, you'll need it fast. You can get more information at the NAPCC Web site, at www.napcc.aspca.org.

Stair-Down

A big thing to consider when Dachs-proofing your home is how to make your stairs Dachshund-friendly. Stairs are hard on Dachshund backs, especially for the Minis because each step is a lot bigger to a 7-pound dog than to a 30-pound dog. If you have stairs in your home, that's no reason to give up your Dachshund dreams. But you do need to take a few precautions.

If you have the space and the resources, a ramp is great for Dachshunds. A ramp is most practical outside, where you can offer your dog an alternate route off the deck. The problem is that some Dachshunds ignore that carefully constructed ramp and take the stairs anyway. (Some gladly use the ramp, though. You just never know.) You can install a gate so the ramp is the only way down for your pet, but now you're getting pretty fancy. Some gates, made for small children or pets, bolt onto walls or decks and have an easy-open swinging mechanism for the convenience of adults. This option is worth it if you can afford it, but it's not for everyone.

Inside is a different story. Most people don't have the space to build a ramp over half their staircase. The best solution is to install those pet gates (or baby gates) at the top and bottom of all staircases. The newer ones bolt to the wall and swing open so you don't have to take the whole gate off to go up and down. Most can be operated easily with one hand. Then, when your Dachsie has to go upstairs, you can pick him up and carry him. And when he's ready to go back down? Pick him up and carry him again.

Some people aren't willing to do this task, of course, and others argue that Dachshunds are built to be natural athletes and should be able to climb stairs. I won't argue. Some Dachsies race up and down the stairs all day long, every day, and never suffer from a back problem. Others may develop back problems, and you won't know whether or not it had anything to do with daily jaunts up and down your staircase.

Deciding whether or not your Dachsie is allowed to climb the stairs comes down to risk assessment. Going up and down stairs can be hard on those Dachshunds who'll probably have back problems anyway, and climbing the steps may trigger an incident. Other dogs, though, will be fine. You can play it safe but expend more effort, or you can expend a lot of effort to prevent something that may never happen. As long as you recognize that you're taking responsibility for your pet, you can make the decision.

Ledges and Couches and Beds, Oh My!

Some Dachshunds are impossible to keep off beds and couches, and when they decide to get down, they get down before you can stop them. Some people build little Dachshund ramps from their beds and couches so their Dachshunds can scamper easily down from high places. Others recognize that their pets are going to jump, and these folks just hope for the best. It's up to you to gauge your individual situation and determine what works for you and your pet. And if your Dachshund does develop back problems, she may very well have developed them anyway. Feeling guilty or imagining what you could have done differently doesn't help anybody.

Still, the smaller your dog, the more stress that jump will cause. If you have a Mini, I advise being extra careful. That's not to say plenty of Standards don't experience a disk incident, but a couch with cushions two feet off the ground isn't such a big jump for a 30-pound dog.

Chapter 7

Dachs-Proofing Your Family

. . . .

In This Chapter

▶ Teaching your family about new puppies and special Dachshund needs

▶ Developing special rules for kids

▶ Making your home truly Dachshund-friendly

▶ Applying Feng Shui to your Dachshund's corner of the world

. . . .

Keeping your home free of poisons and choking hazards is great, but it won't do much good if your toddler barrels across the room and sits squarely on your new puppy. Even an adult can unwittingly injure a Dachshund if he or she doesn't know how to hold one correctly. And that poor, scared little puppy will soon be at the mercy of your family.

Are they loud? Are they boisterous? Is your family life a little chaotic? All families are. But that doesn't mean you can't create a Dachshund oasis for your new puppy, especially when you first bring her home. Read on.

Family Meeting: Dachshund Lessons

Once you secure your home environment, it's time to Dachs-proof the occupants. Not everyone in your family will automatically know how to handle a Dachshund puppy, so a family meeting is in order. The topic of discussion? Life with a new Dachshund.

Make sure that everyone gets in on this meeting. Children especially need to know a few things about Dachshunds before you turn them loose on the poor, unsuspecting puppy. At the meeting, you can enumerate the nine no-no's of Dachshund ownership. The kids get an extra couple of tips, too.

Because of their unusually long bodies, Dachshunds must be picked up and held well supported on both ends at all times. Show your children (and adults, too) how to pick up a Dachshund before they try it on yours. Put one hand under the Dachshund's chest. Put the other hand under the

Dachshund's belly. Lift slowly without twisting your dog and keep both ends fully supported. And never lift a Dachshund by the front end only, allowing her back legs to swing around.

The nine no-no's of Dachshund ownership

I won't go so far as to say that you need to require every member of your family to memorize and recite back to you the following list of Dachshund no-no's, but it won't hurt to post this list somewhere and make sure that everyone has read it at least once:

- **Don't overwhelm your Dachshund.** Dachshunds are relatively small dogs and can be easily scared or confused by lots of people, loud noises, and chaos. Give your Dachshund a place to go away from the family uproar. A kennel or crate is a perfect Dachshund haven.

- **Don't overfeed your Dachshund.** Dachshunds are prone to getting chubby, which wreaks havoc on their spines. Cool it on the treats and people food. Use pieces of kibble out of your Dachshund's daily food ration for treats and training. And if you must give your Dachshund people food, stick to small pieces of raw carrots, broccoli, apples, and berries. (Puppies love chasing a wayward, rolling blueberry around the kitchen.)

- **Don't skimp on quality.** Buy the best food you can find. Ask your vet for recommendations. Dog food quality is often directly related to dog food price, although you may occasionally hear otherwise. The more natural and the more meat, the better. I don't believe it hurts to add some healthy, fresh, whole human food to your pet's diet, either, as long as you adjust kibble portion size accordingly. (See Chapter 8 for more on what kind of food to buy your Dachshund for more information on what to feed your Dachshund, including the homemade-diet option.)

- **Don't be a couch potato.** Dachshunds need exercise (just like you do), so don't neglect that daily walk. Some playtime in the fenced backyard is great for your Dachshund's health, too, and helps keep obesity at bay.

- **Don't ignore your Dachshund.** Dachsies thrive on human attention and affection, plus they look to you for guidance on good behavior. If you decide to bring a Dachshund into your life, decide to spend time training and simply being with your dog each day.

- **Don't let your Dachshund escape.** Dachshunds are proficient diggers and can be pretty clever escape artists. They also can't be trusted off leash near traffic, no matter how well trained you think they are. They are hounds and will follow a scent, oblivious to danger. You are in charge and must keep your Dachshund safely enclosed or on a leash. Otherwise, you could lose your friend.

✔ **Don't assume that your Dachshund can speak English or read your mind.** Your friend needs teaching so he can learn the house rules and proper behavior. That's your job as the human end of the Dachshund-human relationship. Learn how to train your Dachshund and work on it every day. Puppy obedience classes are a great place to start.

✔ **Don't skip the vet visits.** All dogs need routine veterinary evaluations in addition to their vaccinations in the first year. As your Dachsie ages, these checkups become even more important. Keep your pet as healthy as possible by fully utilizing your vet's expertise to catch problems before they turn serious.

✔ **Don't ignore a yelp of pain or any sudden signs that your Dachshund is losing the use of his legs.** When an acute disc herniation occurs, time is of the essence. Waiting it out to see whether it goes away can mean paralysis for your dog. If you can't get him to a vet immediately, put him in his crate and *don't let him move.* (Movement can injure the spinal cord and cause permanent paralysis when the herniation could otherwise have been repaired.) Then get him to the vet or emergency care facility ASAP. (For more on canine intervertebral disk disease and what to do if your Dachshund suffers from disc herniation, see Chapter 17.)

Your vet may have additional helpful tips for family members about life with a new Dachshund. Choosing a vet with Dachshund expertise is best. He or she will know from experience what to look for, watch for, and prepare for.

Dachs-proofing your kids

Kids love Dachshunds, and the feeling is mutual, but kids can sometimes get a little boisterous and rough with a small dog. If all children learned and demonstrated respect for their fellow creatures on this Earth, the world would be a kinder, gentler place. Do your part by Dachs-proofing your kids. What could result but family harmony?

Copy this list and give it to your kids. Read it or explain it to the younger ones. These are rules to live by:

✔ Dogs love to play, but sometimes they need to be alone. We all have our limits. After an exuberant playtime, give your dog some downtime in his den.

✔ Dogs need to have privacy when they eat and sleep. No poking, prodding, or pulling a dog during dinner. Instinct may cause him to respond with a snap. Also, no rude awakenings, please. Dogs need to sleep a lot, and when they're sleeping, it's hands off.

✔ No junk food. Dogs need healthy food and may get sick if given candy, sweets, chips, or other unhealthy food. If your parents generally don't like you to eat something, or if they call it a *special treat,* don't give it to the dog. No, not even when Mom and Dad aren't looking. You wouldn't want your dog to get really sick just because of what you fed him.

✔ Dachshunds — especially Minis and Dachshund puppies — aren't as tough as most kids. They must be handled gently, not roughly. No tug of war for Dachshunds, either. The sharp back-and-forth movements can hurt their backs. Also, Dachshunds are small and short. Never drop them from your arms or from anything else. Place them gently on the ground while supporting both their front and back ends.

✔ If a dog makes any kind of growling noise or if he shows his teeth, leave him alone. He's telling you that he doesn't want to play.

✔ Never, ever pet any dog you don't know very well. If you see a dog wandering around alone, leave him alone and tell a grownup. If you see someone walking a dog and think you'd like to pet him, always ask the owner first; then pet the dog slowly and talk softly. That's the way to make friends with a dog.

Kids can be a dog's best friend or a dog's worst enemy. Some kids are great with dogs and quickly become a puppy's primary trainer. Others, especially those under the age of 7 or 8, find it very difficult to handle a dog carefully and gently. Because Miniature Dachshunds are particularly small and can easily be injured as puppies, most vets and breeders don't recommend bringing a Mini into a household with children who aren't yet in the first or second grade.

Kid-proofing your Dachsie

Of course, when you mix up kids and dogs, the kids aren't the only ones with potential to do some damage. An irritated or injured Dachshund can snap at a small child (or even a large child), and a bite can break the skin.

When bringing a Dachshund into a home with children, introduce her to the kids one at a time. Have the kids approach slowly, pet gently, and talk softly. Eventually, your Dachshund will know everyone and feel comfortable. And remember to show your kids the proper way to hold a Dachshund. It's shown in Figure 7-1.

Bringing a new baby into a home where a Dachshund is already firmly entrenched? Try this: A few days before you bring home the baby, bring home a receiving blanket with the baby's smell on it (don't wash it after the baby uses it) and let the Dachshund get to know the smell on the blanket. Then, when you bring the baby home, hold the baby and dog and let them check each other out. And don't forget to pay your Dachshund lots of attention.

She'll be confused about the change in the family, and she'll wonder why you're suddenly so busy. Reassure her that she still has an important place in the family order. And don't forget to maintain those training sessions.

Figure 7-1:
Hold the
Dachshund
close to
your body
and support
it's legs and
underbelly.

Dachs-proofing your other pets

Got cats? Dachshunds love them, especially Miniature Dachshunds (see Figure 7-2). Got other dogs? Dachshunds love them, too. However, introductions shouldn't be too sudden.

One good way to introduce your new Dachshund and your other pets is to let each pet hang around in a room where the other pet has been for a while before letting them see each other. One vet I know suggests keeping them in separate rooms with a door between them so they can hear each other before they see each other. Curiosity may eventually get the better of any aggressive impulses.

Of course, unneutered males may not get along well with each other, and unspayed females may not, either. Best to have at least one (and I suggest *all*) of your pets altered.

Figure 7-2:
Dachshunds
get along
with cats
just fine.

Photo courtesy of Alli and Pam Henley.

Dachshund-Friendly Décor

Here's the really fun part. For many people, Dachshunds are more than pets. They are a way of life. Beyond Dachs-proofing your home, you can actually design your home around and for your Dachshund. Why not? If you've been in search of a decorating theme, this one's a lot of fun.

Making your home a Dachshund haven

Your home can be more than safe. It can be a Dachshund dream house. When you're Dachs-proofing your home, I recommend that you get down on your belly and look around for potential hazards (see Chapter 6). Well, you can do the same thing to make your Dachsie's dream house — this time getting down there to look for what a Dachshund would like to see.

Low furniture, lots of cushions, a Dachshund-sized sofa, enclosed pet beds that give a sense of security (cat beds are good for Minis), and lots of blankets and quilts for burrowing all make Dachshunds feel at home. Who doesn't love a little luxury?

One of the great things about Dachshunds is that they don't have that typical doggy smell so characteristic of other hound breeds. In fact, Dachshunds usually appear exceptionally clean (unless you've just been tramping through the mud with yours). You might as well just give in and let him up on the sofa!

A feeding station kept scrupulously clean, a low doggy door for outdoor forays, a grooming center (especially for longhairs and wirehairs), and a dish of gourmet dog biscuits (for special occasions only) add the finishing touches to your Dachshund's haven.

Some of your décor can be just for you, even if your Dachshund won't appreciate it. Collecting Dachshund paraphernalia is fun (see the following section). Dog-themed decorating items are even more abundantly available, from wallpaper with dog footprints to dog-printed bedding sets. If you're a dog person through and through (or if you're fast becoming one), why not show your true colors?

Dachshund paraphernalia: A collector's dream!

I've never seen any other breed with more associated paraphernalia. From framed Dachshund folk art to antique Dachshund-shaped boot scrapers, Dachshunds make for a great decorating theme and great collecting opportunities. Scan antique shops and flea markets for Dachshund items. Tell dealers what you're looking for, and they may be able to point you in the right direction. You can also purchase Dachshund paraphernalia on the Web. Check out the following Web sites:

- Distinctively Dachshund at `http://members.aol.com/disdox2/catalog/catindex.html`. This site has some great stuff — from Dachshund-shaped purses and pencil cases, to Dachshund angel Christmas tree toppers, to wood, porcelain, and bronze Dachshund figurines and miniatures, to Dachshund collectible plates and spoons. You can also write or call the company the old-fashioned way: Distinctively Dachshund, P.O. Box 11374, Yakima, WA 98909, 1-888-PET-DOGS (1-888-738-3647). Oh, and they have Basset Hound stuff, too.

- Dachshund Delights at `www.doxidelight.com/fromthe.htm`. This site has Dachshund-themed merchandise and more, displayed with a great sense of humor. Here's the old-fashioned contact info: Dachshund Delights, 8675 Pierce Road, Garrettsville, OH 44231, 1-800-444-9475 (from inside the United States) or 1-330-527-9557 (from outside the States). The fax number is 1-330-527-9558.

Dachsie Feng Shui

Dachsie *Feng Shui?* Am I kidding? Well, sort of. But not completely. For those of you who haven't heard this trendy term, *Feng Shui* is the ancient Chinese art of placement based on Chinese astrology and the purposeful arrangement of the objects and habits of our lives to promote good luck, good fortune, and the best flow of lifeforce energy, or what the Chinese call *chi*.

It seems that everybody these days, from celebrities like Donald Trump to people like you and me, is having his or her home redesigned and decorated by a Feng Shui master. Hey, it's the turn of the century. People are expanding their horizons.

Feng Shui is the ancient Chinese art of placement based on the complex systems of Chinese astrology, the four directions, intuition, and other traditional methods, none of which have anything to do with Dachshunds . . . at least until now.

And why shouldn't your Dachshund reap the potential benefits as well? If it's good enough for you, it's good enough for your Dachsie, right?

Of course, any real Feng Shui master would probably be appalled at my amateur Feng Shui advice — and even more appalled at my application of the concept to dogs. But to me, dogs and people aren't really all that different, so why not? The following tips are those I've gleaned from a couple of different sources and then modified for our Dachshund friends. (If you're interested, check out *Feng Shui Step by Step,* by T. Raphael Simons, and *Sacred Space,* by Denise Linn. But be forewarned: Neither book mentions anything about Dachshunds.)

I apologize in advance to any offended Feng Shui masters. None of this is backed up by any studies on any Dachshunds whatsoever.

✔ When you first bring your new puppy into your house, have a Welcome Ceremony. Take the puppy into each room, walk around the perimeter, and let your puppy take in and learn the energy of your home. You can even say a blessing as you go — something like "We welcome our new friend and dedicate this house to peace and harmony among all creatures human and canine." Or something more your style.

✔ Never place your Dachshund's crate or bed directly facing a door. Doing so will make your Dachshund feel insecure. Your Dachshund should be able to see the door from his resting place but at an angle.

✔ Never place your Dachshund's crate or bed in the bathroom. His health and well being will symbolically drain away. Plus, who wants to sleep in a bathroom? It isn't very cozy.

✔ Placing your Dachshund's crate or bed in the center of the wall directly to your left when you enter a room will make him feel more a part of the family. Placing his crate or bed in the center of the wall directly to your right when you enter a room will help him get along with your children.

If you know your dog's date of birth, you can figure out what element he's associated with — water, wood, fire, earth, or metal. Each element comes with certain characteristics, sort of like our horoscopes. Granted, you may not feel exactly like the description of your horoscope, but it can still be fun to read.

- **Water Dachshund.** Born between November 7 and February 4. Water dogs are intelligent, more reflective than active, and less likely than other Dachshunds to become overweight (although it's not impossible — are you making it too easy?). They are easygoing as far as Dachshunds go. You don't like what they're doing? They'll just do something else, no problem. Water Dachshunds may appear nonchalant, but they are sensitive and will be hurt if you ignore or scold them. Go easy. Water dogs like cold weather and tend to have long lives.

- **Wood Dachshund.** Born between February 4 and May 5. Wood dogs are strong, athletic, and loyal, and they bond strongly to humans. They are also comedians with lots of energy and the wonderful ability to entertain a room full of people. Wood Dachshunds are particularly friendly and loving, and no dog beats them for faithfulness. They may exhibit a temper, however, if they're mistreated or if they think their beloved human is being threatened, so keep small children at bay. Wood dogs don't mind the rain.

- **Fire Dachshund.** Born between May 5 and August 7. Fire Dachsies are particularly spirited, lively, optimistic, and loving. All Dachshunds are courageous but especially the Fire Dachshunds. They can also tend to be particularly rash and impulsive, so watch them carefully when you pass that Great Dane on your daily walk. Your Fire Dachshund may just push him too far this time. Fire dogs love hard and lose hard, so they may not take the loss of a friend, dog or human, very well. Fire dogs love hot weather and are prolific breeders, so get your little male neutered before he spreads his genetic material all over the neighborhood.

- **Earth Dachshund.** May be born any time, but many are born in the last week of July or the first week of August. This sign is harder to pinpoint. Either a dog is an Earth dog or he isn't. You can tell if you've got an Earth dog if your Dachshund is unusually stable, calm, balanced, almost serene. Earth dogs are gentle and dependable, love comfort, and enjoy a walk on a windy day. They aren't easily excitable and are happiest at home on your lap. You may even wonder if they're meditating.

- **Metal Dachshund.** Born between August 7 and November 7. They are forceful and not easily trained because they are quite sure their way is superior to your way. They are perfectionists, as much as dogs can be, and super-confident. They may also tend to get compulsive about their own orderly sense of routine. Good luck breaking the daily grind by taking your Metal Dachshund on vacation. Metal Dachshunds love clear, bright, beautiful days (don't we all?), and when things are going their way, they are particularly joyful that all is right with their world.

And there you have it — Feng Shui for Dachshunds. And only a little bit tongue-in-cheek. I hope that you recognize your Dachsie in one of the preceding profiles. And remember, keep that Dachshund bed in an auspicious location!

Chapter 8

Shop 'Til You Drop: Outfitting Your Dachshund

1 f you love shopping, this chapter is for you. And if you don't, don't despair. Many pet catalogs and the Internet are at your service.

This chapter is about pet supplies — what you need and what you don't necessarily *need* but think would be awfully fun to have. Every dog needs a few basics. And Dachshunds require a few special supplies. And then there are the luxuries. If you can afford them, go for it. If you prefer to keep your dog budget in check, your Dachshund won't mind. All he really wants is attention from you (and a few good meals every day, of course).

Every Dog Needs a Den

One of the most important pet supplies you'll buy — and *should* buy before bringing your new Dachshund home — is a crate. Personally, I don't like the word *crate*. It sounds like something that should contain cartons of milk or oranges from Florida, not a living, breathing, beloved pet. The word also conjures up images of cruel confinement, and that's exactly what a lot of people imagine when they're told they ought to buy one.

Truth is, a crate will become your Dachshund's second best friend (after you, of course). Dogs are den animals, and they feel most secure having an enclosed, familiar place to retire or escape the fray of family life once in a while. So I call crates *dens* instead, because as far as your Dachshund is concerned, that's exactly what they are. Dens are also invaluable housetraining tools, which I explain about in the next section.

Never leave a brand-new puppy in a den for more than two or three hours, even at night. Older puppies can last about four hours, but if you work all day, someone should come home at lunch to give your pet a potty break. Even adult dogs, although they can last eight or nine hours in a crate, would prefer not to spend all day in one. If you're gone every day for nine or ten hours, consider hiring a dog walker or pet sitter to do lunch duty.

Why crates are kind

Remember that commercial where the harried housewife screams, "Calgon, take me away!" and then she's magically transported to a luxurious bubble bath, far from the shrieks of small children, ringing telephones, and malfunctioning appliances? Your Dachshund feels a little like that sometimes. Well, maybe not exactly. No one can say for certain how a dog feels (although some of us are pretty sure we can tell, from time to time). But dogs do get overwhelmed, seem to suffer from stress, and, although social creatures, sometimes prefer to be alone.

But your Dachshund can't take a bubble bath at will and wouldn't want to. Instead, when a dog is feeling overcome by commotion or simply needs some downtime, nothing feels better than retiring into the safety and comfort of the good ol' den.

Once you teach your new Dachshund that the den is home sweet home, you'll discover other ways the den can benefit both you and your Dachshund. The den will help your Dachshund learn housetraining. Dogs don't like to soil where they sleep, so as long as you don't wait too long, your puppy will usually refrain from relieving herself until you take her outside. (Turn to Chapter 13 for more on housetraining.)

Also, if you've got a little beggar under your table, your dog can spend time in her kennel when the family has dinner. It's a lot easier to keep the kids from slipping your Dachshund people food under the table when there isn't a Dachshund under there, nosing around. Putting her in her den at dinnertime is kind to your pet because it will keep her healthier and won't encourage bad begging habits, let alone obesity.

Let your pet spend some time each day in her den even when you are home so that she learns that *den* doesn't equal *you going away.* She may seem to dislike it at first, but once it becomes familiar, her den is sure to be her favorite spot. Unless your dog is sick and needs your help, let the den truly be hers by never putting your hand in there. The less intrusive you are when it comes to your Dachshund's space, the more she will feel secure in that space.

When purchasing a Dachshund den, look for a sturdy, well-ventilated plastic crate with an easy-open door (easy for you to open, not your Dachshund). You want a size just big enough that your Dachshund can stand, sit, lie down, and turn around comfortably, but you don't want one so huge that he can relieve himself in one corner and sleep in another. Fold up a blanket or buy a nice, soft cushion or pad for the bottom, and you're set.

Plastic dens may not be particularly lovely pieces of furniture, but to most Dachshunds, plastic dens feel more secure and safe on the inside than those open-wire kennels, which don't resemble a den very closely. If you already have a wire kennel, drape a blanket over the top and three sides to give your pet a better sense of security. Also, avoid making your dog stand on a wire grate. That's uncomfortable, and puppies can snag their toes. Cover the bottom of the den with something soft and wash it often.

An alternative to crates: Dog beds for Dachsies

If you're talking aesthetics, dog beds (see Figure 8-1) are much nicer looking than plastic crates. Some Dachshunds love them — especially the types that are more enclosed. (Lots of Dachshunds, especially Minis, like those cushy, semi-enclosed cat beds.) If you can get yours used to a bed, that's fine. You can buy some beautiful ones — even furniture-quality wooden beds sized just for small dogs.

Figure 8-1: Some Dachshunds like dog beds.

Photo courtesy of John and Joyce Kane.

But just because your dog sleeps in a dog bed, that doesn't mean she won't also appreciate and use a den. You'll appreciate it, too, when you suddenly need to confine your Dachshund for her own safety, when housetraining becomes a nightmare, or when you find that your Dachshund won't come out from under the kitchen chair because it's the closest thing to an enclosed den she can find.

Other Basic Supplies: A Pet Store Checklist

A den is a must. But what else do you need? Chapter 1 contains a general list, but I want to get a little more specific in this section and cover the options — the must-haves, and the why-nots. Take the following lists to the pet store and have fun.

The must-haves

Following is your list of pet supply staples. These items are pretty nonnegotiable. Your dog needs them. You can spend a little or a lot on, say, a leash or a food bowl. You can even buy them at garage sales or borrow them from a friend who no longer has a dog. But find these things, one way or the other:

- **Food.** Buy as good a food as you can afford (see the section "Kibble, Kibble Everywhere. . . ." later in this chapter, for more about what to feed your Dachshund).

- **Leash or lead.** Dachshunds must be kept on a leash when near traffic in an unenclosed area. Keep your pet safe. You don't need to spend a lot. Four-foot lengths are good for new puppies. When your dog is older, a 6-foot length is perfect. Choose leather or nylon, whichever you prefer.

- **Collar or harness.** A leash isn't much good without one. Harnesses are nice for Dachshunds because you won't risk pulling on their necks. Don't leave a harness on all the time, though. It can rub away at your dog's coat. Collars also give you a little more control, and some dogs seem to prefer them.

- **Food and water bowls.** Any bowl will do, as long as it is unbreakable and heavy enough so that your Dachshund doesn't keep knocking it over when he tries to eat. Weighted bowls, ceramic bowls, and metal bowls are good choices.

- **Shampoo.** Even if you don't use it very often (you don't need to bathe your smooth unless he gets really dirty), you should have shampoo on hand for those times when you do. Use shampoo made for pets, not for people. People shampoo is harsh and can irritate your pet's skin and eyes.

- ✔ **Toothbrush and toothpaste.** It may seem silly to you, but brushing your dog's teeth is essential for her good health. Not only does brushing keep tartar buildup at bay (excessive tartar buildup must be removed by a vet, often under general anaesthetic, which is always a risk), but tooth decay and bacteria in your dog's mouth can actually lead to heart disease and other serious health problems, especially as your Dachshund ages. Bacteria from the teeth can get into the bloodstream, and that spells trouble. Look for a toothbrush and toothpaste made just for dogs. People toothpaste isn't good for your Dachshund. A people toothbrush may work, but dog toothbrushes are longer with more compact, sturdier bristles, and they're angled in a way that makes brushing easier.

- ✔ **Nail clippers.** A dog with long nails risks a foot injury. Long nails on hard surfaces spread the footpads too far apart. They also make walking more difficult. Keep your dog's nails nicely trimmed. Ask your vet to show you how (or have it done professionally once every four to eight weeks). Buy clippers made for dogs, not for humans. Human nail clippers can seriously injure your dog and probably aren't strong enough to cut your dog's nails anyway.

- ✔ **Brush and comb.** Your dog's grooming needs depend on what coat your Dachshund has (see the section "The Well-Groomed Dachshund," later in this chapter, for more on grooming tools).

- ✔ **ID tags.** I don't have to tell you why these are a must-have, do I? Nobody thinks they'll lose their dog, but if you do, your dog can't tell anyone where he lives. Most pet stores have forms you can fill out to order ID tags. Or look in magazines and pet catalogs.

- ✔ **Pet gate.** A must-have if you have rooms where your Dachshund isn't allowed or stairs you want to keep him from descending or climbing. Baby gates, pet gates — same thing.

- ✔ **Toys.** Dachshunds just want to have fun. A few toys are a must-have, even if they're homemade (see the section "Playtime!" later in this chapter, for more on what to give your Dachshund to make playtime fun).

- ✔ **Pet odor remover.** Accidents happen, but if your dog smells a previous mistake on your carpet, accidents will happen again and again. Technology has produced products that truly remove the scent of a past indiscretion. Take advantage. Housetraining will be easier. Ask your local pet store employee to recommend a brand. I like Nature's Miracle.

Most vets and breeders generally do not recommend vitamin supplements. Supplements can throw off the nutritional balance of your pet's diet. Unless your vet specifically prescribes something for your Dachshund, stick with a healthy, complete, nutritionally balanced food recommended by your vet, as well as occasional healthy treats.

The why-nots

Beyond the must-haves are the why-nots, the pet supplies that are more luxury than necessity. If you want to spend the money, why not? Some of the following items will be more appreciated by your pet than others, and some are, admittedly, just for your own amusement and pleasure. But that's worth something, too. Here they are:

- **Gourmet dog treats.** Fancy gourmet dog treats from dedicated dog bakeries are now widely available. If you live in a big city, you may well live near a dog bakery. Browse around and pick out a few special treats for your Dachshund. But remember, don't overfeed, even if the treats are healthy. Many of the gourmet treats are all natural and made of human-grade ingredients, but that still isn't an excuse to let your Dachshund binge. A calorie is a calorie, no matter the source. One treat every day or so should be fine, but you may want to consider decreasing the kibble allowance on those days just slightly.

- **Retractable Leash.** This is a very long leash that retracts into a plastic case with a handle. Retractable leashes are perfect for walks or hikes in parks, forests, or other natural areas where your Dachshund will love to go sniffing about. You can keep him safe while he explores. A retractable leash isn't for everyday use, however, because it isn't good for teaching your dog to heel.

- **Dog bed and other dog furniture.** Yes, they make dog furniture. Little chairs, little beds, *little chaise lounges* — all very lovely and impressive, all pretty expensive. But what better way to make your home a Dachshund haven? Of course, if you drop a bundle on a fancy bedroom set for your Dachshund, be prepared. She may just ignore it and prefer to curl up on the people couch instead. After all, that's where you sit.

- **Fancy collars, bows, sweaters, jackets, coats, and boots.** A Dachshund in clothes? Sure! Doggy fashion is big these days, and boutique-y types of pet stores are full of options. Dress your dog to match his or her unique personality. Behold Figure 8-2.

If you live in a very cold climate, a few articles of clothing are actually more of a necessity than a luxury. Dog sweaters, jackets, coats, or whatever your pet finds comfortable can keep your Dachshund warm on cold winter walks. Dog boots keep ice crystals and rock salt from getting between your Dachshund's footpads (they also protect your pet from sharp rocks and hot surfaces on summer hikes). The question is, can you get your dog to wear them? If yours won't, always wipe your Dachshund's paws with a warm cloth or even a baby wipe. Even when it isn't snowing, rock salt and ice crystal residue can get between your dog's paws.

Figure 8-2:
Is this high
fashion or
campy fun?

Photo courtesy of Vicky Cosgrove.

Tools for Training

You don't need many tools for training a Dachshund. I don't recommend the so-called choke collars, although some trainers swear by them. Most trainers I've met who emphasize positive training methods have abandoned the choke collar for kinder, gentler, and more effective methods.

You do, however, need a harness or collar, a leash, and a handful of treats for each training session. Measure out your Dachshund's food allowance at the beginning of each day and then take kibble out of this allotment for use in training. That way, you avoid extra calories. When the session is over, a couple of bouncing blueberries or a broccoli floret should be ample reward, as long as your dog isn't accustomed to getting the tail end of your éclair or the last couple bites of your bacon cheeseburger.

Look for a harness or collar that is comfortable for your Dachshund. Rolled or flat leather collars are nice, but you may prefer nylon, especially for a puppy, because they're washable and often more adjustable and your puppy is growing quickly. Nylon collars and harnesses are also good for Minis because nylon is so lightweight.

Harnesses are also nice for puppies. With a harness, you're less likely to pull inadvertently on your puppy's neck, especially before he is used to walking on a leash. Remember those delicate spines! For small dogs, begin with a 4-foot leash. When your dog is larger, you can move up to a 6-foot lead. Or, to save money, buy a 6-foot lead and wrap it around your hand once or twice at first.

Remember to check your puppy's harness or collar at each daily grooming session or at least once a week. Puppies grow quickly, and when you can't fit two fingers between your dog's neck and the collar, it is too tight. Loosen it or buy a new one.

Puppy pads

These don't work for everyone, but if they work for your puppy, they can help a lot with housetraining — especially if you don't plan to let your dog outside for each bathroom break. If you use puppy pads, do so consistently and don't use anything else. They're scented to encourage puppies to use them for elimination. But, as I said, not all puppies are convinced. For many, a few layers of newspaper are just fine (and newspaper costs less).

The den: An all-purpose training tool

The best training tool you can buy is a den (crate). Once your puppy has grown fond of her den, you can use it for many purposes, from housetraining and managing other undesirable behaviors to giving your Dachshund a well-earned break after a vigorous and stimulating training session or playtime.

The Well-Groomed Dachshund

If you've got a smooth Dachshund, you don't need much in the way of grooming tools. But longhairs and wirehairs require a little more, especially if you've decided to do all the dog grooming yourself. Talk to your vet or a local groomer for tips on which grooming tools are best, but this section provides a short list of tools for you. (For more info on how to groom your Dachshund, see Chapter 16.) And don't forget the toothbrush, toothpaste, and just-for-dogs nail clippers for every Dachshund.

Even if you plan to groom your Dachshund yourself, you may want to take her to a professional groomer the first time so that you can ask questions and get good advice about which tools to use and what to do. Or ask your vet to show you the ropes.

Smooth grooming tools

Grooming a smooth may be easy, but you still need a few tools of the trade:

- ✔ Soft-bristled brush.

- ✔ Slicker brush or hound mitt, which has bristles sewn onto the palm.

- ✔ Spray oil made for dog coats if you want to make your Dachshund's coat look extra shiny (a common practice for show dogs). You can also use a little baby oil and your hands. But just a little.

- ✔ Moisturizing shampoo and/or conditioner/crème rinse for smooths with dry-skin flakes.

Longhaired grooming tools

Grooming a longhair takes skill and practice. You can always hire a groomer to do it and then keep your dog well brushed between professional groomings. If you insist on learning how to do it yourself, several books give good instructions, but nothing beats watching someone who knows the ropes demonstrate for you. Your breeder may be the best person to show you, but a professional dog groomer might also be willing to show you the basics. You can also talk to breeders at a dog show for tips and demonstrations.

- ✔ Straight scissors

- ✔ Thinning shears

- ✔ Stripping knife

- ✔ Flea comb

- ✔ Soft-bristled brush

- ✔ Shampoo with conditioner or creme rinse to keep tangles at bay

Wirehaired grooming tools

If you don't care about keeping your dog looking like a show dog, wirehairs can get by with electric clippers and a short shave whenever their wiry coats get out of hand. If you want your dog to look ready for the show ring, however, you need a few other tools, including your thumb and forefinger, which you'll use periodically to pluck the longer hairs from your Dachshund's coat (it doesn't hurt him). Just as with Longhairs, you'll learn a lot by watching someone who knows the ropes demonstrate for you. Your breeder, breeders at a dog show, or a professional dog groomer can show you what to do. This list is short, but the grooming process is long:

- ✔ Stripping knife
- ✔ Scissors
- ✔ Clippers with a variety of blades, including a #10
- ✔ Flea comb

Playtime!

Puppies need toys. Play is a puppy's work and the means by which he learns about the world. But not all toys are created equally. The best ones for Dachshunds are along these lines:

- ✔ Something very hard and appealing to chew on, like a hard rubber Kong toy. These are great. They have holes you can fill with dog treats or other tantalizing things, and your Dachshund may work all day at trying to get the treat out of the Kong.
- ✔ Something with more "give" to chew on, like a Nylabone or Gummabone chew toy.
- ✔ Something soft, like a made-for-dogs fleece toy. Sure, your Dachshund may shred it or pull out all the stuffing, but she'll have a whole lot of fun doing it.

  Watch out for dolls or stuffed animals with plastic parts or eyes that can come off and pose a choking hazard.

- ✔ A ball or other objects to chase, if your Dachshund likes to chase or even retrieve.

  Tug of war with a rope toy may sound like fun, but avoid playing this game with your Dachshund. The sharp back-and-forth movement can injure his back, even resulting in paralysis. Stick to ball chasing.

Kibble, Kibble Everywhere. . . .

In the long run, dog food will turn out to be your most expensive pet supply, so don't waste your money. Choosing the right food for your Dachshund may seem pretty tricky. So many brands. Should you choose a natural food? A meat-based or a grain-based food? Does price matter, or should you go for the cheap brand? And what about making your own dog food at home?

The publicity out there about dog diets is indeed overwhelming, and eventually you'll have to make a decision. I can tell you what I've learned after several years of research and writing many articles on the subject. But, in the end, the choice is up to you because the experts don't always agree. The best you can do is find a food that

✔ Your dog likes

✔ You can afford

✔ Your vet recommends

✔ Is nutritionally complete

Which commercial food is best?

If you choose to feed your dog kibble — the easiest option — your choices are astounding. Corn-based, meat-based, hypoallergenic, natural, meat meal, fresh meat, by-product meat, no meat, human-grade ingredients, not human-grade ingredients — *how* do you pick? The first thing to do is learn how to read the label.

Most breeders and vets don't recommend canned food over kibble for several reasons. It is more expensive, it is less nutritionally dense, and it can promote tooth decay. An occasional treat mixed in with your dog's kibble won't hurt anything (especially if you brush your Dachshund's teeth every day), but it isn't nutritionally necessary and may just make you feel better.

✔ Look for a food that lists meat among the first three ingredients, preferably as the number one or two (or both) ingredient. Fresh meat is best. Meat meal can be a high quality protein source. Meat by-products have protein and also things dogs in the wild would eat (bone, skin, cartilage), but some people don't like the sound of *by-products* because you don't know what you're getting, and you really don't. Some people are enthusiastic about vegetarian diets for dogs, but I personally haven't researched the subject enough to recommend it.

✔ Look for words you understand. Lots of chemical names should give you pause. Although not all chemicals are bad for your dog, and many haven't been *proven* to be unhealthy, it makes sense to me that dogs (and people, too) are designed to eat foods as close to their natural state as possible.

✔ Look for a food that is naturally preserved with vitamins E and C rather than chemical preservatives. The verdict is still out on the effects of chemical preservatives, but naturally preserved food is so widely available that I don't see any reason to take a chance.

✔ Any food advertised as being nutritionally complete must include a statement on the label that says it's appropriate for maintenance and/or growth stages (in other words, for adult dogs or for puppies). If your food of choice doesn't say that, it hasn't passed the test and isn't meant to be the dog's complete diet. Even better is a statement that the food has been subjected to feeding trials by the dog food company and has been proven to be nutritionally adequate.

Popular beliefs about food variety

You may have heard that you should never switch your dog's food, or if you do, you should do so gradually. You may also have heard that your dog doesn't require any food but his own brand of kibble and that he should never be given anything else.

Not everyone agrees with this point of view, however. Dogs don't eat the same thing every day in the wild. And, personally, I find it hard to believe that the occasional addition of healthy people food, like fresh veggies, fresh fruit, an occasional sprinkle of minced meat, or a spoonful of yogurt or cottage cheese or scrambled eggs, is going to do any Dachshund any harm — except for encouraging obesity. The trick is to keep the calories down and the nutritional density up. And sometimes, that's quite a trick if you feed your Dachshund too much people food or too many treats. Moderation in all things!

Regarding switching your dog's food gradually, yes, any change in diet should be done gradually. And note that dogs with sensitive systems are more likely to react adversely to dietary changes than normal, healthy dogs.

If you're feeling confused, here is some general advice: Find a good-quality kibble, naturally preserved, with meat listed first or second, that your dog likes. The higher priced foods are probably better. And when in doubt, ask your vet which food she prefers for her own dogs.

What about homemade diets?

Considering making your dog's food at home out of natural, healthy ingredients? Sounds appealing, yes, but it is time consuming. Of course, if you have one 6-pound Miniature Dachshund, you'll spend a lot less time making her food than if you have a house full of Standards.

The only problem with homemade diets is that if they aren't nutritionally complete, your dog can suffer. For example, a dog fed only meat eventually experiences severe health problems. The trick is to find the right diet.

Getting into the finer points of the homemade diet is beyond the scope of this book, but I can recommend a couple of books on the subject that tell you exactly what to do if you want to make your dog's food at home, and I highly recommend both of them. These books are also filled with great general health information on dogs. They are *The Holistic Guide for a Healthy Dog,* by Wendy Volhard and Kerry Brown, DVM (Howell Book House, 1995), and *Dr. Pitcairn's Complete Guide to Natural Health for Dogs and Cats,* by Richard H. Pitcairn, DVM, Ph.D., and Susan Hubble Pitcairn (Rodale Press, Inc., 1995).

Raw or cooked

There's a debate about whether dogs on homemade diets should eat raw meat or cooked meat. People feel strongly about this one. If, after reading up on homemade diets, you feel that your dog would benefit from raw meat, and you have a source for clean, preferably organic meat, great! You probably won't have a problem. If it makes you nervous, cook the meat first. Your dog will still get plenty of protein. Regarding bones, They are messy and make some people nervous, but others think that they're great. Dachshunds have such strong jaws and are such adept chewers that I would hesitate to give a Dachshund even a large raw bone. Any bone splinters can be dangerous for your dog. Never give any dog cooked bones of any size.

If you don't want to go all out with the homemade diet but would like to bake an occasional treat for your Dachshund, check out Appendix B of this book for some fun and healthful recipes.

No matter how much your Dachsie begs, never give her a taste of that chocolate bar or chocolate chip cookie. Chocolate can be fatal for dogs. It can cause dehydration and diarrhea that is difficult to treat and deadly if not caught in time.

People food: The good, the bad, and the ugly

People food: Some of it's good, some of it's bad, and some of it's downright dangerous for your Dachshund. If it will help you to remember, keep a copy of Table 8-1 on your refrigerator.

Table 8-1	The Scoop on People Food
Good People Food	*Bad People Food*
Baby carrots, broccoli florets	Hot dogs or any cured meat
Small pieces of green beans	Any candy, especially chocolate
Fresh or frozen peas	Spoiled food of any kind
Plain yogurt	Sweetened yogurt

(continued)

Table 8-1 *(continued)*

Good People Food	Bad People Food
Low-fat cottage cheese	High-fat cheese
Berries	High-salt food
Small pieces of fruit	Bones, cooked or raw
Small amounts of olive oil	Butter or lard
Canola oil or flaxseed oil	Baked goods — cookies and such
Oatmeal, rice, and whole grains	Any processed food
Fresh low-fat meat, minced	High-fat meat

Budgeting for Supplies

You may be getting a little nervous. How will you afford all this stuff? You don't have to have everything on Day #1. Food and a den are all you really need at first. Grooming tools and toys should follow soon after, though. You can probably spread out your new puppy purchases over a month or two, but do budget for them because your Dachshund is worth it. You've made a commitment to give her the best care, and that doesn't mean ignoring her needs in order to save a few pennies. It means spending what is necessary to ensure her good health and happiness. You would do the same for a child, wouldn't you?

On the other hand, you certainly don't need the most expensive of everything. Tight budgets are a reality for many. Go for the lower priced brands, as long as the quality looks good.

Chapter 9

The First Day

*Y*ou've got the den. You've got the food. You've got the chew toys. And now, much to your joy, you've got the Dachshund. Yikes! Suddenly, the responsibility hits you: You've got a dog. Now you get to take him home and begin your new life — your Dachshund-full life. And, suddenly, you feel like you aren't even sure how to make it home with that tiny, dependent puppy on your lap. Don't worry. This chapter talks you through it all, step by step. In a few short days, you'll be feeling like a pro.

Taking the Ride Home

What was that about riding home with that little puppy on your lap? Whoa, there. First of all, cute as she is, and as much as you want to hold and cuddle her, she needs to be restrained safely in the car. You'd restrain your infant in the car when bringing him home from the hospital, wouldn't you? Even if you wouldn't, there are laws that say you must. In a few states, laws are coming into place that require dogs to be safely restrained inside vehicles, as well.

Most states, however, don't require your dog to be restrained. You can make it a family rule, though, and everyone will benefit if you do. Here's why:

✔ If you get in a traffic accident, you probably won't be able to hold on to your new puppy. She can be thrown around inside the vehicle or can go through the windshield.

✔ Your new puppy can serve as a major distraction, possibly encouraging you to cause a traffic accident.

✔ An unsecured dog can become a missile inside a vehicle during an accident, possibly seriously injuring the people inside.

Nobody thinks they'll get into an accident, of course. Unfortunately, many people do. While researching an article recently on dog seatbelts, I heard story after story of people distracted by their dogs — people who swerved over the line and crashed into another car, killing its occupants; people whose dogs were killed when thrown around or out of a car during a crash; people killed by a dog being thrown around inside a car during a crash; and even people in minor accidents whose dogs jumped out of the car when the car was stopped and were killed or caused accidents by running across the road.

I can't think of a single argument not to buckle up your puppy, especially since dog seatbelts and pet carriers are so widely available and inexpensive. The two main types are harness seatbelts that attach to the car's seatbelts, with or without tethers that attach to the harness and pet carriers with slots so a car seatbelt can hold them securely in place. Pet carriers are probably best for brand-new puppies because they may feel more secure and protected to a nervous Dachshund, but either type is safe. (Pet carriers are also good for older Dachshunds who tend to chew destructively. Don't think they aren't capable of chewing up the seats when you're concentrating on navigating through rush-hour traffic.)

Following is a list of harnesses and/or tethers that are well made and effective:

- **The Hold-a-Dox harness.** Based on this company's Hug-a-Dox harness made just for Dachshunds (they transfer pressure to the chest and put less strain on the dogs' delicate backs), this version has a fitting through which you can string your car seatbelt. You can find both the regular and seatbelt-fitted harnesses on the Web at www.doxidelight.com/harness.htm. The e-mail address is doxidelite@nacs.net. Or you can contact the company the old-fashioned way at Dachshund Delights, 8675 Pierce Rd., Garrettsville, OH 44231. Phone: 800-444-9475.

- **Batzi Belts.** These tethers attach to the seatbelt and then to your Dachshund's harness. They are inexpensive and well made. You can order the tethers from Batzi Enterprises at the Web site www.batzi.com. The e-mail address is info@batzi.com. Or use the old-fashioned method: 6717 NW 53rd Terrace, Gainesville, FL 32653. Phone: 888-738-2358 or 352-372-1793. Fax: 352-372-9958.

- **The Kwik Klip Car Safety Harness.** This harness is available from a company called CARE (Canine Automotive Restraint Equipment), which has an excellent Web site that could convince just about anyone to buckle up any dog in any vehicle. Find it at www.canineauto.com. The e-mail address is service@canineauto.com. Or write or call CARE at 420 E. 120th Ave., Unit B-2 #435, Thornton, CO 80233, 303-280-3087.

According to a 1997 American Animal Hospital Association Pet Owner Survey, 35 percent of pet owners take their dogs and cats on vacation with them. And 39 percent take their pets on day trips — camping, on picnics, to the park, or to the beach. Buckle up, everyone.

Welcoming Your Dachshund

Once you arrive safely at home, you can welcome your Dachshund to the family. A real welcome is in order. Life has just changed dramatically for both you and that little dog in your arms, so there's nothing wrong with making a bit of a fuss. You don't want to overwhelm your new dog, of course, but you do want to show him around, acquaint him with his new turf, and do what you can to let him know that he's in a loving and safe environment.

Giving the grand tour

First on your list is the grand tour. This event is for you as well as your new pet, helping you to realize and acknowledge the changing nature of your family. Take your Dachshund from room to room and show her what is hers. Your new Dachshund will want to see the Dachshund dining area, the sleeping quarters, the toys, the . . . but hold on a minute. Aren't you forgetting something? That little puppy probably has to piddle. Make the piddle place your first stop.

First stop: Elimination station

Dogs like to eliminate in the same place all the time, if they can. If you provide your puppy with a spot in the yard just for this purpose and take him there as soon as you get home, even before you go inside the house, you'll set the groundwork for housetraining success.

Pick a spot in the yard, put your puppy down, and let him sniff around and explore. He may pick a different spot, but unless it's the middle of your flower garden or some other objectionable place, let him choose. If he eliminates, praise him. If he doesn't, give it a few minutes. Then take him inside but don't put him down on the floor. Bring him back out 10 or 15 minutes later and try again. Keep this up until he does his duty. If you can keep him from having an accident indoors the first day, you've made great progress.

Crate training, or the method of using the den to teach your puppy how to control his bladder, is explained in more detail in Chapter 13. For now, take your puppy outside to his elimination station frequently for the first few days, especially on day one. Soon he'll learn what that special spot in the yard is for.

Some people prefer to paper-train their Dachshunds, especially if they prefer not to take the dog outside, live in very cold climates where the snow is typically higher than the Dachshund, or are in some way unable to take the puppy outside. That's fine. Just pick a spot, spread out a newspaper, and take your Dachshund there. A scented puppy pad may encourage elimination. Put it over the newspaper for added protection.

Your breeder may have used newspapers for the puppies to eliminate on, so even if you aren't paper-training your Dachshund in the house, don't line the den with newspapers. They may signal to your Dachshund that the den is the elimination station.

The Dachshund dining room

Next up, the dining area. Kitchens and bathrooms are good for puppy food and water bowls because, frankly, puppies aren't the neatest eaters. Set up a big water bowl (though not too big — your puppy shouldn't have to strain to get a drink), keep it full at all times, and keep the food bowl clean.

On the first day, after your puppy has eliminated in the yard, bring your puppy in and feed him. Puppies need to eat more often than adult dogs, so feed yours at least three times a day. (Make sure that you don't feed more than the daily amount recommended by your vet, including treats.) When you get home, after the initial shock, your puppy will probably be hungry.

A new puppy has a lot on his plate, so to speak, so he may not be very hungry the first day. However, new puppies, especially minis, can't afford to go for a day or two without food. If your puppy refuses to eat anything for more than 12 hours, or acts listless, tired, or very shy or scared, call your vet immediately. He could be sick, and might require treatment.

The rest of the home

After a nice meal, your Dachsie pup is probably ready to explore the rest of the house. You'll show him his sleeping quarters soon, but for now, take him into all the rooms in which he'll be allowed. If he is a young puppy, this may mean he's already seen it all. If not, show him the other Dachshund-safe areas of the house. By now, your Dachshund may have figured out there are some other interesting creatures around. Time for introductions!

Letting Dachsie meet the family

After your puppy gets the lay of the land, it's time for him to meet the inhabitants. Introduce the members of your family one by one. Your Dachshund can become overwhelmed if everyone crowds around at once, so let each family member (especially kids) approach slowly and gently, speaking in a quiet, soothing voice.

Some puppies are fine with a little chaos, but introducing your new member to the family one at a time gives her a chance to sniff each person's hand, check out each person's face, and enjoy a stroke or two. This approach may help your puppy learn who's who with a little more ease. Don't pass your puppy around just yet. Let her sniff from the safety of your arms or the floor. Children, especially, may not handle a new puppy in a way that makes her feel secure.

What if my new Dachshund is an adult?

Adult Dachshunds entering a new home experience the same stress as new puppies. They may or may not be better trained than a new puppy. They don't know where they are or with whom they are about to share a life. They don't know where to eliminate, where to eat, or where to sleep. And they probably need to get used to a brand-new den. Follow the same instructions for a new Dachshund of any age, and your new Dachshund will soon be a happy and well-adjusted member of your family, assuming that he was happy and well adjusted before. (If not, you may have other issues to deal with. See Chapter 13.)

Letting Dachsie meet the other pets

If you've got another dog or cat or two, don't throw them all together right away. Confine your pets before bringing your new Dachshund into the house; put them in a room with something that has your new puppy's smell on it — a blanket or mat from his den maybe. Then let your new Dachshund sniff around your house at least for an hour or so while the other pet or pets are confined. Once they've detected each other by scent, you can bring them face to face, but hold each pet for a while first to keep the situation controlled.

Don't forget to respect your original pet's space. Your dog or cat needs reassurance that the new puppy isn't a replacement but an addition.

Allowing for nap time

After the initial tour, potty break, snack, and introductions, your new Dachshund is probably exhausted. Time for a nap. This is your first opportunity to get your Dachshund used to her den. Put the den where you plan to keep it and let your puppy sniff around. Throw a few pieces of kibble inside and let her go in after them. Don't slam the door behind her. Let her come in and out for a few minutes. If it's been awhile, take her outside to her special spot for one more chance to eliminate. Then put a soft blanket, cushion, or mat inside the den, insert your Dachshund, and close the door.

You may hear whining. You may hear crying. You may hear frantic barking. Reassure your puppy in a gentle voice that everything is okay but that it's now time for a nap. Leave the room. Be strong. Let her whine. She may not know she needs a break, but she does. Leave her there for at least 20 minutes — longer if she falls asleep.

When she wakes up, let her out immediately so she doesn't associate the den with too much unpleasantness at first. Take her directly outside to her special spot and then back in again. Now you can play or try your first training session — something very simple, such as raising a piece of kibble above your puppy's head to make her sit as you say "Sit" and then praising her when it works. (Chapter 14 has more on basic commands, including Sit.)

 Puppies, like babies, are relatively simple creatures. They need sleep, food, water, love, and guidance. As long as you provide these five things on that first day (and for the rest of your puppy's life, although later her needs will expand), you are on the right track.

Getting Through the First Night

The day has gone well, and now night approaches. You've heard about nights with a new puppy, and you're nervous. Understandably. Don't expect to get much sleep. That way, if your puppy sleeps through the night, you'll feel lucky. If he doesn't (which he probably won't), you won't be disappointed.

Approach the first night with optimism and a sense of duty, and you'll do right by your puppy. Taking your puppy out a couple of times during the night is a labor of love and well worth the payoff in the end. A dog who never has the chance to eliminate in his den is typically housetrained much sooner than a puppy who's confined longer than his bladder can stand.

Sleep? Who needs it?

The first night with a new Dachshund puppy, or any new dog, carries its share of burdens and joys. One of the burdens is typically a lack of sleep. You go to bed, you get up, you take the puppy out, you go back to bed, you get up, you take the puppy out, you go back to bed, you get up . . . and in between, who can sleep with that whining and crying?

People with new babies don't sleep much either, but, fortunately, your puppy will probably learn to sleep through the night much sooner than a human infant learns. And if your Dachshund is older, he'll learn even more quickly because he's simply getting used to a new situation.

You may spend the first night pulling out your hair, wondering what you've gotten yourself into. But don't call the breeder just yet, begging for her to take your puppy back. A few strategies can help you sail through that first night, and the nights to come, with ease.

Figure 9-1:
Sleep? We
don't need
no stinking
sleep!

Photo courtesy of Judy Rosensteel.

The crying game

One of the hardest parts for dog lovers to endure is the whining. Your Dachshund cries, moans, howls, pleads, and begs. She wants to sleep with *you*. How can you resist? She sounds so pitiful, so pathetic, so lonely. If you were in that kennel, you'd want someone to take you out and cuddle you, too.

But you aren't in that kennel, and your Dachshund puppy isn't a human. Dogs prefer to sleep in enclosed, den-like places. Yours simply hasn't grown accustomed to his yet, and he won't if you don't give him the chance.

If the crying keeps you awake, you can always move your Dachshund to another room, although he'll probably be happier in the room with you. If the whining gets frantic, get up and take your puppy out to his special spot in the yard or on the newspapers. Otherwise, do so every three or four hours if your puppy is awake. Don't wake him up to take him out. He needs to learn to sleep through the night.

Once your Dachshund is trained to sleep through the night without needing to go out, you may as well give in and let him sleep under the covers with you, unless you really object to the idea. Truth is, under the covers is where most Dachshunds sleep, whether their humans originally intended things that way or not. They want to be near you and they love being underneath things. They are insistent. They are persistent. They very likely *will* break you. And when winter comes, you'll be glad they did because there are few things in this life cozier than a warm, snuggly Dachshund on a frigid January morning.

Puppy whining is a lot like infant crying. Puppies don't know the rules yet, and they have no other way of expressing their needs than through whining and crying. Some of those needs are more urgent than others, and it's up to you to figure out which is which. You'll both learn. In the meantime, take your puppy out often enough so that he isn't forced to urinate in his den; then take a deep breath and put in those earplugs.

You aren't being cruel; you are being kind. It just doesn't feel like it. And if you do slip up and he has an accident, don't kick yourself. Change your puppy's bedding and resolve not to let it happen again.

In and out, in and out

In general, your puppy probably needs to go out every two to three hours during the night if she is about 8 weeks old — less often if she's older. That doesn't mean she won't *ask* to go out more often, however. She is lonely and scared, and she doesn't like being shut in that unfamiliar place.

Some puppies may last longer. Maybe you'll get lucky. Some even sleep straight through the night or only need to go out once. If yours is more demanding, don't despair. Your puppy will soon learn, and in a few days, you'll be able to stretch the times between nighttime outings to four, six, and, hallelujah, eight hours. Most puppies learn in a week or two, and some puppies learn right away.

Adult dogs need to eliminate approximately four times per day, although some get by with fewer trips to the elimination station. Young puppies need to go more often but almost always eliminate sometime within an hour after eating, due to the *gastrocolic reflex,* the internal mechanism that governs the elimination process. Get to know your puppy's timing, and you'll know exactly when to take her outside after meals. All dogs undergo the gastrocolic reflex, but adult dogs are better able to control the urge to eliminate.

Good habits to get into

You can do a few things to help your puppy sleep through the night without having to eliminate:

- ✔ Unless your puppy seems unusually thirsty, limit water consumption after 7 p.m.
- ✔ Take your puppy outside to eliminate right before you put him down for the night.

- ✔ Take your puppy out first thing in the morning, at the same time every day. (You can always go back to sleep on the weekends, but your puppy may not be able to hold it if you decide to sleep in.)

- ✔ Check your puppy's bedding frequently in the early days. If he gets used to sleeping on wet bedding, he'll be more inclined to continue having accidents in his crate.

- ✔ Keep reminding yourself that you are teaching your puppy to control his bladder and establish good habits. Then, once he's learned, you can relax the reins a bit. In fact, you'll probably even be convinced to let your Dachshund sleep with you.

A fully housetrained Dachshund may still want to sleep in his den, although most choose you and your bedcovers any day. If you like the companionship, once your dog is housetrained, it won't hurt anything to let him sleep under the covers with you. Press Dachshund owners around the world, and most will probably admit that they've got a Dachshund bed warmer themselves.

The Next Morning: Starting the Routine

It's morning . . . already. The sun is up, and you've made it through the first night. Maybe it wasn't even so bad. Today is your first full day with your new friend. And it's the day for setting up the routine you'll all live with most of the time.

Don't wait and don't think you should make the first few weeks special for your Dachshund. If you can take time to be home more often, that's perfect, but don't center your entire day around your new dog. When things go back to normal, your dog won't understand the sudden change.

Dogs are creatures of habit, and they love routine. Let your new Dachshund know, from the very first, what the schedule will be. Everyone will get along more easily and happily that way, and your new dog will be glad to know what to expect.

Setting up a family routine

Your new family routine should be a lot like the old family routine. You simply need to add a few steps here and there. If you are a list person, write your family's schedule on a piece of paper; then insert the following items where they make sense:

- ✔ Take puppy out (first thing in the morning).
- ✔ Give puppy breakfast.

- ✔ Take puppy out (about 20 minutes after breakfast).
- ✔ Do puppy's grooming session.
- ✔ Do puppy's morning training session.
- ✔ Pet puppy.
- ✔ Give puppy lunch.
- ✔ Take puppy out (about 20 minutes after lunch).
- ✔ Do puppy's afternoon training session.
- ✔ Take puppy for a walk.
- ✔ Give puppy dinner.
- ✔ Take puppy out (about 20 minutes after dinner).
- ✔ Pet puppy.
- ✔ Take puppy out (right before bed).
- ✔ Put puppy to bed.
- ✔ Take puppy out (when necessary, middle of the night).

Yep, your daily routine just got more complicated and will take a little more time. That may mean less time for television or talking on the phone or whatever else you do with your leisure time, but that's the commitment you made when you decided to bring a dog into your life.

But incorporating your puppy's routine into your own is fun. Having a Dachshund around makes life better — just ask any devoted Dachshund owner. Your time spent will be well worth it.

Becoming creatures of habit

Because dogs respond well to schedules and routines, establishing a daily order is an important part of making your dog feel like her universe is secure and in order. In addition to establishing the routine, however, you need to make sure that each item on your list occurs at approximately the same time each day.

Keeping a schedule isn't easy on some people, but it is important for your Dachshund. So try your best. Take him out at the same time each morning, feed him at the same times each day, and train, groom, walk, and pet him consistently — always in the same order, always at about the same time. This kind of life is heaven for a dog and establishes a firm foundation that will make relating to and training your dog much, much easier.

Spend some quiet time a few times each day (preferably at about the same times each day) with your Dachshund, petting and talking to her in a gentle voice without any demands or expectations. Tune out everything else and focus on your pet. You and your new friend will both learn to anticipate these bonding sessions. Your Dachshund will grow to feel safe and secure in your presence, and you may experience some wonderful stress relief. Five minutes twice a day is plenty. It may well be the best five minutes of your day.

Grooming: Don't wait

You may be tempted to wait awhile before grooming your Dachshund, especially if you have a smooth. Isn't that too much to do on the first or second day?

Not at all. Grooming is a crucial part of your Dachshund's routine. It keeps your pet healthy, accustoms her to handling by you or anyone else (most importantly, your vet), and alerts you to any lumps, bumps, bald spots, parasites, or other health problems before they become too serious.

On the first full day you've got your friend at home with you, groom your Dachshund at the appointed time. Even if you choose to have your longhair or wirehair professionally groomed, daily maintenance sessions with you are important for your dog's health and serve as a great get-acquainted or stay-acquainted time.

The following routine is just a suggestion. Feel free to modify the order as you like but include all the relevant steps:

1. **Tell your Dachshund it's grooming time and bring him to the grooming spot.**

   Good choices are the bathroom countertop, the back porch, or a table in a room that can stand a little Dachshund hair.

2. **Gently massage your Dachshund from head to toe, feeling for any lumps, bumps, or irregularities.**

   If you do this task every day, you'll catch any changes as soon as they occur. And don't forget to examine your Dachshund's coat and skin for changes.

3. **Pick up each foot and wiggle each toe, feel the footpads, and then gently examine and rub each ear.**

   These are typically sensitive areas, and if your Dachshund is used to having them touched, he'll be much easier for your vet to handle.

4. **If your Dachshund's nails need clipping, clip them.**

   Regularly clipping off the tips of your dog's nails shouldn't be a problem. On the very first vet visit, ask your vet to show you how to clip your Dachshund's nails so you can do it yourself. It isn't hard once your dog is used to it, and it doesn't hurt as long as you don't cut down too far.

   Your vet can show you how to avoid cutting the *quick*, the small vein in your dog's nail. When nails are clipped frequently (about once every two to four weeks — less often if your dog walks on cement frequently), the quick retracts somewhat and you don't have to worry about cutting it. If you are lax in your clipping duties, though, the quick tends to extend closer to the tip of the nail. In dogs with light nails, you can see the quick and should avoid cutting it because stopping the bleeding can be difficult. In dogs with dark nails, you have to guess. If you do clip the quick, your dog may yelp and you'll have to stop the bleeding. Keep a product on hand for that purpose (available in pet stores).

5. **Brush your dog's coat with a soft-bristled dog brush.**

   Check for any sign of parasites as you brush. If you are very fastidious, you can end the brushing portion of the grooming session with a flea comb once-over.

6. **Brush your dog's teeth with toothpaste made for dogs.**

7. **Apply a pest-control product if it's time (see Chapter 16 for more information on pest control for your Dachshund).**

8. **Praise your pup for behaving so well.**

Training on the first day

Training is something that shouldn't wait. Why not begin training on the very first day?

Training should be fun for both you and your Dachshund, and good habits can only be learned through your instruction. Positive reinforcement is a great way to teach puppies the rules, and training sessions that use positive reinforcement are enjoyable for everyone. Check out Part III of this book for info on how to train your Dachshund.

Remaining calm and patient

Dachshunds are adorable but quite stubborn little creatures, so cultivating the virtue of patience is a necessity for any new Dachshund owner. Just when you think they'll never learn, they do. (Or they decide to give in and do what you want.)

Being impatient, getting irritated, or, worse, getting angry at your new pet doesn't help teach your Dachshund how to behave. It only teaches your Dachshund how to fear you. If you feel yourself getting irritable or angry, stop the training session immediately or give your Dachshund a break in his den. If you think you simply can't stand to clean up one more accident, rethink your housetraining techniques. If you can't stand to clean up the chewed garbage one more time, move the garbage can to a place where your puppy can't reach it.

Sure, impossible behavior from your new puppy can be frustrating, but in most cases, the behavior that really needs changing is yours. Your puppy obviously isn't getting the message, and you may need to reexamine your strategy. It's up to you to manage your puppy's behavior in a way that will help improve the behavior to your liking. You are in charge. You can do it.

There's never a good reason to strike a dog. Hitting doesn't make sense to dogs and only makes you appear dangerous and unpredictable. If you feel yourself losing control, separate yourself from your dog and calm down. Then take a new approach.

The Big Payoff

When you and your Dachshund have finally worked out the rules and understand each other, life suddenly becomes sweet. You'll wonder what you ever worried about. You have such a *good* dog, you tell your friends. Pat yourself on the back. You've done a great job at managing and training your new Dachshund. And give your Dachshund a pat on the back, too. He's tried hard to please you, and he's learned a lot. He *is* a good dog after all.

Part III
The Obedient Dachshund

The 5th Wave — By Rich Tennant

"WE'VE HAD SOME BEHAVIOR PROBLEMS SINCE GETTING 'SNOWBALL', BUT WITH PATIENCE, REPETITION AND GENTLE DISCIPLINE, I'VE BEEN ABLE TO BREAK ROGER OF MOST OF THEM."

In this part . . .

Training: It's the key to a healthy relationship with your Dachshund. After describing the Dachshund personality and helping you understand your role as a trainer, I show you how to housetrain your Dachshund. Then I provide helpful advice on how to teach your Dachsie all of the behaviors that any good dog should know. I conclude this part with coverage of dog shows and competitions.

Chapter 10

Dachshund Defiance:
What It's All About

*Y*ou've heard it from this book and probably from a lot of other places if you've been doing your research: Dachshunds are notoriously stubborn. You may also have heard the words *defiant, willful, obstinate, headstrong,* and *intractable.* All true, yes, and in some Dachshunds more than others.

Depending on your perspective, however, these are all signs of intelligence — of an independent thinker who is far more than an obedient automaton. Ask any Dachshund devotee about the Dachshund's stubborn streak, and you'll probably elicit a smile. Instead of angering those who love him, the stubborn Dachshund engenders affection, even pride, because the Dachshund's obstinate nature is anything but malicious. Your little pup is simply smart as a whip.

Signs of Intelligent Life

I've heard trainers, breeders, and behaviorists describe two types of intelligence in dogs: the kind of intelligence that makes a dog highly and easily trainable (Border Collies, Shelties, and Blue Heelers are this kind of intelligent, for example) and the kind of intelligence that manifests itself as the ability to think without the necessity of human intervention. Dachshunds tend to fall into this second category, so don't be fooled into thinking your stubborn, seemingly untrainable puppy is stupid. *Au contraire*. The problem may just be that your Dachshund is *too* smart.

Most dogs want to please the people they love but not to the point of severe boredom or through senseless repetition or through the performance of an activity that doesn't seem to have a point. Dachshunds revel in fun, but what's so fun about standing in the middle of the living room floor being told to sit, stand, sit, stand, sit, stand, sit, stand. . . . Keep training sessions short, frequent, fun, and challenging. If you're bored, your Dachshund is probably bored, too.

Dachshunds may not be humans, but they aren't robots, computers, or animals that enjoy a life of servitude, either. They want to be with you; they want something interesting to do with their time; they want to enjoy their food, their sleep, and their playtime; and they're happy to learn tricks and do what you ask, as long as it makes sense to their doggy minds.

So the first thing to remember when approaching your Dachshund for that very first training session is that training must be fun, must have rewards, and must be something you and your Dachshund do every day together — something both you and your Dachshund anticipate with relish.

Why Dachshunds Are Independent Thinkers

Different dog breeds have been bred for different reasons. Some have been developed to be very in tune to their human's every need — working in close partnership to herd livestock, for example. Some have been developed to be strong, protective working dogs. Some have been developed to curl up and look pretty on the laps or in the sleeves of royalty on various continents.

Field trials: Independent thinking in action

Watching a Dachshund field trial is a great way to observe the Dachshund's independent nature in action. In Dachshund field trials, Dachshunds compete in pairs to follow the scent of a rabbit. (The rabbit isn't caught or killed; usually, it's not even seen by the dogs.) Once the dogs catch the scent, or *line*, of the rabbit, the handlers aren't allowed to intervene in any way to direct the Dachshunds. The dogs must do it all on their own, followed by the watchful judges, who determine which Dachshunds are most capable of following the trail.

Dachshunds (and many other hunting and tracking breeds) have been bred to think for themselves (see Figure 10-1). Traditionally, the best Dachshunds were the ones that could follow a scent without constant supervision, that could go into a badger den and corner a badger on their own, that could bark to alert their human companions that the prey was cornered in a wholly joint effort — man and Dachshund against badger or rabbit or wild boar.

In other words, Dachshunds — even the Minis — were made to perform reliably and intelligently without too much human intervention, pure and simple. Therefore, the best way to get through to a Dachshund, so that she can know your house rules and what you desire from her, is to learn how to speak her language.

Figure 10-1: This pensive-looking Dachshund is a free thinker.

Photo courtesy of Gail Painter.

You Can't Obey What You Don't Understand

If only you could tell your new puppy, "Listen here, Gertrude. When you feel the urge to eliminate, please let me know ahead of time and I'll let you outside." Or "This is the deal, Otto. When I say 'Sit,' you plant your rump on the ground and stay there. And when I say 'Come,' you run right over here as fast as you can. If you do, I'll really like it a lot."

Sadly, dog training isn't that easy. But it isn't that hard, either. The first thing you have to realize is that your Dachshund doesn't speak English. Okay, sure, you know that. But have you really considered what that means? It means that your Dachshund isn't being defiant the first time you say "Sit" and he just stares at you with a look that says "What planet are you from?" He just doesn't know what you're talking about. His mother didn't tell him "Sit." How is he supposed to understand?

And, even if your Dachshund has learned that when you say "Come" in the living room and he walks over to you, you'll probably give him a treat, he doesn't necessarily understand that when he smells a juicy squirrel dashing through the park and runs madly after it, and you shriek hysterically, "Get back here right *now,* you bad dog!" that you expect the same response from him as you did in the living room.

Teaching your Dachshund what behavior you expect when you say certain words takes a little bit of work and lots of consistent practice. (And no matter how much you practice, your Dachshund may still chase that squirrel, so keep the leash on outside.) It also takes a certain degree of *showing* before the telling alone will work.

Never hold a grudge against your Dachshund. After a few seconds, your dog has no idea what you're angry about. He only knows that you're angry. If you decide to punish him for chewing your shoe by keeping him locked up for two hours or ignoring him all day, your punishment will be ineffective and even destructive because your Dachshund will learn to fear you or avoid you rather than listen to you.

Talking Dachshund

So how do you talk Dachshund? First, you have to see the world from your Dachshund's point of view.

Imagine that you're a Dachshund, scampering around about 8 inches off the ground. You have suddenly been uprooted from the home you knew, and here you are in a strange place with a strange new creature that towers above you and keeps uttering strange, undecipherable sounds. The creature seems very nice, offering food and petting you. The voice sounds well intentioned, and sometimes you get treats.

But sometimes the voice gets mad, irritated, scary. Sometimes the creature appears dangerous, waving his arms wildly, yelling. Sometimes the yelling seems to be at you, but you can't imagine why. You'd like to do whatever will make the creature talk nicely, and you'd sure like some more of those treats. If only you knew what to do to elicit that behavior from your human.

Oh, well, you might as well go on exploring your new environment, relieving yourself when you have to and chewing on whatever you find that looks tempting. After all, you don't have anything else to do — until somebody communicates with you in a way you understand.

Don't just praise your dog when he does something you ask him to. Also praise him when he is doing something well or right when you didn't ask. Constant positive reinforcement of good behavior is integral to developing a good relationship with your Dachshund. If you spend the whole day yelling "No!" and "Bad dog!" but never rewarding your Dachshund for the things he does right, your Dachshund won't learn the self-confidence that's so important to a well-trained and happy pet.

Stay calm and upbeat

If you want to relate to your Dachshund, the first and most important thing you can do is stay positive. Getting angry when your Dachshund eats your loveseat or leaves a puddle on your antique quilt is understandable, but it also won't do any good. Leave the room, get angry, get over it, come back, and resolve not to let it happen again because (and you may not want to hear this) the whole thing was your fault anyway.

Your Dachshund isn't malicious. He doesn't hold a grudge. He doesn't try to wreck your stuff or disobey you. When he does something wrong (wrong according to your rules), it's only because he didn't understand that he wasn't supposed to do that thing under those circumstances.

If you are always (or at least usually) calm, positive, upbeat, and happy when teaching your Dachshund what he can and can't chew, eat, and eliminate on, as well as what fun things you and he can do together, he'll get your meaning much more quickly. Dachshunds are all about reward. What can they do to get one, and then what can they do to get another one? It's that simple. Yelling is not a reward. A slap on the rump is not a reward. Rubbing his nose in an accident is most certainly not a reward. But a treat? A pat? A walk? An enthusiastic — even bubbly — "What a good, sweet, darling little puppy dog you are!" Now *that's* a reward, and that's how you relate to a Dachshund.

Show and tell and reinforce

Of course, sometimes you need to show your Dachshund what to do. For example, taking your Dachshund to his elimination station every hour or so the first day you have him home is *showing* him. Associating his action with a word or phrase, such as "Go potty," is how showing leads to *telling*. Praising him and/or offering him a bit of kibble when he does his duty is *positive reinforcement*. Together, these three actions result in a Dachshund who knows what you want and is glad to give it to you.

The most effective method, in my opinion, for showing, telling, and reinforcing what is expected of your Dachshund is lure-and-reward training. A lure, such as a piece of kibble or a treat, is used to guide your Dachshund into the desired position as you tell him the name of the position — Sit, Lie Down, Bow, or whatever. When the position is achieved, Dachsie gets the treat. Show, tell, and reinforce. Now that's not so difficult.

Accentuate the positive

There are lots of ways to train dogs, and most people use a combination, depending on the situation. The most common methods of training are positive reinforcement, negative reinforcement, punishment, and extinction. *Positive reinforcement* rewards desired behavior with something the dog wants, such as a treat or praise. *Negative reinforcement* rewards desired behavior by removing an unpleasant condition — like when you release a choke chain when your dog sits. *Punishment* discourages undesired behavior by inflicting something undesirable, such as a swat or a scolding. *Extinction* specifically doesn't reinforce undesired behavior — like when you ignore your Dachshund when he jumps up on you.

Positive reinforcement used in conjunction with extinction is now considered by many contemporary trainers to be the most effective method of training. When your Dachshund does something you want him to do, reward him immediately. When he does something he isn't supposed to do, don't reinforce the behavior. Completely ignore him. He'll hate that.

Of course, if he is doing something dangerous or damaging, you have to stop him immediately. Whisk him outside before he eliminates on your carpet and remove his jaws from your table leg — even accompany your removal of him with a firm "No!" But for heaven's sake, don't make a big deal about it. He won't understand, he'll get scared, and even if he does learn not to chew the table *in your presence* (because that is the only time he gets punished for it), he won't understand that he shouldn't *ever* chew on the table.

And forget punishing him an hour, or even five minutes, after his transgression. Dogs associate punishment with whatever they are doing *at that moment*. If you come home from work and see three little piles in various parts of the living room, and you start screaming at your Dachshund while he happens to be taking a drink of water or resting peacefully, he'll think you're punishing him for taking a drink of water or resting peacefully. Or he'll just think you're crazy.

Rewards for a good dog

Tired of the same old pieces of kibble for positive reinforcements? You can use many things to reward your Dachshund. Here are some ideas:

- Different food treats. Small pieces of veggies and fruit, a spoonful of plain yogurt or olive oil with dinner, pieces of whole-grain cereal (oat rings or wheat biscuits, for example), or bits of scrambled eggs will keep your Dachshund excited about training.

- A game of fetch or a run around the yard.

- An extra grooming session now and then (if your Dachshund loves to be brushed).

- A walk with you (the *ultimate* reward for a job well done).

Some trainers don't believe in using food rewards, but Dachshunds are highly food motivated, so as long as your rewards aren't causing your Dachshund to become overweight, food is a great way to train a Dachshund. It isn't bribery — at least not in a bad sense. We are all motivated by rewards. Motivating dogs with food is like paying people for working at their jobs. We all like a kind word from our bosses, but we like a nice big bonus in our paychecks even better. Why should our Dachshunds be any different?

One of the most important things to remember when learning how to communicate with your Dachshund is consistency. If you praise your Dachshund for obeying your command one day and then ignore him for obeying your command the next day, or if you refuse to let him on your bed one day and then let him on your bed the next day, he won't get it. Make the rules and stick to them. If you must change them, keep them changed. Dachshunds don't understand waffling, and the result will be a dog that doesn't know what you want because as far as your Dachshund can tell, *you* don't even know what you want.

Understanding Dachshund

To communicate well with your dog, you must learn to speak Dachshund *and* understand Dachshund. That means you need to relate to him when you desire certain behaviors, and that you also need to understand why he behaves as he does.

Dachshunds aren't complicated. (And neither are people, really.) They enjoy pleasurable activities. They require food, water, sleep, and affection. They absolutely love to go on walks, play outdoors, chase squirrels, retrieve balls (but not necessarily give them back to you), sleep under the bedcovers with you, and curl up on your lap when you relax to watch television. They'll do just about anything for your undivided and rapt attention.

They don't enjoy being hungry, in pain, overly tired, uncomfortable, or frightened, and they absolutely hate it when you are displeased with them —

especially if they don't know why. They don't want to be ignored. They want to be the center of your universe, and they sincerely believe they deserve to be.

They don't know what "Sit" means until you show them. But they are smart, so once you show them, they'll understand. They don't know why you want them to do boring, repetitive things when they could be off sniffing around or having lunch. But they'll do those things if the reward is big enough. They want to know *why* they shouldn't pull on the leash. So if you make it clear that pulling on the leash means no walk and that trotting politely by your side means a long walk, they'll be happy to oblige.

And that's about it. If only raising kids were that easy! (Actually, positive re-inforcement works on kids, too, but that's a different book.). Now all you have to do is practice, practice, practice, keep it fun, keep it happy, and keep it rewarding for *everyone* involved. (You won't want to train your Dachshund if it isn't rewarding for you, either; we're all motivated by positive reinforce-ment.) Pretty soon, you'll have a well-trained pet, and people will wonder how you did it. Just tell them you are fluent in the language of Dachshund.

Some dogs seem to be completely untrainable. Then well into the first year, their owners suddenly discover that these dogs are deaf, an affliction more common in piebald Dachshunds than in other colors. If you are having seri-ous training problems with your Dachshund and you think he could have a hearing problem, take him to your vet right away. Too many undiagnosed deaf dogs have been repeatedly punished for not obeying a command they never heard. There are alternate methods for training deaf Dachshunds, which you can learn from a professional trainer with experience in this area.

The Wide Range of Normal

Despite all the generalizations you'll hear about dogs and Dachshunds, the fact is, every Dachshund is different. Some are more stubborn than others. And some are jollier or bigger performers or more retiring or less likely to enjoy children or more inclined to snap at strangers than others.

You can read every book on the planet about Dachshunds, dog behavior, and training, but until you get to know the personality of your own Dachshund, you'll only have half the story. People are all different, too, and every home environment is different. Any individual Dachshund in any individual home is going to result in a unique and special situation.

Nature versus nurture

Your Dachshund inherited certain traits and tendencies from his parents. He may be particularly smart or quick or laid-back. But nurture plays a big part as well. Everything you do, everything you say, and the way you and your Dachshund live together help shape his personality in ways that will affect his ability to learn, his desire to please you, and even his zest for life. Talk about a big responsibility.

Lots of the rules of this book apply lots of the time, but even if you do everything the way you think you should, your Dachshund may tend to be particularly stubborn and hard, requiring sharper corrections (though never physical ones). Or maybe you've got a sensitive fellow who practically faints with joy if you smile in his direction. You'll probably never need to raise your voice even slightly with this one, and you may never even need to use food as a positive reinforcement for training. Maybe yours doesn't want to sleep in your bed at all. Maybe she already knows what you mean when you say "Come," and you hardly have to train her. Maybe he pushes your limits to see how much he can get away with, even when he knows exactly what you want — just out of curiosity or tenacity or because he's particularly precocious.

All you can do is live and learn together, stay positive, give yourself a time-out when you get angry (and you probably will get angry from time to time). Keep at it. You and your Dachshund have a bond of mutual love, respect, and affection, even if you may not always like each other at a given moment.

When training problems mean health problems

In some cases, training problems or certain unusual behaviors may indicate a health problem. Apart from individual differences, be on the lookout for any of the following behaviors and alert your veterinarian. Better to catch a health problem in the early stages than to ignore it until it becomes something life threatening. Call your vet if your Dachshund

- Never obeys your commands when he can't see your face.
- Was housetrained but suddenly begins to have accidents inside the house.
- Behaves aggressively for no good reason, like growls or snaps at people who aren't posing a threat, especially if you've trained your Dachshund not to bite or if he has never exhibited aggressive behavior before.
- Suddenly becomes shy around people when he wasn't previously.
- Suddenly seems forgetful or confused, possibly bumping into furniture (more common in older dogs).
- Suddenly refuses to come, go on a walk, or move at all.
- Yelps when touched.
- Suddenly becomes very destructive, fearful, or hysterical when left alone.

All these behaviors may seem at first to be training issues but could be signs of a serious health problem, possibly of an acute nature. Don't hesitate to call your vet. She is there to answer your questions and keep your Dachshund well.

The Canine Behavioral Consultant: Your Ally

If your dog exhibits behavioral problems, seems untrainable despite your best efforts, or has any of the problems listed in the preceding section and your vet has ruled out a medical problem, consider contacting a canine behavioral consultant. No, it isn't like taking your pet in for psychotherapy. Dogs can suffer from very real and serious behavioral problems and a canine behavioral consultant or animal behaviorist is specifically trained to deal with these problems.

A canine behavioral consultant may not have all the answers, but a good one may know just what to do when you've exhausted other avenues. Certainly consult one before giving up on your pet. Sometimes the most serious-seeming problem is really a simple matter.

To find a good canine behavioral consultant or animal behaviorist, contact The American Dog Trainers Network. Its Web page, at www.inch.com/~dogs/behaviorists.html, lists animal behaviorists and canine behavioral consultants. You can e-mail the network (you must include your telephone number, or they won't respond) at dogs@inch.com. You can also call the network's help line with your training and behavior questions: 212-727-7257 between 1 p.m. and 3 p.m. EST, seven days per week. ***Note:*** If you leave your message *before* 1 p.m. and request a return call, your call will be returned collect. For those of you who still like to write regular letters, sorry. They don't accept communication via regular mail.

Don't be shy about calling a behaviorist or behavioral consultant. Lots of people do, and lots of people are very glad they did. Many dogs have been saved through simple behavior modification techniques. Most dogs surrendered to animal shelters are there because of behavioral problems their owners couldn't or wouldn't handle. Don't let your Dachshund suffer this fate. Learn the language, train, hire a professional when necessary, and immerse your dog in lots of love. Now you're talking Dachshund.

Chapter 11

Who's Training Whom?

In This Chapter

▶ How your Dachshund's inborn tendencies affect his capacity for getting trained

▶ The power of Dachshund wiles — and how to put your own wiles into play to get him trained

Sometimes, despite your best efforts, you'll wonder who's training whom when you get to the end of a long day of Dachshund disobedience. Training a Dachshund can indeed be a challenge, and it helps to keep reminding yourself who's the boss, as well as how to be the boss.

Your Dachshund won't mind being the boss, but he really would rather that you do the job. In any case, somebody has to be boss, and if you won't do it, your Dachshund will. Believe me, you don't want to spend your days subject to the capricious nature of this tiny tyrant. You must take charge, and this chapter shows you how.

Know Your Dachshund

The first step toward taking the reins in the dog-human relationship is to know your Dachshund. All Dachshunds have certain qualities and instincts. Knowing them and taking advantage of the characteristics of the breed help you take control and maintain it.

Each persona discussed in this section is probably a part of your Dachshund's overall personality. Some personas may sound more like your pet than others. Whichever types seem dominant in your dog, use those tendencies in your training and play sessions. This is one of the advantages of owning a purebred dog. Although each Dachshund is different, in some ways, they're all the same. Each characteristic discussed in this section carries with it certain training challenges. There are also certain games each Dachshund persona enjoys, as well as certain types of competition each type excels at, if you want to pursue those things.

Dachshund field trials

If your Dachshund is a natural tracker, consider competing in Dachshund field trials. For a brochure containing the Dachshund field trial rules and regulations, send $1 to the American Kennel Club, 5580 Centerview Drive, Suite 200, Raleigh, NC 27606-3390. Or read the rules and regulations online at `www.akc.org/dic/events/perform/ftdach1.cfm`. You can also call, fax, or e-mail the AKC to request this information: 919-233-9767 (phone), 919-233-3627 (fax), `info@akc.org` (e-mail).

The hunter/tracker

Dachshunds were bred to hunt, to track a scent, and to follow their quarry, with unwavering persistence, until the prize is won. What does this mean for you?

- **Training challenge:** If your Dachshund detects a scent while you're working, training, playing, or walking together, it'll take every ounce of doggie willpower for him not to dash off after it. Many of them aren't able to resist. If your Dachshund runs away, it's your fault for not keeping him on his leash in an open area. You should know that he's a hunter and a tracker, and you can't argue with instinct.

- **Great games:** This type of Dachshund enjoys games that mimic a hunting or tracking situation. Show him a small ball, let him sniff it, and then throw it as far as you can. Watch him do his stuff. The tricky part is convincing him to give it back to you so you can do it again, but after he learns that returning the ball to you means another go-around, he'll probably be more than willing.

- **An edge on the competition:** Use your Dachshund's tracking ability for advanced training in field trials, den trials, and utility trials (an advanced stage of obedience competition). Dachshunds love to have challenging work to do, especially when it uses their natural instincts to good advantage. Seeing a Dachshund in action, using his natural instincts, is a sight to see, and once you try it, you may find that you're hooked. (For more on training your Dachshund for competition, see Chapter 15.)

The digger

If you have a Dachshund and your backyard fence isn't buried at least a foot underground, you probably know all about the Dachshund's penchant for digging. Some Dachshunds dig more than others, but in general, they all love it, once they discover how fun it is. What does this mean for you?

- ✔ **Training challenge:** Your Dachshund can behave in the most maddening ways: digging under your fence and running off, digging up your flower beds and vegetable gardens, and even attempting to dig through your shag carpeting, your couch cushions, and your bed mattress. What's a person to do? If you're aware of this particular Dachshund penchant, you have no excuse not to prepare. Line the bottom of your fence with bricks or rocks or even pour a foundation under the fence. Grow your garden somewhere else or put a fence around it (dig a foot-deep trench and sink the fence into it or your Dachshund will dig under this one, too). And, if your Dachshund insists on digging in a specific area on your carpet or furniture, break out the Bitter Apple spray and take action. Be vigilant and prevent destructive digging before it gets too destructive. And don't get mad if your Dachshund digs. You can't argue with instinct, and she isn't doing it to make you mad. She just thinks it's really, really fun.

  If your Dachshund loves to dig, but you can't afford to pour a foundation under your fence, all is not lost. Line the base of your fence with cinder-blocks to make digging more of a challenge; then keep the yard full of fun things to do — even places to dig that aren't near the fence. In extreme cases, your Dachshund may not be able to go in the backyard unsupervised, but a little extra vigilance is a small price to pay to keep your Dachshund safe.

- ✔ **Great games:** If you don't mind a rather rugged backyard, you can encourage certain, specific digging. Inside the house, show your Dachshund a toy. Let her sniff it. Go into your fenced yard, bury the toy in a hole, and cover it up. Let your Dachshund out. See how long it takes her to find it and dig it up. Do it again. What a way to spend an afternoon. What joy when your Dachshund uncovers the toy. Your Dachshund will be in heaven.

- ✔ **An edge on the competition:** Dachshunds are born for den trials and earth dog trials. If your Dachshund really likes to burrow under things (and what Dachshund doesn't?), you probably have a natural. Earth dog and den trials don't take much training. They are considered events that utilize a dog's natural instinct and are not for exhibiting special skills developed by training (although that bury-the-toy-in-the-yard game will probably help to hone your Dachshund's natural instinct). The AKC and the AWTA (American Working Terrier Association), as well as many regional or local Dachshund and Terrier clubs, hold these competitions. Only Terriers and Dachshunds are allowed. (Check out Chapter 15 for more information on how to get involved.)

Earth dog trials

If your dog loves to dig and has a keen sense of smell, she'd probably love to compete in Earth dog trials. To read the complete American Kennel Club rules and regulations for Earth dog trials, check out the AKC Web site, at www.akc.org/dic/events/perform/earthdr.cfm. You can also write, call, fax, or e-mail the AKC to request this information in printed form: American Kennel Club, 5580 Centerview Drive, Suite 200, Raleigh, NC 27606-3390; 919-233-9767 (phone), 919-233-3627 (fax), info@akc.org (e-mail).

The athlete

Dachshunds may have delicate backs and may not appear particularly buff, but many are superior athletes (see Figure 11-1). Dachshunds were built to work, not to sit around looking pretty. Even the Minis were designed to follow quarry into smaller dens, not to be Toy versions of the Standard. No lap dogs in Dachshund land (although they do love your lap). What does the Dachshund's natural athletic ability mean to you?

- ✔ **Training challenge:** Dachshunds like to move, exercise, and use their natural athletic ability, so if you're a sedentary person, you'll have to find a way to make sure that your Dachshund gets enough exercise. Miniatures can often get enough activity running around inside the house or apartment. Don't expect them to sit still all day, though. They aren't made for it. Standards really do need more space in which to run. Backyard time and a walk or two or three are in order. A Dachshund who doesn't get enough exercise may turn his energy to more destructive efforts. The Dachshund's tendency toward obesity makes exercising your short little athlete even more important. Sure, you can turn your Dachshund into a couch potato, but that's not healthy for him. It's good for you to get out there and move, too, so why not benefit both of you and give your athlete a natural outlet for his abilities?

Athletic as they are, there are certain activities Dachshunds probably shouldn't do too often. If a sport or activity involves running around sharp corners at high speed, shaking the neck as in a boisterous game of tug of war, jumping down from high places, or racing up and down steep stairs, discourage your Dachshund from getting too rowdy. You want to keep his back in good shape.

✔ **Great games:** Dachshunds love to play. They are excellent runners, and although it isn't good for them to jump too often, some really enjoy jumping up to catch a ball (or grab your dinner off that low counter). Let your Dachshund refine his natural athletic abilities by playing active games. Throw a Frisbee and let him chase it. Set up an obstacle course and let him maneuver it to find a favorite toy, ball, or food treat. And don't forget the all-important walk. Your Dachshund loves to be on the move, and when your daily exercise is over, your natural athlete will be more than happy to relax, kick back, and allow you to pet him to sleep.

✔ **An edge on the competition:** Don't be fooled into thinking that your Dachshund can't compete in such athletic activities as obedience and agility competitions in addition to those areas of competition reserved for Dachshunds, such as field and den trials. Dachshunds have achieved the highest obedience titles, which takes tremendous athletic ability. And although Dachshunds aren't typically the first breed people think of when they think of agility (a competition in which dogs maneuver an obstacle course), Dachshunds can and do participate in agility competition as well. Your local dog club may have other events your Dachshund can participate in. If you think organized athletics is fun, and your Dachshund enjoys that kind of thing, go for it.

Figure 11-1:
This Dachsie looks like a natural athlete, does he not?

Photo courtesy of Rozina Smith.

The actor within

Your Dachsie is a real clown and is happiest when all eyes are on him. You wonder whether anyone will pay attention to you again because since you brought home your Dachshund, he's the star of the household, and he likes it that way, thank you very much. What does this mean for you?

- **Training challenge:** If you don't make training fun, and if it isn't all about your Dachshund, forget it. What does a born performer want with tedium? Nothing. Take advantage of your Dachshund's showy side and make a big deal out of good behavior. The best way to reward bad behavior is to completely ignore it. Your born performer wants to be center stage and hates being ignored even more than being yelled at, so take advantage.

- **Great games:** If it pleases your little show pup (and it probably will), teach her some really flashy tricks, sure to elicit oohs, aahs, giggles, and applause from spectators. Tricks are sure to become a favorite part of your scene-stealing Dachsie's repertoire.

- **An edge on the competition:** You may want to look into a fun competitive activity called canine freestyle or canine musical freestyle. This competition involves a choreographed routine that includes both you and your Dachshund as participants. Any dog can compete, but Dachshunds love to show off, and if yours is good at obedience but you both like the idea of something flashier, freestyle may be right up your alley. Even if you are a little shy, your Dachshund can do most of the fancy footwork. (Check out the canine freestyle organizations listed in the nearby sidebar or contact your local Dachshund club or dog club for event opportunities in your area.)

Dachshund racing? No no no!

Back in the 1960s, Dachshund lovers wondered whether their dogs would enjoy racing on the kind of track used by Sighthounds for lure coursing. The Dachshunds *loved* it. Dachshund racing quickly became a fun, informal, and very popular weekend event all around the country. Unfortunately, the sport became so popular that Greyhound racetracks began to exploit the event to promote their flailing industry. Dachshund owners and breeders now urge all people who care about the future of Dachshunds to refuse to participate in Dachshund racing of any kind. The dogs may love it, but they will inevitably suffer from careless breeding and abuse if it becomes too profitable. Please don't support Dachshund racing. Do it for the breed so that Dachshunds won't suffer the same fate as the unfortunate Greyhound.

Canine freestyle events

For more information on canine freestyle events, contact and/or join either of the following organizations (both have great information on their Web sites about freestyle in general and membership in each organization in particular):

✔ The World Canine Freestyle Organization Ltd., at www.woofs.org/wcfo. The mailing address is P.O. Box 350122, Brooklyn, NY 11235-2525. Or e-mail, call, or fax the organization: wcfodogs@aol.com (e-mail), 718-332-5238 (phone), 718-646-2686 (fax).

✔ The Canine Freestyle Federation, at www.canine-freestyle.org/. Receive complete CFF regulations for $5 or as part of the complete membership package when you join. Contact CFF corresponding secretary Monica Patty, 21900 Foxden Lane, Leesburg, VA 20175. You can also ask questions about canine freestyle by e-mailing CFF at directors@canine-freestyle.org.

Those Dachshund Wiles. . . .

So you're dealing with a hunter, a tracker, a digger, an athlete, and an actor destined for whatever stage you'll give him. The combination results in a unique set of what I like to call Dachshund wiles.

Dachshund wiles are something hard to define and yet exceedingly powerful. They make up the force that mysteriously compels you to hand over a full half of your hot dog to your devious little darling, even when you're still hungry. They keep you from answering the phone when your Dachshund is curled on your lap. They keep you from staying angry at your Dachshund for more than about five seconds. And their powerful emanations somehow propel you, each and every night, to the very edge of your bed, reserving most of the space on your king-sized mattress for your 8-pound Miniature Dachshund.

A force to be reckoned with, indeed. And certainly a force to consider when attempting to teach your Dachshund about how to behave. What can you do in the face of such a power? Learn how your Dachshund uses his wiles, and you'll learn how to put some of your own wiles into play.

How dogs manipulate

Dogs aren't dumb. Furthermore, they are programmed for survival. The survival instinct manifests itself in many ways, especially in the more intelligent creatures. Your Dachshund is downright creative in his mastery of the survival instinct for his own benefit.

Dogs need certain things, like food, shelter, warmth, and companionship. They also desire certain things, like more food, more warmth, and a whole lotta companionship. Dogs don't like other things, like hunger, standing out in the rain, or being ignored. They are social animals, domesticated to enjoy the good life, and oh, how they love suppertime.

It only makes sense, then, that your Dachshund will do whatever he can to get more of what he wants and less of what he doesn't want. Any creature does this. Some are simply more effective in their techniques than others. Your Dachshund will soon learn, all on his own, what behaviors encourage you to hand over the goods (treats, kind words, snuggles) and what behaviors encourage you to go off the deep end or refuse to offer any more treats.

Are you a pushover? Your Dachshund will soon learn whether a certain cute expression accompanied by a slightly cocked head and perked ears will melt your heart and cause you to toss just one more gourmet dog cookie in your Dachshund's direction. If you're not careful, she'll come to learn that barking, nipping, or jumping results in treats and attention. (To your Dachshund, even negative attention, like yelling, is better than being ignored.) Always remember to reward the good behavior, not the bad.

In other words, you must turn the tables on your clever little pet. If she recognizes that begging only gets her ignored, but that lying quietly in the corner during dinner elicits that much-desired behavior in you — namely, you serving her dinner — you've got the upper hand. When she realizes that barking and jumping on you results in nothing but that a well-behaved greeting when you arrive home — with eager wagging tail but no jumping — gets her lots of praise, stroking, and kisses, you'll be manipulating her in the best way.

After your Dachshund is well trained, you'll be able to bend the rules now and then. However, if you make it a habit to enforce rules only when you have the energy, you may as well forget the rules altogether. Your Dachshund won't understand your inconsistent enforcement as having anything to do with rules. He will only understand that he doesn't know how you'll react when he does something, so he won't even try to anticipate. He'll just do what he wants to do.

Why you must be in charge

If you don't decide from day one to be in charge of your Dachshund's behavior, he'll take you for a ride. You'll be a slave to his whims, his bad habits, and his begging, barking, chewing, housebreaking mishaps, and other behaviors that you never dreamed you'd endure.

Raising a Dachshund is hard work. It takes vigilance, consistency, and a refusal on your part to give in. Of course, being consistent and firm, and steeling yourself against those Dachshund wiles, is easier for some than for others. You'll be a step ahead of the game if you first figure out your personal training style, including your strengths and, more importantly, your weaknesses. (Check out Chapter 12 to determine your own personal training profile.)

Chapter 12

Determining Your Trainer Profile

*E*veryone has a unique nature and personality, and attempting to practice any daily behavior that goes against your personality is probably futile. If you're crazy about chocolate, a diet of tofu and bean sprouts won't last for more than a day or two (just ask me — I know). You have to find a diet that makes sense for your personal tastes and level of willpower.

Same thing with dog training. If you're a great big sap, and one look at that little puppy is enough to drop you to your knees because you're so overwhelmed by his cuteness, a strict, regimented, authoritarian style won't work for you. You'll probably end up with a Dachshund in your bed, and you'll probably spend lots of money on fancy treats and expensive sweaters at the local doggy boutique, feeling guilty all the while that you're doing something wrong.

On the other hand, perhaps you love dogs and they're a big part of your life, but you feel that consistency and good behavior are paramount and have no trouble making a set of rules and enforcing them. Your Dachshund can whine or bat her big dark eyes at you all day, but you know that extra treats will make her chubby, and you have no intention of giving in.

Part of the challenge of training a dog, especially a Dachshund, is to recognize that your personality and training style will impact your training effectiveness. This chapter helps you determine your individual training style and develop a training strategy that's tailored to your strengths and weaknesses.

Understanding Your Personal Training Style

An analysis of your relationship with your Dachshund isn't complete without a little self-examination (see Figure 12-1). For some people, training dogs is easy. Others can't seem to train the most willing and tractable of pets. What is it about human behavior that is sometimes so contrary to communicating effectively with animal behavior?

Different people have different training styles. Play-based training or short drills, food rewards or praises and pats, learning tricks or unlearning bad habits — all are effective as long as they are consistent, loving, practiced daily, based on positive reinforcement rather than punishment, and fun for you and your Dachshund.

Figure 12-1:
Are you the kind of trainer who can get a Dachsie to endure this?

Photo courtesy of Adam Hare.

Determine your training profile

You can be better prepared to train your Dachshund if you figure out what your personal tendencies are beforehand. Answer the following questions to determine your trainer profile. If some of the questions aren't relevant yet (for example, if you haven't tried housebreaking yet or haven't started train- ing yet), imagine how you think you'd react in the situation.

1. You just brought your new Dachshund puppy home with you, and you are introducing her to her new Dachshund den. She doesn't want to go inside. What do you do?

   A. Throw in some treats, push her inside gently but firmly, and shut the door. She'll get used to it.

   B. Throw in some treats and then ignore her. If you aren't interesting to play with, the treats will seem more attractive and she'll go in eventually.

   C. Think to yourself, "The crate looks so cold and uninviting. Maybe if I take her out enough times during the night, she won't pee in the bed."

2. You and your family are just sitting down to a nice family dinner. Where is your Dachshund?

   A. In his crate. He won't even get a chance to learn how to beg in your house!

   B. Lying quietly nearby, on the kitchen floor. You are determined not to reinforce any begging by giving him table food, but you hate to have him miss out on the family dinnertime.

   C. Under the table, front paws on your lap. He knows he'll get a little nibble. How can you help but slip him just a tiny morsel of roast beef? It doesn't seem fair that you get to eat such good food and he doesn't.

3. You give your Dachshund treats

   A. During training when she fulfills a request.

   B. To reinforce any good behavior.

   C. Probably too often, but when she looks at the dog cookie jar that way, with such longing, you can't resist.

4. Housebreaking has been

   A. A breeze. You crate-trained your Dachshund, and he learned in a week. He never had a single accident inside.

   B. Fairly successful. You're still working on it, but he's getting the pic- ture. He still makes a few mistakes, but you clean them up right away and try to be as vigilant as possible.

   C. Um, well, pretty much unsuccessful. You aren't sure your Dachshund gets the concept yet. You can't get yourself to keep him in that crate for very long, even when you aren't supervising him, because you can't bear the whining and crying. You feel so sorry for him, so you let him out. You've missed quite a few opportunities to get him outside in time, but you don't mind cleaning up the messes all that much.

5. Your training sessions are

   A. Strictly regimented, at the same time each day, with a planned schedule of what you will cover in each session.

   B. Daily, but they're pretty informal and fun.

   C. Pretty much nonexistent. You keep forgetting to have actual training sessions, but whenever you think of it, you ask your Dachshund to sit or stay or do whatever seems fun at the time.

6. Your goals for your Dachshund are

   A. To train her for competition, either in obedience, agility, field trials, or wherever her talents are.

   B. To have a well-behaved family pet that knows and follows the house rules most of the time.

   C. To have a buddy and best friend. You aren't too concerned with whether she can do tricks. You just want her around for cuddling.

7. Your vet tells you your Dachshund is overweight. What do you do?

   A. Immediately restrict his food intake and increase the length of his walks.

   B. Cut back on the treats and begin measuring his kibble so that you don't overestimate, plus you become careful about walking him every day instead of skipping the walk when you don't feel like it.

   C. Buy lower-calorie treats and try to cut back on his food, but when he acts like he's starving, you often give in and give him just a little bit more. You think to yourself, "He does love his food so! Maybe if I let him out in the backyard more often, he'll get more exercise."

8. Your Dachshund barks at everything — passersby on the street, trash blowing by, and even you when she wants something like a treat or some attention. How do you handle it?

   A. Begin strictly refusing to reinforce barking by completely ignoring her when she barks or putting her in her den when she gets too loud, especially if she is outside disturbing the neighbors. No one should have to listen to such excessive noise.

   B. Recognize that Dachshunds bark but that excessive barking isn't necessary. You keep the blinds shut on the front window and ignore her when she barks at you. You make her come inside if she barks in the yard. Otherwise, you pay attention because she may be alerting you to something.

    C. Think to yourself, "Dachshunds bark. What about it?" You don't mind so much. Besides, if you get evicted, you can always move out to the country where people understand about barking dogs.

  9. In your home, nighttime consists of

    A. Peace and quiet, with your Dachshund curled up in his den, sleeping through the night (after the first few weeks).

    B. An occasional trip outside, but mostly your Dachshund sleeps nicely under the covers with you.

    C. Broken sleep. Every time your Dachshund makes a noise, you wake up and take him out or give him a toy to chew. You've even found yourself playing with him at 3 a.m. because he wanted to play. You aren't getting much sleep, but you feel like your Dachshund needs the attention. You only hope he'll grow out of this stage sooner or later and sleep through the night so you can, too.

  10. During the day when you're at work

    A. Your Dachshund stays in her den or in an enclosed, pet-proofed area. You either come home for lunch to let her out or hire a pet sitter or dog walker to cover the lunch hour.

    B. Your Dachshund stays in the kitchen with a baby gate keeping her out of the carpeted areas. Sometimes she chews things, but you're working on it. You come home for lunch as often as you can. When you don't, you usually have a mess to clean up.

    C. Your Dachshund gets free reign of the house. You feel so guilty leaving her that you feel she deserves to shred the trash and have a few accidents. You can't blame her.

Letting your Dachshund run free when you're away can result in more than just property damage. Your Dachshund can be seriously injured or poisoned if he ingests certain types of trash or other foreign objects or substances. Dachshund-proof any room in which your Dachshund will be left unsupervised for any length of time. Better yet, let him snooze in his den when you're away.

Develop a personalized game plan

After you answer the questions in the preceding section, you need to see where you stand. Count up your answers and determine whether you have mostly As, Bs, or Cs. Then read the applicable training-strategy discussion that follows. If you have about an equal number of any two letters, read both training-strategy discussions.

If you have mostly As

You're a highly disciplined, efficient, and consistent pet owner. You've probably always been a schedule person, and you encourage discipline and respectful behavior in everyone around you — spouse, children, and pets. For you, a dog is simply another family member that's expected to follow the rules and behave in an acceptable manner. If anyone can bring out the best in a Dachshund, it's you. Dachshunds crave consistency and want to know the rules.

Consider training your Dachshund for professional competition, if your dog has what it takes. *You* certainly do. Take advantage of your tendencies by keeping your Dachshund on a strict schedule, a healthy diet, and regimented training sessions. Systematic training is great. You get a lot accomplished in the minimum amount of time.

Your one challenge? Remember to be *fun*. Consistency and schedules can get tedious if you don't maintain your sense of humor when others aren't quite as disciplined as you are. When your Dachshund slips up, gently nudge him back on track. Don't get angry or irritable when he doesn't measure up to your high standards. Instead, keep working with him. He'll get it, and if he can trust you to be kind and loving in your firmness, he'll do anything for you.

If you have mostly Bs

You're the kind of dog owner most breeders are looking for. You know what your pet needs, and you do your best to give it to her. Sometimes you get busy, sometimes you get off schedule, and sometimes you bend the rules. In general, though, you are a responsible and loving Dachshund companion who tries hard to teach your pet what it means to behave and have a fulfilling family life.

Your training sessions are fun and full of play, which Dachshunds love. Your pet will surely respond quickly to your requests once she learns what you want. Your challenge? To keep a schedule and to remember to train *every day*. Dogs thrive on consistency and regularity even more than humans do, so a routine is important for your dog even if you don't always follow one. You're doing a great job, however, and your Dachshund is lucky to have a pet owner as caring and responsible as you are.

If you have mostly Cs

You're probably fully aware that you are not in charge of your Dachshund. She's in charge of you. You'd better either prepare for a life of servitude or change your ways. Don't be offended. I used to be in this category, and I know change is possible. Difficult, yes, but I don't mean that you have to alter your personality. For the sake of your Dachshund, you do have to summon up some inner strength and take charge. Sure, she's sweet. Sure, she's charming. Sure, she's just about the cutest little thing you've ever seen in your life, and you love her to death. All the more reason to do what's best for her, and that doesn't mean letting her run the show.

Dogs (like children) will challenge you at every turn but want nothing more than to know, without a doubt, what the rules are. They also want to know what to expect on a daily basis. Even if you can't manage a consistent and regular schedule for yourself (I can't, either), at least make a list of things you do each and every day for and with your Dachshund: three meals (measure that kibble, please, or you'll overestimate), one grooming session, one or two walks, and two or three short training sessions. So these things don't happen at the same time each day? Fine. Just make sure that they do happen each and every day. You owe it to your pet because she depends on you for structure. Lots and lots and lots of love is great, but it isn't enough to make your Dachshund happy, healthy, and secure.

Many dogs are surrendered to animal shelters because their owners never bothered to fully housetrain them and then got tired of cleaning up after them. The next time you think crate-training or any other housetraining method involving confinement is cruel, remember that surrendering your Dachshund to an animal shelter is much crueler. Do the kind thing and housetrain your Dachshund with consistency and vigilance.

Going to Obedience Classes (For Your Dachshund and You)

No matter how good you are at training your Dachshund at home, obedience classes are a great experience for both you and your Dachshund. Every dog should experience them, as long as the trainer is a good one. A seasoned dog trainer will probably give you ideas and strategies that hadn't occurred to you. He or she can help you deal with individual problems or tendencies of your own pet — something no book can do. Also, learning good behavior in a place other than your living room and in the presence of other dogs will help your Dachshund see that training applies everywhere, not just at home.

According to a report released by the National Council for Pet Population Study and Policy in 1998, of all the dogs surrendered to animal shelters, 43 percent had not been spayed or neutered, 33 percent had never seen a veterinarian, and a whopping 96 percent had not attended any kind of obedience class or formal training.

Not all obedience classes are the same, however. Look for a teacher who advocates positive training methods rather than rougher methods, such as the use of a choke chain, and certainly avoid those who use leash jerks for corrections. Those things aren't necessary for training Dachshunds, in the opinion of many contemporary trainers. If used incorrectly or too harshly, they can also injure your Dachshund's back.

Ask the trainer running the obedience class to explain his or her personal philosophy of training. (If he or she is too busy to be interviewed, look elsewhere. Wouldn't you do the same if your child's teacher refused a parent-teacher conference?) What are his or her influences? What methods have proved most effective? Does he or she have any experience training Dachshunds?

If you hear terms like *lure-and-reward training, clicker training,* or *play training,* that's a good sign. But watch out for comments about leash jerking, hitting of any kind, or any other physical type of discipline.

Lure-and-reward training is a method of training in which a lure, such as a treat or piece of kibble, is used to physically guide your dog into position, such as a sit. *Clicker training* is a method of training in which a click from a plastic device (called a *clicker*) is associated with a food treat. Eventually, the click itself becomes rewarding to the dog and is used as a positive reinforcement for desired behavior. *Play training* is a method of training in which practice of certain commands is disguised as play.

You can also ask your vet for recommendations. Or call the Association of Pet Dog Trainers, an organization devoted to better dog training through education and a great advocator of positive training methods, at 1-800-PET-DOGS and ask for the names of trainers in your area who use positive training methods. They also have a Web site at www.apdt.com with a dog trainer search engine. Ask for a trainer's references *and* check them. Sometimes a recommendation from a satisfied customer (or a warning from a dissatisfied customer) tells you more than the trainer ever could.

And don't forget your intuition. If a trainer just seems wrong, for whatever reason, keep looking. If you feel good about a trainer and his or her methods make sense to you and seem humane, kind, and in the best interest of the dogs, sign up.

Going to obedience classes when your puppy is about 3 months old creates a firm foundation for future training, teaching both you and your Dachshund good habits and providing a structure to follow at home. Then, if your Dachshund and you love it, you can continue on with more advanced classes — possibly even training for professional competition.

Good luck and don't delay. Start training your Dachshund today.

Chapter 13

Teaching the House Rules

*I*t's time to get down to some training tips that you and your Dachshund can really sink your teeth into. You've been worrying about these house rules, haven't you? What new puppy owner doesn't? Bad behavior is one cause of puppy and dog abandonment to animal shelters, and the saddest part is that the puppies and dogs aren't even to blame. They pay the price for their owners' lack of knowledge and/or commitment.

But that's not going to happen to your Dachshund because you're fully pre-pared to teach your Dachshund how to behave himself in a human world. Right? *Good.* Time to get to it.

Housetraining

Admit it. This is your biggest worry. Nobody likes to mop up puppy pee and scoop up puppy poop. Wouldn't it be great if your puppy never had a single accident in the house?

It's possible. Difficult but possible. Most importantly, if you do slip up (notice I say if *you* slip up, not your pup), don't give up hope. Clean up the mess, clean it well, and resolve not to let it happen again.

Few sights please a new puppy owner like the sight of a puppy doing his duty in the proper location. Others may find this preoccupation slightly repulsive, but when your puppy squats or starts to poop, don't be surprised if you suddenly begin to cheer out loud. Each successful potty venture puts you one step closer to housetraining success, and when you've housetrained a Dachshund, you know you've accomplished something major!

Eliminate elimination battles

For some puppies and even adult dogs, housetraining is a long, protracted battle between dog and human, which sometimes lasts for months. No one should have to put up with that — human or dog. And who wants to? You can eliminate elimination battles with a little foreknowledge and about a week or two of extreme vigilance. Talk about a big payoff. When your Dachshund is sleeping through the night and asking politely to be let out during the day, you know you've got it made.

Understand the elimination process

Puppies don't eliminate at random. A very specific process happens inside them (and inside dogs and even humans of all ages, but most apparently in puppies and babies) called the *gastrocolic reflex,* which is the internal mechanism that governs the elimination process. Eating triggers this reflex. The body makes room for new food by expelling the remains of old food in the colon. The result? Somewhere between 5 and 60 minutes after a puppy eats, she needs to eliminate.

Every dog is different. Some puppies need to eliminate right away, and others take awhile. Each individual puppy usually eliminates after about the same length of time following each meal, however, so in those first crucial days, watch your puppy carefully. Determine how soon after a meal he usually has to go. Keep track for a couple of days, and you'll have a good idea.

Remember that timing is everything

After you know your puppy's typical *e-time* (elimination time), you're ready for action. Feed your puppy, and about five to ten minutes before you know she probably has to go, take her calmly outside to her elimination station. Let her sniff around. When she starts sniffing and circling, sniffing and circling, you've met with success.

E-time has nothing to do with the Internet! It is a term I use to signify the amount of time it usually takes for your individual puppy to need to eliminate after a meal. In most puppies, the e-time is between 5 and 60 minutes.

Be hyper-aware of the sniff-and-circle routine. It's your key to the moment when elimination is imminent. If it happens indoors, you have about 3 seconds to get your puppy to the proper place. Many a Dachsie owner has whisked his or her puppy outside with puppy eliminating all the way to the door. It's not pretty, but it's the price you pay for missing the timing.

Your detailed guide to housetraining

You can read and read, but you still may not have a clear-cut idea of exactly what to do to housetrain your Dachshund. Well, here you go. Memorize these detailed guidelines or post them on your refrigerator (and if you decide to paper-train your Dachshund — or, like one senior owner I know, allow him to use the extra shower stall as his own — the same guidelines apply, except that you whisk him off to his *inside* elimination station):

✔ Before bringing your puppy inside the house for the very first time, take him to his elimination station and stay there until he does his duty.

If he won't eliminate, take him inside, put him in his den, close the door, and tell him in a gentle voice that you'll be back. Then return in 15 minutes and try again. Don't take him anywhere else in the house until he has eliminated in his special spot.

✔ Every two hours during the day for the first week, take him out to his special spot.

If he doesn't go, bring him in and put him in his den (nicely — don't get mad or none of this will work). Then return every 20 to 30 minutes and try again until he goes. (**Note:** Your puppy may have a stronger bladder, and you may find that you can take him out every three or four hours instead of every two. But start with two-hour intervals until you know your Dachshund's individual tendencies.)

✔ Within 30 minutes after a meal, take him outside until he goes.

Once you learn your puppy's e-time (see the section "Remember that timing is everything"), you can alter this step to fit your puppy.

✔ For the first week, take your puppy out every four hours during the night.

Set your alarm if you have to, but your Dachshund will probably wake you up. (If he is sleeping soundly, you can wait it out, but don't miss the opportunity when he wakes up.)

✔ Always take your puppy out first thing in the morning, at the same time each morning (sorry, that means on weekends, too), and immediately before bedtime, at the same time each evening.

Continue this habit throughout your Dachshund's life.

✔ Never, ever miss the sniff-and-circle routine.

For the first couple of weeks, be extra vigilant. It could happen any time, even when an elimination session isn't scheduled. After your Dachshund is housetrained, still keep the concept in the back of your mind. We've all been known to forget about letting the dog out every now and then. And note that after an extra-big meal, sometimes your Dachshund will need more outside time than usual. Whenever you see it, out she goes.

✔ For the first couple weeks, keep your Dachshund in uncarpeted areas whenever she is out of her den.

Cleanup will be much easier, and the scent won't last like it will in a carpet. (Or purchase a reliable odor remover specifically designed for pet odors.)

✔ If your Dachshund makes a mistake, remember that *it's your fault, not your Dachshund's.*

Don't get mad. You *can* behave with urgency when whisking your Dachshund outside if you catch him in the act. But don't yell at him, don't show your temper (even if you are extremely irritated, which you very well may be), and for your dog's sake, don't hit him or rub his nose in his transgression (or, I should say, *your* transgression). Don't beat yourself up about it, either, but most importantly don't blame your dog. He won't get it. He really won't. It will just make things worse.

Dachshunds are fastidious, clean animals, lacking in that familiar hound smell. They don't want to eliminate in a manner that displeases you, and they don't want to mess up their living environment. They only need a little guidance from you to do what makes everyone happy. Be a patient, consistent, and loving housetrainer, and the job will, eventually, be accomplished.

To help you keep track of when to take your Dachshund outside in the first week, make a copy of the following chart and circle the appropriate time of each successful elimination accomplishment. The chart lists times in two-hour intervals throughout the day and four-hour intervals throughout the night, assuming that your Dachshund gets up at 7 a.m. and goes to bed at 11 p.m. Times are approximate. Modify them for your own schedule.

DAY 1	DAY 2	DAY 3	DAY 4	DAY 5	DAY 6	DAY 7
7 a.m.	7 a.m.	7 a.m.	7 a.m.	7 a.m.	7 a.m.	7 a.m.
9 a.m.	9 a.m.	9 a.m.	9 a.m.	9 a.m.	9 a.m.	9 a.m.
11 a.m.	11 a.m.	11 a.m.	11 a.m.	11 a.m.	11 a.m.	11 a.m.
1 p.m.	1 p.m.	1 p.m.	1 p.m.	1 p.m.	1 p.m.	1 p.m.
3 p.m.	3 p.m.	3 p.m.	3 p.m.	3 p.m.	3 p.m.	3 p.m.
5 p.m.	5 p.m.	5 p.m.	5 p.m.	5 p.m.	5 p.m.	5 p.m.
7 p.m.	7 p.m.	7 p.m.	7 p.m.	7 p.m.	7 p.m.	7 p.m.
9 p.m.	9 p.m.	9 p.m.	9 p.m.	9 p.m.	9 p.m.	9 p.m.
11 p.m.	11 p.m.	11 p.m.	11 p.m.	11 p.m.	11 p.m.	11 p.m.
3 a.m.	3 a.m.	3 a.m.	3 a.m.	3 a.m.	3 a.m.	3 a.m.
7 a.m.	7 a.m.	7 a.m.	7 a.m.	7 a.m.	7 a.m.	7 a.m.

Don't fall prey to these common housetraining mistakes:

- ✔ Missing puppy's sniff-and-circle routine.
- ✔ Leaving puppy unattended before he is fully trained.
- ✔ Not taking puppy to the same place for elimination each and every time.
- ✔ Allowing puppy to eat or drink water after about 7 p.m. (If she is really thirsty, let her drink water but be sure to take her out again before bedtime.)
- ✔ Not taking puppy out immediately before you put him in his kennel for the night.
- ✔ Letting puppy sleep outside her crate for the first week.

Biting, Gnawing, Chewing, and Other Toothy Indiscretions

Puppies bite, and if you didn't know it before you brought your Dachshund puppy home, you surely know it now (see Figure 13-1). Sometimes called *mouthing*, puppy biting is really just oral exploration. Great for puppies. Not so great for new shoes, chair legs, wall moldings, and the human fingers that are so often the subject of their inquiry.

Figure 13-1:
Watch out
for this
creature.
Without
training,
he'll chew
on you and
everything
you hold
dear!

Some people think that puppy mouthing is cute and like to excuse it because it's a puppy's way of exploring the world. But you won't think the behavior is so cute when your puppy is an adult dog and is still shredding your possessions and nipping at people whenever they annoy him.

Puppy teeth are sharp as needles. That's one reason to discourage mouthing of human flesh, but there are other reasons. Important reasons:

✔ Letting your puppy chew on your fingers teaches him that chewing on your fingers is okay. You aren't doing your puppy any favors. Others won't be as indulgent as you, but your puppy won't know that. He'll only know that chewing fingers must be fine because you let him do it.

✔ Your puppy can't do too much damage when she gnaws on you, but when that puppy is bigger — even a full-grown Mini — she'll be accustomed to using her mouth. If she is suddenly startled or hurt, she may be more inclined to bite than a dog that's been trained from the beginning never to apply canine teeth to human flesh.

✔ Because puppies love to chew everything, it's up to you to make it very clear which things are okay to chew and which aren't. Your puppy must learn that a few select objects are chewable — and nothing else. This rule sets the stage for good oral behavior for the rest of your puppy's life.

If your Dachshund was never a big chewer but suddenly becomes destructive or chews obsessively (including self-chewing), she may have a medical problem. Visit your vet and have her checked out. Skin problems, epilepsy, separation anxiety, or any number of other disorders may be the cause. Some dogs suffer from a condition similar to obsessive-compulsive disorder in humans, which causes them to chew obsessively. Most of these conditions can be effectively treated.

Nip it

The first important measure you must take to nip indiscriminate mouthing in the bud is to never allow your puppy to chew on your fingers. If he tries, don't let him. Keep your hands away from his mouth. If he accidentally gets a mouth full of fingers, quickly remove them and say "No!" If he never gets a chance to chew on you, he'll be less likely to give it a thought.

Same thing goes for other objects your puppy shouldn't chew — furniture, shoes, paper, etc. Keep all small, loose items that could be choking hazards out of puppy's reach. Keep your shoes in your closet and keep the closet door shut. Prevention is best.

You can't store your sofa away for the first year of your puppy's life, however. Same goes for the dining room chair and tables and any other large piece of furniture your Dachshund takes a fancy to. Don't let your puppy chew these things. If he insists, liberally apply some Bitter Apple spray according to the instructions and always make use of a well-placed chew toy.

Use a well-placed chew toy

Some Dachshunds chew more than others and some Dachshunds aren't interested in any toy but their favorite. For the exuberant chewers, make use of a well-placed chew toy at every opportunity. Store Gummabones, Kongs, Nylabones, and other safe, sturdy chew toys all over the house so that whenever your Dachshund gets too interested in chewing your fingers, toes, shoes, or furniture, you can immediately remove him with a firm "No" and then hand him an acceptable option. When he chews the toy, heap on the praise. "What a good dog!"

Nylabones and *Gummabones* are brand names for chew toys that flake off in tiny pieces so they don't pose a choking hazard. *Kongs* are hard rubber, semi-cone-shaped hollow toys that can be stuffed with biscuits or other treats — even a dollop of peanut butter — creating hours of challenge for your Dachshund. (Wash frequently.)

Your detailed guide to bite prevention

Ah, just what you've been waiting for. Here are the detailed guidelines to follow with your new puppy in order to say good-bye to painful puppy bites and destructive chewing:

- ✔ From the first moment you meet your new puppy, never, ever let her chew on you or anyone else.

- ✔ From the first moment you meet your new puppy, never, ever let him chew on anything you wouldn't want him to chew on when he is an adult.

- ✔ Keep chew toys in every room your puppy is allowed, plus one in her den at all times and one in the car if she travels with you.

  Whenever she even thinks about chewing something forbidden, pop a chew toy in her mouth. She'll soon associate the chewing urge with a chew toy.

  And if you catch her in the act, pull the old switcheroo: Remove her from the bad object and replace it with the good chew toy.

- ✔ Not sure when he feels like chewing? *Watch* him.

  Some puppies start to chomp their jaws and look around.

- ✔ Never fly off the handle because your puppy has chewed something forbidden.

  You either left it out when you shouldn't have or weren't supervising her. Guide her toward the good behavior and don't reinforce the bad behavior by making a big fuss.

That's it. The tricky part is to be eternally consistent. Always enforce the rules. If you miss an enforcement opportunity, move on. Every now and then won't hurt. Certainly don't punish your Dachshund and resolve never again to let him chew anything he shouldn't chew.

Help! He's a demolition machine!

Some people complain that their Dachshunds destroy things when left alone. If you have a destructive chewer, you have two options: Live with it or keep your Dachshund in his den when you're away. He won't mind if you do the latter, as long as you don't keep him in there for more than four or five hours without a break (come home for lunch or hire someone). In fact, he'll be safer in his den. Destructive chewers are more likely to choke, strangle themselves, or get poisoned. You could be saving much more than your stuff. You could be saving your Dachshund's life.

Your Little Barker

If you have a Dachshund, you have a barker. Not much you can do about it. Dachshunds bark for many reasons — some of them reasonable and some of them unreasonable. It isn't fair to get annoyed or angry at your Dachshund for barking. But obsessive or unnecessary barking is something you can address and, in most cases, resolve.

Barking too much can actually be harmful for your Dachshund's health. If she barks obsessively, she puts herself under a lot of physical stress. Obsessive barking can also be a sign of a health problem or a sign that your Dachshund is particularly insecure or fearful.

Barking is more than harmful for your Dachshund. It's harmful for you. At best, you'll find yourself continually irritated with your Dachshund. At worst, your neighbors will not be happy with you, and if you live in an apartment, you could be asked to leave, or even evicted, if the noise becomes too bothersome to other tenants. Owners of nuisance barkers have even been subjected to lawsuits.

The only reasonable approach to a little barker, then, is to keep her from becoming a public nuisance and keep her from driving you, and herself, crazy. But how do you do it? The first step is to understand why your Dachsie is barking.

Understanding why Dachshunds bark

Dachshunds bark more than some breeds because barking was part of the original Dachshund plan. When used in hunting, a Dachshund would corner its prey and then bark loudly and sharply to alert its human to come and finish the job. The Dachshund's bark had to be heard across sometimes great distances.

So, even if you don't hunt with your Dachshund, you'll still reap the, ahem, *benefits* of centuries of breeding. Your Dachshund's bark is loud and sharp, no matter why he is barking. It isn't his fault, but it is something you should be prepared for.

Removing the cause of the barking

Centuries of breeding aside, you shouldn't have to listen to barking all day, and you should be able to stop barking by removing the cause. Doing so involves determining the cause first, of course. Dachshunds bark for lots of reasons:

✔ Someone is invading their territory (their house, their yard, their humans). Or something resembles a threat, and they think you should be alerted.

✔ Something resembles prey (a squirrel, a cat, a piece of trash blowing down the street).

✔ They want to get out of wherever you've put them (a pen, a den, a room with a gate or closed door, a yard with a fence).

✔ They want to get your attention, or they want you to return after you've left.

✔ They are really excited.

✔ They are suspicious or fearful of someone or something, such as a visitor or a noise (for example, a ringing phone or doorbell).

✔ They are bored.

Some of these reasons are justifiable, even desirable. If a stranger is invading your property, you probably want to know about it, and your Dachshund is just the guy to tell you. In such a case, you can determine who the invader is. Then you can either show your Dachshund that the person is okay by letting in the visitor, or you can call the police. Praising your Dachshund for alerting you to the presence of trespassers (good or bad ones) is perfectly acceptable. "Thank you, good boy! Now you can be quiet." This is the kind of barking you want to encourage.

But if your Dachshund barks unreasonably, you don't want to encourage it. First, remove the cause of the barking:

✔ If your Dachshund barks at everything that moves outside the front window, you need only keep him from looking out the front window. Draw the blinds or close the curtains. Or keep your Dachshund in another room.

✔ If your Dachshund is suspicious or fearful of particular noises, eliminate her exposure to these noises. Turn down the ringer on the phone, disconnect your doorbell and post a Please Knock sign on your door, or put your Dachshund outside or in her den when you know someone will be coming over.

If your Dachshund is very fearful of certain sounds, like the phone or doorbell, but you don't want to do anything as drastic as taking your phone off the hook or disconnecting your doorbell, you can try *desensitization,* a technique in which the dog is repeatedly exposed under controlled and secure conditions to the object of fear. Only try desensitization under the supervision of an animal behaviorist, however. You don't want to traumatize your Dachshund.

✔ If a squirrel is teasing your Dachshund in the backyard, let your Dachshund inside.

✔ If the neighborhood kids are teasing your Dachshund through the fence, shame on them. Call their parents.

✔ If your Dachshund barks frantically whenever you leave him alone, begin keeping him in his den when you're away. But also practice keeping him in his den when you are home so that he knows it's a safe place and doesn't always indicate your absence. (Talk to your vet about remedies for severe separation anxiety if this is a problem.)

✔ If your Dachshund is really excited, calm him down. (A few happy barks uttered out of sheer joy when you and your Dachshund are playing together won't hurt anything.)

✔ If your Dachshund is bored, give him something to do. Sometimes a few favorite toys and a Kong stuffed with a couple of biscuits are all it takes.

Sometimes, though, you can't remove the cause of your Dachshund's barking. You can't keep cars from driving by your house or people from walking down your street. You can't keep the mailman from coming up your walk each day, nor can you stop the phone from ringing.

You can't become a hermit and move out to the country, miles from anyone else, just because your dog barks. (Well, maybe you can, but you probably don't want to.) So after you've eliminated all the causes you can, your next step is to train your dog not to bark.

Generally, I would never recommend having your dog *debarked* — a surgical procedure that alters your dog's vocal cords to lessen the volume of barking — unless the only alternative is to abandon the pet or face legal action. Shock collars and citrus spray collars designed to discourage barking punish a dog for behaving according to instinct. But in severe cases of obsessive barking, these kinds of collars may be helpful and are preferable to debarking. Talk to your vet for more information but don't be too quick to use any of these solutions. Give training a fair chance first.

Manipulating your Dachshund's instincts

Imagine this scenario: Your Dachshund is sitting perched on the back of the couch, his favorite place from which to view the world. Unfortunately, however, every time someone walks or drives by your house, he lets loose a volley of barks that have you jumping out of your skin.

Now imagine that every time your Dachshund starts barking, you start yelling, "Stop it! Shut up! Quiet! I can't stand it anymore!" while waving your arms around, maybe even jumping up and down. After all, you are really, really irritated.

But do you know how your Dachshund sees your actions? Remember, your Dachshund doesn't speak English. To her, all that yelling sounds an awful lot like barking. Without realizing it, you are supporting and reinforcing your Dachshund's behavior. She's thinking something to the effect of, "Wow, I'm powerful! When I bark to scare off those cars, my human follows my lead and barks, too. And it works! Those cars run right past our house! What an effective team we are!"

Wait a minute. That wasn't the result you were looking for. You wanted your Dachshund to stop barking. You thought you were discouraging her, when all the while you were inadvertently showing her what a superb watchdog she is. Whoops.

Training your dog not to bark requires an effort contrary to your human instinct. First, when she barks, you must show no emotion whatsoever except, perhaps, for a quiet disdain. Gently remove her from view of the stimulus and out of earshot of the neighbors. If she stops barking, turn on the charm and praise her. If she keeps it up, put her in her den and walk away. Completely ignore her until she stops barking. When she stops, let her out of her den and praise her, play with her, and reward her. As long as she is barking, however, *don't* react.

If she habitually barks at visitors, keep her in her den whenever someone is expected over. You may hear her barking from her den. It's her instinct to alert you that someone is coming, so don't be angry. She's just doing her job.

Once the visitor is inside and your Dachshund has calmed down, you can let her out — on her leash, if necessary, to keep her controlled. If she starts to bark, send her right back inside.

In the case of mailmen, ringing phones, and other regular stimuli that you can't avoid and can't necessarily anticipate, a disdainful "No" when the barking starts and immediate banishment to the den may help. Then again, it may not. At least you can answer the phone to stop the ringing. And the mailman probably doesn't hang around in front of your house for too long.

In other words, there are two major keys to training your Dachshund not to bark unreasonably:

- ✔ Remember that some barking is justified and desirable.
- ✔ Never, ever react to unreasonable or undesirable barking in any way except to dispassionately remove your Dachshund from the source of the barking when possible.

That isn't so hard to remember, is it?

Jumping

Dachshunds get so excited. They want so desperately to capture your attention. They want to see what's going on, and that's hard to do when you live so close to the ground. "How can I help but jump up? It's a fascinating, stimulating, and exhilarating world up there above my head!"

Don't buy it for a minute. Your Dachshund doesn't have to jump up on you or anybody else, ever. She can see just fine, and you, as her tall friend, have the responsibility of getting down to her level every so often. It's only fair, if you don't want her to try to ascend to your level.

Fortunately, Dachshunds aren't very big, so they won't knock you down if they jump on you. Jumping is, nonetheless, bad manners, and your friends and neighbors may not think it's as cute as you do. Train your puppy not to jump from day one, and everyone will be impressed with how well mannered and restrained your little Dachshund is.

How you inadvertently encourage jumping up

If your Dachshund jumps, he does it because you encourage it. Yes you do. Encouraging jumping is all too easy. All it takes is a look, a smile, or any sign of pleasure or even attention that very first time your Dachshund applies his front paws to your lower legs.

Here's another scenario for you: You get home after a long day. You can't wait to see your new puppy. You open the door, and she comes bounding joyfully toward you. Your face lights up as your puppy leaps up against your legs. How *cute*. You smile. You say, "Good dog!" And you scoop your puppy into your arms. You're both in heaven.

And you've just "told" your puppy that she gets a great big reward if she jumps up on you. Now she'll do it again and again and try it on others and keep doing it until she's full grown. If you suddenly get mad at her when she does it, she won't understand why. She'll think you are unpredictable and maybe a little bit scary. But she won't think, "Oh, I guess now I shouldn't jump up anymore."

How to reteach your jumper

If you've already reacted with positive reinforcement to your jumping puppy, don't despair. It's not too late to reteach your Dachshund that jumping is no longer allowed. Getting mad isn't the way to do it, however.

Every single time you come home, or even into a room, and your puppy runs to you and jumps up, you need to do something very difficult: Completely ignore him. Don't talk to him and don't look at him. Pretend he isn't even there. Wait it out. He'll be confused at first. He'll probably try to jump with even greater fervor. Eventually, he'll give up. Don't give up before he does.

When your puppy stops jumping on you, turn toward him and really pile on the praise. Get way down low so he can see your face. That's what he was trying to do, anyway. "Helloooo, puppy! Whatta good doggy! I missed you soooo much!" Pet him, offer him a treat — whatever will make him happy.

You've just rewarded him for *not* jumping.

If, in the process of your praises, he jumps on you again, completely turn it off: Ignore him again. Don't look at him and don't speak. When he stops jumping on you again, praise him again, giving him all your attention.

Your puppy may not get it immediately, but after a few times, he'll get it. After that, never, ever reward him or pay any attention to him at all when he jumps on you. As soon as he stops, however, immediately turn your full attention on him with all the praise and petting you can muster.

If your puppy jumps on other people when they come to visit, have them do the same thing. Instruct visitors before they come inside about the plan. If the puppy jumps, the visitor must completely ignore the puppy. When the puppy ceases jumping, the visitor can meet, greet, and pet the puppy.

If you resolve jumping up in puppyhood, your adult Dachshund won't be a jumper. Hooray for you. You've got a well-mannered Dachsie. People will like to come to your house because you've got the dog that doesn't jump all over everyone.

Remember that jumping off of high places can be dangerous for your Dachshund's back. Give your Dachshund other options for getting down off of high places like beds and couches — a ramp, a lift from you, or a soft pillow to land on. Keeping your Dachsie off the beds and furniture is much harder than keeping him from jumping off. Most Dachshunds will manage to jump off of high places once in a while, despite your best efforts. Just do what you can to minimize it and keep your Dachshund well exercised and at a healthy weight so that his back can most effectively withstand the pressure of an occasional jump.

Working with the Adult Dachshund

If you've adopted an adult Dachshund, she may already be housetrained, she may never bite or chew inappropriate things, she may not bark inappropriately, and she may know never to jump up on people. Or she may need a little work on any or all of these areas.

Teaching an adult Dachshund is essentially the same as teaching a puppy. All the steps and methods that work for puppies work for adults, too. Sometimes adults take longer to learn because they are changing old habits. Other adults learn much faster. Maybe they used to be housetrained, got out of the habit, but remember quickly. Or maybe they are very eager to please you, so they try extra hard to learn the rules.

In any case, don't assume that your adult Dachshund is untrainable. You know that line about not being able to teach an old dog new tricks? Forget it. Old dogs are great and are perfectly capable of learning good house manners.

If your adult Dachshund seems to be having severe problems with behavior — won't housetrain, barks obsessively, bites or growls, or jumps up uncontrollably despite your good efforts not to reinforce bad behavior — first call your vet to rule out a medical problem. Then consider a professional trainer and/or an animal behaviorist or canine behavioral consultant. Your adult Dachshund may have past issues of abuse or neglect, or he may never have been trained in any way. A professional can help you address these issues and resolve them in the Dachshund's best interest.

Good luck, and may your Dachshund soon be the best-behaved dog on the block.

Chapter 14

Basic Training

● ●

In This Chapter

▶ Understanding the benefits and limits of obedience classes

▶ Giving basic puppy lessons: Sit, Stand, Down, and Come

▶ Giving lessons of the leash: Walk and Wait

▶ Troubleshooting your training problems

▶ Always remembering that training lessons should be fun

● ●

*O*nce you've conquered the house rules, you can move on to more fun training activities. Personally, *you* need a dog that is housetrained and doesn't bite or destroy things, but your Dachshund needs stuff to do — a purpose in life. A dog who can sit, roll over, speak, lie down, and heel on command feels she has important *work* and loves learning the tricks that impress family, friends, and neighbors.

But training isn't all about fun and games. It can also be a matter of life and death. If your untrained Dachshund slips out the front door between the legs of someone who isn't paying attention, and if she then dashes for a squirrel across the street, all you can do is hope a car isn't coming. But, in the case of a well-trained Dachshund very familiar with the Come command, you just may be able to get your Dachshund to turn around before she hits the street. Unfortunately, you may not be successful because the instinct to give chase is strong in the Dachshund. But the better trained your Dachshund is, the greater are her chances for survival.

Add to that the fact that most Dachshunds abandoned to shelters aren't trained, and you've got more than sufficient reason to start teaching your Dachshund some basics today. This chapter is here to help.

Obedience Classes: Something to Consider Seriously

You may be fully committed to training your Dachshund at home. Good for you. But that doesn't mean you and your friend won't both benefit immensely from a good obedience class. Obedience classes expose your Dachshund to other dogs and other humans, as well as teach your pup that he must follow your lead no matter where you are. Classes can also give you some great new tips and tricks that you may not find in your training books. Teachers can address specific problems you may be having, and if you find a teacher with a method you love, you may find that you and your Dachshund can go up, up, up to the highest echelons of obedience competition.

Even if you register for nothing more than a puppy kindergarten class, you'll be glad you did it. You and your Dachshund both need training and a structure for your daily sessions.

Puppy kindergarten is a term used to describe classes for young puppies or dogs that have never had any obedience training. These classes focus on teaching owners basic management skills, like housetraining, socializing puppies, and gently guiding puppies through very basic commands such as Sit.

Finding a good teacher is important. Look for someone who uses positive training techniques rather than negative techniques or punishment, such as swats and leash jerking. Also look for someone you feel comfortable with, whose style you can relate to. Then be prepared to do a good deal of work.

Obedience classes work best when you work every day with your Dachshund on your own at home. Once a week in class is not sufficient training time. When your teacher tells you to practice twice a day for 10 to 20 minutes — every single day — she means it. Otherwise, you'll find that obedience classes have little if any effect on your Dachshund's behavior. Beyond the essential element of a positive and fun approach, obedience training is all about two key concepts: consistency and persistency.

Two training sessions each day are ideal, but even one 20-minute session per day (adult dogs usually can't concentrate for much longer — puppy sessions will be much shorter) goes a long way toward establishing a training ritual for you and your Dachshund. Make it just as important as brushing your teeth (and brushing your Dachshund's teeth). Do it every day, and you won't regret it.

But what do you *do* every day? A good obedience class instructor will give you lots of suggestions — even a detailed format for your homework. If you haven't registered for your classes yet, or you just want some variation, you can also try the puppy lessons in the following section.

Puppy Lessons

This section covers some basic lessons you can teach your Dachsie. Each is simple, short, and fun — perfect for a puppy just learning the ropes or an adult dog that hasn't ever experienced a training session before.

For every puppy lesson, be sure that you have a ready store of your puppy's food (taken from his daily allowance) or very small treats so you can immediately reinforce good behavior.

Getting a puppy's attention

The first lesson involves getting your Dachshund's attention. Puppies are notoriously distractible. How on Earth are you going to teach your puppy to sit, let alone get him to pay attention to you long enough to hear you say the command *Sit?* First, you teach your puppy when it's time to listen:

1. **Pick up your puppy and look him in the eye while saying his name.**

   Some puppies will look you in the eye immediately — even hold your gaze for a few seconds before twisting around to see what else is going on that might be of interest. Others will look anywhere but.

2. **Do one of the following:**

   If yours looks at you when you say his name, praise him and give him a treat.

   If your puppy won't look you in the eye, start making funny (nonthreatening) sounds. Whistle, click your tongue, and say "Beep beep!" or "Toodleoodleoodle" or whatever other funny sound amuses you. (Remember, this should be fun for you, too.) *Note:* Don't use your puppy's name for this one yet. He probably hears it all the time, and you're looking for a new sound that will capture his attention. Then, as soon as he looks at you, smile happily and say "Good dog!" and give him a treat.

3. **Repeat Steps 1 and 2 one or two times.**

4. **Now try the exercise with puppy on the floor, you sitting in front of him.**

   When he gives you his attention, be enthusiastic. Play with him joyfully, give him a treat, pet him gently — whatever he really loves.

   If, in Step 2, you had to go with the second option — making funny sounds — continue with the rest of these steps.

5. **Once your Dachsie reliably turns his attention to you when you make your funny sound, add his name to the sound.**

   Do this, for example: "[*whistle*] Hans!" or "Beep beep, Hans!" Continue to reward him enthusiastically every time he gives you his attention.

6. **Repeat Steps 4 and 5 several times every day.**

7. **After several days, begin to drop the funny sound and only use your Dachshund's name.**

   Continue to reward him whenever he gives you his full attention.

You can also practice this lesson during walks, in the car, in the park, or wherever else you are with your Dachshund. Eventually, he'll learn that when you say his name, it's in his best interest to pay attention to you because something great is sure to happen.

You can, of course, name your dog whatever you like. Short names (or short nicknames of long names) that are fun and easy to say are most effective for training, however. Peter, Max, Trixie, and Sport make better choices than Bartholomew, Zachariah, Veronica, or Mary Margaret (although Bart, Zach, Vicky, and Meg would all work well).

Teaching the Sit command

Once your Dachshund has learned to pay attention to you when you address him, you can begin to add other words to his name to signify different behaviors. But how do you get your Dachshund to know what you want him to do? Through the magic of lure-and-reward training.

Even before your Dachshund knows her name, you can lure her into a sit with a piece of kibble or a treat. You can even try this lesson with puppies that you're visiting at the breeder's, to see which ones are most responsive to you:

1. **Put your puppy in front of you, preferably up on a table so that you can be close to her eye level.**

2. **If she isn't standing, lift her up to a standing position.**

3. **Pick up a piece of kibble and hold it in front of your puppy's nose, as shown in Figure 14-1.**

   Put it just close enough for her to see and smell it but not close enough for her to grab it.

4. **Once your puppy notices the treat, slowly raise the treat up in the air and slightly over your puppy's head.**

   How can she resist? She must try to follow it. But to do so, she'll have to raise her head. And to raise her head, she'll have to sit.

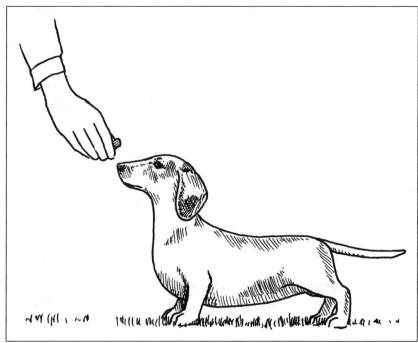

Figure 14-1:
Let your
Dachsie see
and sniff the
kibble.

5. **As your Dachshund sits, say "Sit" in a relaxed and friendly manner and then immediately praise her.**

   "Good sit! Whatta good dog!"

6. **When she is fully seated, give her a treat without delay.**

   "Whatta good dog! Whatta good little Gretel!"

7. **Repeat Steps 1 through 6 once or twice and then try the exercise on the floor.**

   Eventually, your puppy will associate the action with the word, but don't rush it. Give it at least a couple of weeks, and if she doesn't get it, go back to the lure for a while longer.

8. **Once she's very familiar with the Sit command, practice *holding* the sit for 15 seconds.**

   In other words, once she's in the sit, don't give her the food immediately. Hold it over her head while you say "Wait" in a friendly and relaxed tone. Wait for 15 seconds to give her the treat.

9. **Gradually, over the course of several weeks, increase the time between the sit and the reward to 5 minutes; then increase the wait little by little after that.**

   Sit, wait, reward.

   Later on down the road, when you want your Dachshund to sit for longer periods of time — say, throughout the family dinner or while you watch television or work on your computer — you can say "Sit, Wait" and then go about your business. When you give your pup the treat, she's released.

For long sits, accompany the treat reward with a release command, such as "Okay!" or "Go Play!" Eventually, you won't even need the treat. Your Dachshund will be happy to sit and wait for you. Of course, she'll always be happy to take a treat off your hands, too, so you needn't abandon the treat if you enjoy offering it.

Practice the Sit command a couple of times every day, with varying lengths of Wait (from no wait at all to long waits of 10 to 15 minutes for the well-trained Dachsie). You can stop periodically throughout your daily walk for a sit and a treat. Also use the Sit command whenever you want your Dachshund to behave with restraint at home or in public. The more often you use this command throughout the day, the faster she'll get it and the better behaved she'll be.

The long sit is fine for periods up to 10 or 15 minutes. Any longer, however, and your Dachshund will probably want to relax into a long down (see the section "Teaching the Down command").

Teaching the Stand command

You teach your Dachshund the Stand command exactly the same way that you teach the Sit command. Begin by luring your puppy into position, associate the action with the word *Stand*, reward him when he stands, and then eventually add a Wait command so your Dachshund stands for extended periods until being released with an Okay command.

Stand is great for grooming, for dog shows, or for pauses during walks when you want to chat with a neighbor. Follow the same steps that are used for Sit (in the section "Teaching the Sit command"), except lure your puppy into position in the following way:

1. **Put your puppy into a sitting position or have him sit by giving him the Sit command.**

2. **Once he's sitting, hold a piece of kibble in front of his nose until he notices it.**

3. **Pull the kibble in a straight line parallel to the floor away from his nose.**

   To follow it, he'll have to stand up.

4. **As he stands, say "Stand" in a relaxed and friendly manner.**

5. **When he is fully standing, praise him and immediately give him a treat.**

   "Good stand! Whatta good Butch dog! Whatta good stand!"

6. **Add the Wait command, as described earlier in the steps for the Sit command, and then the release command.**

   What a well-behaved Dachshund you have!

No matter how consistent and persistent you are in your training sessions, if you don't make training fun for your Dachshund, you can forget it. A positive attitude, lots of happy praise, and a sense of excitement — "Can you believe we actually get to have this much fun?!" — are all essential elements to any Dachshund training session. If you have an old-fashioned notion of discipline, it's time to get modern. The old adage "No pain, no gain" doesn't serve you here. And, remember, the surest way to tell whether your Dachshund is having a blast is to determine whether *you* are having a blast. If it's fun for you, it's probably fun for your Dachsie.

Teaching the Down command

Down is good for getting your Dachshund under control. It's a more submissive position than the sit and can help to calm your Dachshund when she is getting overexuberant. Down is also an excellent position for extended waits. Practice the long down when you watch TV, you work at your computer, the family is having dinner, or friends are visiting and they've had enough Dachshund fun and are ready for adult conversation.

Teach the Down command after your Dachshund has mastered Sit:

1. **Tell your Dachshund to sit; reward her; and then bring another piece of kibble into view, just in front of your Dachshund's nose.**

2. **When you have her attention, slowly lower the kibble to the floor in a diagonal line, away from your puppy's nose.**

   If she follows it with her nose but doesn't lie down, move it slightly away from her so she has to lie down to reach it. If your Dachshund stands up to follow the kibble, moving out of the sit, take the kibble away and start over with the Sit command.

3. **As she goes down, say "Down" in a friendly and relaxed tone.**

4. **When she lies down, give her that treat and pile on the praise.**

   It may take a few tries for your Dachshund to figure out what you mean, but when she gets it, go at it: "Whatta good Frieda! Gooood down! Gooood doggy!"

5. **Once your Dachshund understands and reliably lies down, add a Wait command.**

   Gradually extend the time between the down and the reward — the same as with the long sit (see "Teaching the Sit command" for details).

   Add a release command (like "Okay!") after a long down and practice often. Whenever you plan to be in one place for more than 5 minutes, practice the long down.

You can practice the long down during pauses on your daily walk, but don't make your Dachshund lie down on hot pavement. Let him practice the Down command on the grass.

Teaching the Come command

Come is the most essential command in your Dachshund's repertoire. That doesn't mean he'll always obey it. You're doing pretty well if he *usually* obeys it. However, he must learn it because it can save his life someday.

It's easy to get most puppies to come. Puppies are curious, and they love people. Squat down or lie down on the floor, open your arms wide, and look excited while calling for the puppy: "Come here, Preston! Come on over here, cute little Preston puppy! Look what I've got for any cute little puppies who come to seeee meeee!"

The older a puppy gets, however, and the more familiar *you* get, the less likely you'll seem like the most interesting thing in the room. Your puppy may think, "Oh, yeah. That guy. But I've never seen that new shoe over there before!" When you get some serious competition, like a rabbit in the garden or a robin on the driveway in full view of the picture window, forget it.

So how do you teach your puppy that "Come!" means *come* and always means *come,* whether he feels like it or not? Habit, pure and simple. Practice the Come command every day, again and again, whenever you get the chance. Always reward it. If your Dachshund sincerely believes that every time he comes to you, something great will happen (such as the pacifying of his eternal hunger for treats), you've made yourself more interesting than that new shoe and even, perhaps, more interesting than the little critters in the yard — at least for a few moments.

1. **Get down close to your Dachshund's eye level — about 5 or 6 feet away.**

2. **Open your arms wide and, with as much excitement and joy as you can muster, say "[*puppy's name*], Come!"**

   Wave a treat in the air, if necessary. If he comes without seeing the treat, give him one anyway to reward him.

3. **When he comes to you, heap on the praise.**

   Really heap it on — this is the big one. "Whatta good good good doggie! What a well-behaved perfect little puppy! Whatta good come! Whatta good dog!" Pet, kiss, play, offer a treat — make it worth your Dachshund's while.

4. **Move back another 5 or 6 feet and then try it again.**

   If your puppy follows you before you've said "Come," say "Come" as he's following you. "Come, Spot! Whatta good Spot! Come! Thatta boy! Come, Spot!"

5. **Do it again and again, until your Dachshund loses interest.**

   Probably five times is the most you'll get in at once. Then do it again later. And again and again and again.

Once your Dachshund understands the Sit and Wait commands, you can combine them with your Come command lessons. Have your Dachshund sit, tell him to wait, and then walk away. Then say "[*puppy's name*], Come!"

Here are two very important things, so listen up:

- ✔ Never go for one day without practicing the Come command a few times. Your goal is to have the sound of the word *Come* induce such a familiar and practiced response in your Dachshund that he obeys without even thinking about it.

- ✔ If you only use food rewards for one command, Come is the one. If your Dachshund is enthusiastically rewarded in a way that makes a big impression *every single time* he comes when you call him, he'll be more likely to obey you every single time you call him.

Leash Lessons

This section's set of commands are for when you and your Dachshund are walking together — you on one end of the leash and your Dachshund on the other. The daily Dachshund walk is an immensely enjoyable experience, provided that your Dachshund is well behaved. Otherwise, it can become an irritating and trying task that you'll probably soon abandon.

Lure-and-reward training doesn't work with these lessons because they involve behaviors or actions that you can't really lure your Dachshund into. However, a few simple, alternative strategies will make your Dachshund's walk all it should be. See every walk with your Dachshund as a training opportunity. Practice the following lessons each and every time you and your puppy venture out.

Collars are more likely to strain and even injure your Dachshund's neck than a harness that fits around her torso. A harness can give you more control over your puppy and may be more comfortable for your Dachshund than a collar. Check your local pet stores, online pet supply companies, and mail-order pet supply catalogs for harnesses.

Teaching the Walk command

Few things are more irritating than a dog that continuously pulls on her leash throughout an entire walk around the block, and few things are more humiliating than being dragged around the block by a 9-pound wiener dog. Teach your Dachshund how to heel by positively reinforcing heeling behavior, and walks will soon become a joy:

1. **Put your Dachshund's harness (or collar) and leash on her; then take her outside.**

2. **Stand next to your Dachshund with the leash in your right hand and the Dachshund to your left. The leash should hang loosely in front of you.**

   Stand still. Don't talk to your Dachshund. Don't look at your Dachshund. She'll probably pull a little, wander around a little, and sniff a little. Eventually, she'll get bored. (If she doesn't, move to a more boring location — say, the middle of a wide cement driveway.)

3. **When she quits moving around and stands or sits next to you, look down happily and say "[*puppy name*], Walk" and begin walking.**

   "Oh, joy!" your Dachshund thinks. "A walk! Hooray!" Off she dashes.

4. **The moment — no, the *instant* — you feel the tension on that leash tighten, stop.**

   Stand perfectly still. Don't look at your Dachshund. Don't talk to your Dachshund. Don't even say "No!" Just stop.

   But this isn't what your Dachshund expected. She thought you were going for a walk. What gives? "C'MON!" she's thinking. "Let's go!" Don't budge. Finally, your Dachshund will give up and come back to you.

5. **When she comes back to you, praise her and begin walking.**

   "Good dog! Let's walk!"

   "Hooray!" She'll lunge ahead again.

Most people are familiar with
smooth Dachshunds, but there are
two other coat types: longhairs,
such as the Miniature Dachshund
(above), and wirehairs (below).

For a longhaired
Dachshund, daily
grooming is a must.

Smooth Dachshunds are perfect
for people who don't have the
time or patience for grooming.

Cream Dachshunds can range
from gold to almost white.

This black-and-tan
color combination
is common in many
dog breeds.

Some red Dachshunds look almost brown, but
Dachshund people still call these dogs "red."

A double-dappled Dachshund is a dappled
Dachshund with patches of white.

Though there's no denying a piebald
Dachshund's beauty, they are
disqualified from competition in every
country except the United States.

Dachshund puppies tend to chew, so provide them with plenty of chew toys.

Your Dachshund's daily routine should include plenty of socializing with people.

Puppies are notoriously distractible, but with a little training, you can get them to pay attention.

Puppies need to eat more often than adults, so feed yours at least three times a day.

These wirehair pups demonstrate the Dachshund's lively, curious temperament.

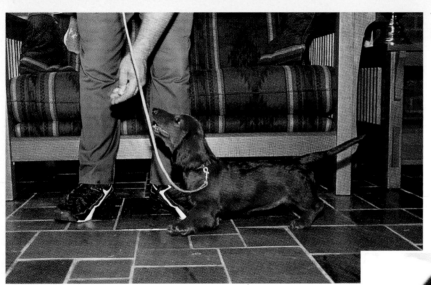

Training will help make your Dachshund a better companion.

The Dachshund's compact legs serve as powerful excavators. Dachshunds can dig out any-thing and dig into or out of anywhere — including snow.

Daily walks and even the occasional swim will keep your Dachshund healthy.

Make sure that the vet you choose has experience with Dachshunds.

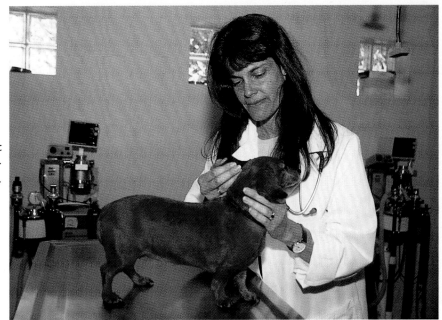

If your Dachshund is very close to the breed standard and has champions in her pedigree, she may do well competing in a dog show.

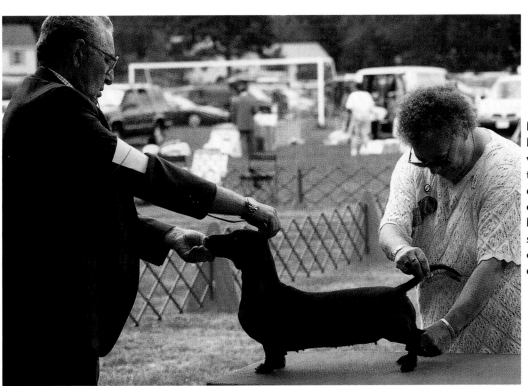

Dachshunds love to be in the middle of everything.

Going on an errand? Take your Dachshund along.

Dachshunds feel at home when they have blankets and quilts for burrowing.

6. When she lunges ahead again, stop again.

Dead still. Don't move. Now your Dachshund may be getting pretty frustrated, but let her figure this one out. When she stays by your side, you move, and the two of you get to walk. Yippee! But, when she pulls and lunges on the leash, you stop. No walk. Boring. Tedious. Everything a Dachshund hates.

7. Keep this stop and go routine up until she gets it.

If she doesn't get it today, she'll get it soon. Every time she stays at your side, say "Walk" and walk. That's the big reward — one of the biggest in your Dachshund's mind.

Here are a few Walk command tips:

✔ Never, ever move when your Dachshund pulls on the leash. Never make an exception. Even when she is 10 years old, if she pulls on the leash, stop. Ignore her and don't move until she is back at your side in a mannerly way. As long as she stays at your side, the two of you can stroll as long as you like.

✔ Once your Dachshund has learned to stay by your side on walks, you can throw in a few literal curves. Walk in an arc to the right and to the left, walk backward, walk in a circle, walk in a zigzag. See how well she can learn to tune in to your movements — even anticipate them. If, at any time, she makes a wrong move or puts any tension in that leash, always, always stop.

✔ Once your Dachshund figures out the game, this command can become great fun. It can also serve as an excellent foundation for more advanced obedience work, including the fun and creative freestyle competition.

✔ Once your Dachshund has mastered the Walk command, you can pick up the pace and change the command to Run. But don't run too fast or for very long with your Dachshund. Because their legs are so short, Dachshunds have to work twice as hard as other dogs to keep up with you.

Teaching the Wait command

If you've been working on the long sit and long down, your Dachshund is probably already familiar with the command Wait. You can use this one on your walks, too — at crosswalks or when you stop to chat with a neighbor. Positively reinforce your Dachshund when he waits patiently at your side in a sit or a down.

Practice the Wait command on a walk after your Dachshund has mastered the Walk command:

1. **While on your daily walk, whenever you approach a crosswalk or any other excuse to stop, say "[*puppy name*], Wait" and then stop walking.**

   If your Dachshund keeps moving, stand completely still and ignore him, just like you did when teaching the Walk command.

2. **As soon as he figures out that you've stopped and comes to wait at your side, tell him to sit or lie down.**

3. **When he sits or lies down, praise him and offer him a treat.**

4. **When you're ready, give the Walk command again and start walking as before.**

Practice the Wait command a few times on every walk, in conjunction with a Sit command or a Down command each time. The neighbors will be so impressed!

Troubleshooting 101

It's easy to read about dog training. It sounds so simple, so obvious, so effortless. Then you sit down and try it, and it doesn't always go the way the book says.

Often, though, the problem is that you aren't in the right mood. Or you just don't have the energy to enforce certain rules consistently. Or you don't train regularly, so your Dachshund forgets. Following are a few common problems and how to address them. And, remember, if you are really having problems, go to obedience class. Better yet, if you want to spend the bucks, hire a personal dog trainer to come to your home for a few sessions. You'll soon be back on track.

✔ **Your Dachshund won't listen.** People tend to get impatient with training. They want to jump ahead to the good stuff and not spend the time on the basics. Sorry, but without the basics, none of the other stuff will "take." Go back to Lesson #1 — getting his attention. If you don't have your Dachshund's attention, you can't get anything else done. Start at this very basic place again until he learns that when he hears his name, something fun and good will come from your direction. Move up slowly from there. And, remember, your Dachshund won't listen to anything you have to say if you say it like you are extremely annoyed or bored. But you've got something fun to say? Something great? Something so exciting that no Dachshund would ever want to miss out? Now you're talking. (And your Dachshund is listening!)

✔ **Your Dachshund won't follow the lure.** Impatience on your part may be the culprit. You hold the treat in front of your Dachshund and raise it up. Your Dachshund looks up, sits halfway, and then stands. Do you say, "Close enough!" and give her the treat? Sitting halfway isn't close enough, and you've just rewarded your Dachshund for doing something incorrectly. Don't give her that treat, not even once, unless she does something the way she's supposed to. It's not cruel to withhold a treat. It's only cruel to withhold your affection, and you aren't doing that, are you? If you find yourself getting frustrated because she won't follow the lure, she won't want anything to do with your not-very-fun, so-called game. If she doesn't get it on the first few tries, try again tomorrow. And the next day. Some Dachshunds are slower to learn, but yours really does want that treat, so keep trying until she understands. It may also help to train her before a meal when she's hungrier; the treat will be an even bigger motivation.

✔ **Your Dachshund has a very short attention span.** Of course he does, especially if he's a puppy. Don't worry if your training sessions are no longer than a couple of minutes at first. A few tries at Come, a play break, and one or two Sit commands make a perfectly respectable training session for a young puppy.

✔ **Your Dachshund refuses to come.** Try training in an area with fewer distractions. You have to be the most exciting thing around for Come to work. If your backyard has lots of other yards, dogs, and wildlife in view, forget it. Practice Come in the bathroom (put the trash away) or other relatively empty room, with no other people or pets around. Also try training before a meal when your Dachshund is hungrier or just after a nap when your Dachshund may be more alert and well rested.

✔ **Kibble isn't good enough.** Different Dachshunds are food-motivated to varying degrees. If pieces of your Dachshund's regular kibble just aren't motivation enough, try healthy homemade or store-bought treats broken into small bits. Or try small pieces of healthy people food, like raw veggie or fruit pieces, oat cereal circles, or, for the Dachshund who needs that extra push, very small slivers of cooked poultry or meat (avoid the processed meat, like hot dogs and lunchmeat).

✔ **You keep getting angry.** Puppies can be so frustrating. If you can't keep your cool, though, training simply won't work. It will only hurt your relationship with your Dachshund. Try training at a different time of day, when you might be in a better humor. If you always train your Dachshund as soon as you get home from work, maybe you should take some time to wind down first. Then train before bedtime. Also, maybe your training sessions are too long. Start with sessions that are only a couple of minutes long. How irritated can you get in two minutes? If you are still having problems, you may need to get to the root of your irritation. If something else is bothering you, practice some serious stress management so you don't take out your human troubles on an innocent, if rambunctious, little Dachshund.

Still having trouble with training? Call that trainer. Professional trainers have lots of experience with dogs just like yours, and they make a living out of helping people just like you. Many will even come to your house to conduct training sessions for your dog and for you, too!

Keep working, keep trying, and never lose that sense of humor. Most training traumas can be resolved if you stay creative and ask for professional help when you need it.

The Importance of Play

I can't emphasize enough how important it is for you and your Dachshund to keep training sessions cleverly disguised as play. Whatever you do together should be fun. If you get bored, your Dachshund is probably bored. If you are getting angry, your Dachshund is probably getting frightened.

Although Dachshunds can be stubborn, the way around their hard-headedness is not through intimidation or violence. Manipulate with charm and teach with joy, and you'll soon convince your Dachshund that doing what you say is what he wants more than anything else. With a little patience and a pervasive sense of humor, you can do it. And your Dachshund can't wait for you to try.

Accessorizing Your Dachshund

Daily walks are important to keep Dachshunds strong and healthy. But don't forget to dress your Dachsie for the occasion. Visors or sunglasses are great for hot summer days, and Dachshunds get chilly when temperatures drop — especially the smooths. Invest in a doggy sweater or jacket to keep your wiener dog warm all winter (see Figure 14-2).

Check your nearest full-service pet store or pet boutique for dog clothes or surf the Web. Because Dachshunds are an unusual shape, your best bet is the places that custom-make clothing. A few good sites that custom-make sweaters and coats are Dachshund Delights, which make sweaters for Dachshunds, at www.doxidelight.com/sweaters.htm; Foggy Mountain Dog Coats (check out the formal velvet coat — *tres chic!*), at www.dogcoat.com. and Haute Dog breed-specific sweaters, including the Doxie, made just for you-know-who, at www.hautedog.com/.

Figure 14-2:
A doggie
jacket will
keep your
Dachsie
warm and
fashionable.

Photo courtesy of Doris Stoll.

Chapter 15

The Makings of a Champion

*W*ow! It turns out that your Dachshund is great at this training stuff. She loves to learn new tricks, and the two of you have great chemistry when it comes to training sessions and learning the ropes of obedience. Maybe you have a champion in the making. If you're looking for something to do in your spare time that includes your Dachshund, why not consider a little friendly competition?

The more you explore dog competitions, the more you may be surprised at how endless your options truly are. You can do the dog show circuit, you can compete in obedience, and you can participate in field trials, agility trials, and earthdog tests. For the truly well-rounded Dachshund (and I don't mean chubby), a versatility award is perhaps the ultimate accomplishment.

But how do you get from interested dog-human team to champion dog-human team? First, you train.

Training for Competition

If a particular dog sport or area of competition interests you, the first thing to do is attend some events where the sport or competition is featured. Your local all-breed dog club or your regional breed club will probably have information about the events that interest you. Give them a call. You can also look for books specifically devoted to your area of interest, to tell you how to get started.

Depending on where you live, you may also be able to take a class that will help you and your Dachshund train. Advanced obedience classes are widely available, and so are certain specialty classes.

One type of class helps you and your dog train for the Canine Good Citizen award. Although not technically a competition — any dog can earn the award if he passes the test, regardless of how many other dogs also earn it — the Canine Good Citizen award is an excellent place to begin. It proves that your Dachshund has mastered certain elements of good behavior and self-control that will help him in the future with more advanced endeavors.

Taking the Canine Good Citizen Test

The purpose of the Canine Good Citizen test is to encourage all dog owners to teach their pets good manners and proper behavior. If every dog were to learn the skills necessary to pass this test, surely the vast numbers of dogs abandoned to animal shelters would decrease, and so would the cases of dog-related injury in this country. Because the test aims to benefit all dogs and all people, any breed and any mixed breed of dog may take the test and earn the award. Unlike many other types of canine competition where pure-bred status is a must, the Canine Good Citizen test is an equal opportunity test.

"Hey! I'd like to be a CGC tester"

If you'd like to administer the Canine Good Citizen test to other dogs and their owners, write to the American Kennel Club for a free information kit or to purchase a Canine Good Citizen test kit: The American Kennel Club, Attn: CGC, 5580 Centerview Drive, Suite 200, Raleigh, NC 27606, 919-233-9767 (phone), info@akc.org (e-mail). If you have any questions about the AKC's Canine Good Citizen program, you can call the AKC's Canine Good Citizen Department: at 919-854-0175 or 919-854-0176. The fax number is 919-854-0151.

Any dog, classes or no classes, can take the test for the Canine Good Citizen award. You can train your Dachshund for it at home. Knowledgeable members of local dog clubs, 4-H clubs, or other clubs whose interest includes the well being of our canine friends usually administer the test. It involves ten tests, each determining how well your Dachshund can perform according to basic good manners:

- **Accepting a friendly stranger.** Your Dachshund must remain quiet and well behaved when a friendly but unknown person approaches, speaks to you, and shakes your hand. While you and the stranger talk pleasantly, your Dachshund must stay next to you and not show any sign of guarding you, of shyness, or of moving toward the stranger.

- **Sitting politely for petting.** In this test, your Dachshund must sit at your side while someone he doesn't know approaches and pets him on the head and body. The stranger must then walk behind and around you and your Dachshund. Your Dachshund must not act shy, aggressive, or resentful toward the stranger.

- **Appearance and grooming.** The purpose of this test is to show that your Dachshund can be safely and easily examined and handled by a stranger, such as a vet, groomer, or friend. The evaluator combs or brushes your Dachshund and gently examines her ears and each front foot. Your Dachshund must accept such handling without acting shy or aggressive.

- **Out for a walk on a loose leash.** You must demonstrate your control over your Dachshund for this test. Walk with your Dachshund on either side of you on a loose leash — meaning, no pulling on the leash for either of you. During your walk, you must make one left turn, one right turn, one about turn, one stop during the middle of the test, and another stop at the end. Your Dachshund must stay in a good heel (practice that Walk command in Chapter 14) and may either sit or stand during the stops.

- **Walking through a crowd.** Your Dachshund must demonstrate his self-control in a public place for this test. You and your Dachshund must walk around and by at least three people, during which time your Dachshund may display interest but not excitement, shyness, or resentment. You may direct, encourage, and/or praise your Dachshund during this test, but he must not pull on the leash and must remain at your side.

- **Sit and Down on command, staying in place.** This test determines your Dachshund's knowledge of basic commands. Ask your Dachshund to sit and to lie down. You may make the command more than once and may use more than one word. (You can include your Dachshund's name in the command, for example, or add words of encouragement.) Next, you must ask your Dachshund to stay and then walk down a 20-foot line away from your Dachshund, during which time he must stay in place, although he can change position (move from lying down to sitting, for example).

✔ **Coming when called.** Your Dachshund must demonstrate her understanding of the Come command. In this test, you must walk 10 feet from your Dachshund, with or without the Stay command. Turn to face your Dachshund and call her to you. She must come when called.

✔ **Reaction to another dog.** For this test, your Dachshund must demonstrate his good manners around another dog. With your Dachshund on a leash, you must approach another handler with another dog on a leash, who are approximately 10 yards away. You and the other handler must stop, shake hands, talk pleasantly, and then continue past each other for 5 yards. Both dogs should show casual interest in each other but shouldn't leave their respective handlers' sides and shouldn't act shy or aggressive.

✔ **Reaction to distractions.** Distractions are a part of life, and in this test, your Dachshund demonstrates how confidently he handles them. The evaluator sets up some common distractions, such as a book being dropped to the floor or a jogger running by. Your Dachshund must show some natural curiosity in, and may even appear startled by, the distraction. But he must not act aggressive or fearful, try to run away, or bark at the distraction.

✔ **Supervised separation.** The last test determines how well your Dachshund can behave when you aren't around to influence him. The evaluator says something to the effect of "Would you like me to watch your dog?" and you agree. Hand the leash to the evaluator and walk out of sight. The evaluator holds your Dachshund's leash for 3 minutes. Your Dachshund needn't maintain a sit or down position, but she shouldn't bark excessively, whine and cry, howl, pace, or act very nervous. Slight agitation is acceptable, since your Dachshund really has no idea where you went.

During the Canine Good Citizen test, you have one chance at each test. If you fail, better luck next time. You may attempt the test again at a later date. Some of the sections of this test are harder for Dachshunds than others, but many Dachshunds have earned their Canine Good Citizen award, and yours can, too. All it takes is practice, daily training sessions, and patience, patience, patience. Then, once your Dachshund has her CGC, why not shoot even higher?

Showing Your Dachshund: Isn't She Lovely. . . .

Maybe you think you've got the most beautiful Dachshund you've ever seen, like the one in Figure 15-1. You may be right! If your Dachshund is very close to the breed standard — especially if he has champions in his pedigree — he may do well in, and sincerely enjoy competing in, a dog show.

Photo courtesy of Gail Painter.

The dog show circuit these days is mighty competitive, however. Most of the people competing with their dogs are breeders or professional handlers who are working on championships for their breeding stock. Although some people do it just for fun, earning championships — and especially national standing — isn't cheap, takes lots of time, and can become addictive. If your Dachshund does well in dog shows and you catch the bug, you may find yourself wanting to become a breeder. If you are willing to do the work and invest the time and money to improve the Dachshund breed, *great*. Otherwise, you may want to think twice about doing the dog show thing.

Also remember that dogs competing in AKC-sanctioned dog shows can't be spayed or neutered. Also, many dog owners hire professional handlers (costly), and if you aren't very familiar with the dog show ropes, you may feel intimidated.

Dog shows come in several types. *Specialty shows* are for dogs of a specific breed. Each national breed club has a specialty show each year. For example, the Dachshund Club of America has a specialty show in which only purebred, registered Dachshunds may compete. *Group shows* are for dogs from one of the seven groups of purebred dogs. Dachshunds belong to the Hound Group and participate in a Hound Group show, competing against all other hounds, like Basset Hounds, Beagles, Greyhounds, and Foxhounds. *All-breed shows* are for dogs of any of the many breeds recognized by the AKC. *Fun matches* and other informal shows are less competitive and lots of fun. These shows are held by clubs working on earning the right to hold AKC-sanctioned shows or clubs that just want to have a good time. Different shows have different requirements, so check with the club hosting the show. These shows often have other events, such as agility trials, tracking contests, and other fun dog events, and are great fun to attend as a spectator.

Local dog clubs often hold more informal fun matches, where dogs can be shown but don't actually earn points toward championships. These matches can be great fun for everyone, especially beginners and the Dachshund who likes to strut her stuff and please the crowd but doesn't want a full-time job on the show circuit.

Before you decide how deeply you'd like to get involved in *conformation shows* (dog shows that judge a dog by how closely it conforms to the breed standard), you'll want to attend a few. Look for dog shows sanctioned by the American Kennel Club or the United Kennel Club (UKC) or look for less formal shows sponsored by local or regional dog clubs.

During an AKC-sanctioned dog show, dogs compete to earn points toward the title of champion. Once a dog earns his Champion of Record title, he can put the coveted *Ch.* in front of his name.

The *United Kennel Club (UKC)* is the second oldest and second largest all-breed dog registry in the United States. The UKC recognizes and registers a wide variety of purebred dogs and also sponsors many types of dog events, like conformation shows, obedience trials, agility trials, and field trials.

In all-breed shows, dogs who have earned their championships compete against all other breeds for several different awards, including Best of Breed, for the best dog in the show of each breed; Best of Winners, a competition between the best male and female dogs in the show; and Best of Opposite Sex, for the best dog of the opposite sex from the one winning Best of Breed. Then each Best of Breed dog competes against the others for the ultimate award, Best in Show.

Purebred groups

The AKC recognizes seven different groups of purebred dogs: Sporting dogs, bred to hunt game birds on land and in water; Hound dogs, used for hunting by sight or scent (this is the Dachshund's group); Working dogs, used to pull, guard, or search and rescue; Terrier dogs, bred to eliminate vermin; Toy dogs, bred to be companions; Non-Sporting dogs, which don't fit into other categories; and Herding dogs, bred to assist shepherds and ranchers with livestock.

The dog show world has indeed become a highly specialized arena, but visiting one is fun. It can also be the ideal place to meet Dachshund breeders — even find the Dachshund puppy of your dreams. If you are determined to enter your Dachshund in dog shows, however, first learn everything you can. Talk to your breeder, talk to veteran handlers (many dogs are breeder-owner handled), and attend as many shows as possible. Buy the program and read it, cover to cover. Make sure you coordinate your schedule so you don't miss the Dachshund competitions. And have fun. If a dog show isn't fun for you and, especially, for your Dachshund, you're both better off spending your time in some other way.

Trying Obedience Competitions: Surprise Them All!

Maybe beauty contests aren't your speed. But if your Dachshund loves to perform tricks, and you're great at teaching them, obedience competition may be. Although still mighty competitive, obedience competition can be lots of fun for Dachshunds and their humans, even if you don't plan to become a breeder.

If you'd like your Dachshund to earn an obedience title or two, you need to attend an AKC-sanctioned obedience competition. Otherwise, look for less formal obedience events sponsored by your local dog club.

The point of obedience trials is to show that your Dachshund has truly learned how to be a well-mannered and useful companion. Advanced obedience work includes tests of tracking ability, a Dachshund specialty. (These tests are hard work, so both you and your Dachshund should be in good shape.)

To earn an obedience title, your Dachshund must earn over half the points in each specified exercise under three different judges at licensed or member obedience trials. The titles you can earn in obedience competition are

- Companion Dog, or CD
- Companion Dog Excellent, or CDX
- Utility Dog, or UD
- Utility Dog Excellent, or UDX
- Obedience Trial Champion, or OTCh.
- Tracking Dog, or TD
- Tracking Dog Excellent, or TDX
- Variable Surface Tracker, or VST
- Champion Tracker, or CT

In general, dogs must earn each title successively. You can't skip to a UDX without earning a CD, a CDX, and a UD first. Then, after a dog has earned a title, he can use it with his name, like a degree. *Ch. Whirlwind's Teeny Weenie, UDX,* for example, has excelled in both conformation (the *Ch.*) and obedience (the *UDX*). Only list the most advanced title in any category.

To get started in obedience or to find an obedience and/or tracking club in your area, call the AKC, check out the AKC Web site's geographical listing of show and obedience clubs (www.akc.org/dic/clubs/states/), or call your local dog club.

Spayed or neutered dogs may participate in obedience trials. However, puppies less than 6 months of age, females in heat, and lame, deaf, or blind dogs may not compete. Dogs who attack other dogs or appear dangerous or overly aggressive are disqualified.

Competing in Field Trials: Dachshund Destiny

Dachshunds are one of only a handful of breeds eligible to participate in field trials, and Dachshund field trials are different from field trials for other dogs, like retrievers. The purpose of field trials is to give breeds designed for field work the opportunity to exercise their natural abilities.

Dachshunds are best at tracking small game through dense brush and alerting hunters to the location of the game. In a field trial, this scenario is re-enacted under controlled conditions (no wildlife gets hurt). Dachshund field trials are based on Brace Beagle field trials, in which a pair, or *brace,* of dogs track a rabbit. In the context of a field trial, a brace is a pair of dogs that compete together.

Field trials are usually held in a fenced area so the Dachshunds can't escape or become lost, and the rabbit isn't killed. Some field trials divide the male and female Dachshund competitions; others don't.

When the contest begins, a Field Marshall calls each brace to attention. Then volunteer brush beaters scare up a rabbit. Whoever sees the rabbit first shouts, "Tally Ho!" After the rabbit has been spotted and has scurried away, the Dachshunds are brought to the place where the rabbit was spotted. Each handler encourages his or her Dachshund to find the *line,* or scent, of the rabbit. As soon as the Dachshund catches the scent, the Dachshund is released; the handler must stop giving instructions but may follow the dog — behind the judges only. When the judges have seen enough to judge the Dachshund's ability to follow the scent with persistence and enthusiasm, they ask the handlers to pick up their dogs.

The ultimate goal of field trials, beyond having a great time, is to earn enough points for the title Field Champion. Versatile Dachshunds who attain the title of Field Champion and are Champions of Record in conformation are considered dual champions. These same Dachshunds who also earn an obedience championship are considered triple champions.

A *dual champion* is a dog who has earned both a conformation champion title and a field champion title. A *triple champion* has earned a conformation champion title, a field champion title, and an obedience champion title.

Visit a field trial or two to see what it's all about and ask the people running their Dachshunds how you can train your Dachshund for competition. Usually, you're rewarded with friendly people and lots of great advice. To find a field trial in your area, contact the AKC, check out the AKC Web site's geographical listing of field trial clubs (`www.akc.org/dic/clubs/other/fieldcb.cfm`), or call your local dog club.

Competing in Agility Trials: Poetry in Motion

Agility is hot these days because everyone loves to watch it. Who can resist a bevy of dogs jumping, running, and tunneling through an obstacle course? The dogs can't resist it, either. If your Dachshund is athletic, and you think she'd enjoy agility, consider training her for agility work and competing for titles.

Agility helps both you and your Dachshund stay in great shape. It's also the perfect outlet for your little performer. Any dog may participate in an agility trial, whether or not she or he is registered or spayed or neutered.

Some Dachshund owners may be nervous about training their Dachshunds to do agility because of the jumping. Luckily, jumps are adjusted for the height of the dog, so a healthy, athletic Dachshund at his ideal weight should have no problem with the jumps. But, if your Dachshund has had back problems before, or you believe that he is at risk for disc disease, stick to obedience or another less up-and-down activity.

Dogs can earn a number of titles in agility competition, each more difficult to achieve than the one before:

- ✔ Novice Agility (NA)
- ✔ Open Agility (OA)
- ✔ Agility Excellent (AX)
- ✔ Master Agility Excellent (MX)
- ✔ Master Agility Champion (MACH)

The obstacle course in an agility trial varies depending on the level of competition, but all levels include contact obstacles with certain areas the dog must touch when going over the obstacle, jumps, and different versions of hoops and tunnels the dog must go through. Dogs must achieve the obstacle course in a set amount of time (also depending on the level of competition) and must successfully maneuver on, in, over, or through each obstacle. The obstacles used are

- ✔ **The A-frame.** Your Dachshund must go up one panel of the A-frame and go down the other panel, touching the contact zone, in whatever direction the judge orders.

- ✔ **The dog walk.** Your Dachshund must go up one ramp, cross a center section, and go down the other ramp, touching both contact zones, in whatever order the judge specifies.

- ✔ **The seesaw.** Your Dachshund must ascend the plank, cause it to seesaw the other way, and then descend, waiting on the opposite side to touch the ground before getting off the seesaw, after touching the contact zone.

- ✔ **The pause table.** Your Dachshund must jump onto the table, pause for 5 seconds in a sit or down position (according to what the judge decrees), and then dismount.

- ✔ **The open tunnel.** This flexible tube must be positioned so that your Dachshund can't see the end of the tunnel when he enters. He must go in one end of the tunnel (the one the judge indicates), go through the tunnel, and come out the other side.

- ✔ **The closed tunnel.** This tunnel has a rigid entrance connected to a soft chute. Your Dachshund must enter the tunnel and exit through the chute.

- ✔ **The weave poles.** Your Dachshund must go between the first two poles from right to left, then move from left to right between the second and third poles, then move from right to left between the third and fourth poles, etc.

- ✔ **The single bar jumps.** Your Dachshund must jump over the top bar without knocking it off, in the direction the judge specifies.

- ✔ **The panel jump.** Your Dachshund must jump over the top board without knocking it off, in the direction the judge specifies.

- ✔ **Other single jumps.** Courses can also include other types of single jumps for your Dachshund to jump over.

- ✔ **The double bar jump.** Your Dachshund must jump over both top bars without knocking off either one, in whatever direction the judge specifies.

- ✔ **The triple bar jump.** Your Dachshund must jump over three bars of gradually increasing heights without knocking off any, in whatever direction the judge specifies.

- ✔ **The tire jump (or circle jump).** Your Dachshund must jump through the tire opening in the direction the judge specifies.

- ✔ **The window jump.** Your Dachshund must jump through the window opening in the direction the judge specifies.

- ✔ **The broad jump.** Your Dachshund must jump over a series of obstacles of varying heights without touching them, entering between marker poles placed near the front and exiting between marker poles placed near the back.

Agility is so much fun that you may find it becomes an every-weekend activity for you and your Dachshund. Why not? Your Dachshund would rather spend his weekends playing with you than doing just about anything else. To find agility competitions in your area, call the AKC, check out the AKC Web site's geographical list of agility clubs (www.akc.org/dic/clubs/other/agilitycb.cfm), or call your local dog club.

Competing in Earthdog Tests: Born to Burrow

Dachshunds love to dig. But you already know that. If yours is a digger extraordinaire, she may have the right stuff for earthdog tests. Most Dachshunds do.

Earthdog tests are lots of fun, too, and any AKC-registered Dachshund (or Terrier) 6 months of age or older may participate, including spayed and neutered dogs.

In an earth dog test, a den is set up by digging a trench, placing a 9-inch by 9-inch wood liner in the trench, and covering it with earth. The tunnel and trench have certain twists and turns, as required by the level of competition, and at the end of the tunnel are bars separating a caged rat from the dogs. The tunnel can also be opened at the end so you can lift your Dachshund out when he's finished. Tunnels for the higher levels of competition have false exits, false entrances, and false scented dens.

For the competition, your Dachshund is released and must enter a specially constructed tunnel, following it through to the end where the rats are caged, and then he must bark, scratch at, and otherwise work the quarry for a specified amount of time.

Beginners can start out with the Introduction to Quarry test (not required for more advanced levels of competition). This test requires that the dogs get to the rat within 2 minutes and work the quarry continuously for at least 30 seconds. This test can help you determine whether your Dachshund is a natural at earth dog tests.

Diggin' dogs

Lots of dogs like to dig, but not all breeds are eligible to participate in earthdog tests. The following breeds are classified as eligible by the AKC: Dachshunds, Australian Terriers, Bedlington Terriers, Border Terriers, Cairn Terriers, Dandie Dinmont Terriers, Fox Terriers (smooth and wire), Lakeland Terriers, Norfolk Terriers, Scottish Terriers, Sealyham Terriers, Skye Terriers, Welsh Terriers, and West Highland Terriers.

More advanced levels of competition and titles are as follows:

- ✔ **Junior Earthdog (JE).** For this test, you must release your Dachshund 10 feet from the den entrance. She has 30 seconds to reach the rat from the time she is released, and then she must work the quarry, staying within 12 inches of it, continuously for 30 seconds. Tunnels for this level of competition are 30 feet long with three 90-degree turns.

- ✔ **Senior Earthdog (SE).** For this test, you must release your Dachshund 20 feet from the den entrance. He has 90 seconds to reach the quarry from the time he is released, and he must work the quarry continuously for 90 seconds. Tunnels for this level of competition are also 30 feet long with three 90-degree turns, but they also include a 7-foot-long false exit and a false den consisting of a 4-foot-long side tunnel with no exit and a heavily scented bedding area with no rat.

- ✔ **Master Earthdog (ME).** For this test, two dogs are worked together. You must release your dog 100 feet from the real den entrance (this may soon change to 300 feet). For this test, however, the den entrance is blocked, and a false den entrance is also available. Dogs must reach the real den entrance and bark to be let in. Dogs who bark at the false den don't qualify for this title. The first dog to reach the real den is temporarily removed so the second dog can have a chance to find it, too. Then the first dog is allowed in the tunnel and must reach the quarry within 90 seconds and work the quarry for 90 seconds. While working the quarry, the judge simulates digging sounds on the top of the den with a piece of wood for 30 seconds, and the dog should not be distracted by this noise. The first dog is then removed, and the second dog is given a turn.

The tunnel for the Master Earthdog test is the same as the tunnel for the Senior Earthdog test except for the blocked entrance. A 20-foot scent line leads to the entrance, and a false entrance is placed somewhere along the scent line. Also, within the tunnel is an 18-inch section that narrows to a 6-inch passageway, and the tunnel also contains a 6-inch-diameter PVC pipe obstacle suspended in the tunnel with 9 inches on each side of the pipe's center line.

Earthdog tests are relatively new, and Dachshunds love 'em. To find opportunities for earthdog competitions in your area, call the AKC, check out the AKC Web site's geographical listing of earthdog clubs (www.akc.org/dic/clubs/other/earthcb.cfm), or call your local dog club.

The New Versatile Dachshund

Dachshund breeders, like many other breeders, are becoming increasingly concerned that Dachshunds be both beautiful and healthy, both show stoppers and athletes, and always able to perform the functions for which they were bred. In an attempt to encourage versatility rather than overspecialization in Dachshunds, the Dachshund Club of America has established a versatility program that awards a Versatility Certificate (VC) to Dachshunds who distinguish themselves in several areas.

To earn a VC, a Dachshund must have 18 or more VC points obtained from a conformation show and at least three of the following five groups: field trials, obedience (including the Canine Good Citizen award), tracking, earthdog tests, and agility.

Depending on the titles or points earned in each group, a Dachshund earns varying numbers of VC points. A triple champion (championships in conformation, field trials, and obedience) automatically qualifies for a Versatility Certificate.

Versatility awards are a great idea. They encourage well-rounded Dachshunds, and the hope is that breeders will avoid breeding just for looks, field abilities, or obedience skill but equally in all areas. The more wide-ranging a dog's abilities, the healthier and stronger he tends to be. Plus, a Dachshund with such a variety of important jobs is a busy, happy, challenged Dachshund.

So what are you waiting for? Start training your pup for the big leagues, and someday you may scarcely remember those days before you were a Dachshund person.

Part IV
The Healthy Dachshund

The 5th Wave   By Rich Tennant

Apparently what happens is, they try to push a tree over. When they find out they can't, they go running off in frustration.

In this part . . .

You find out what it takes to keep your Dachshund happy and healthy. I also describe in detail the back problems that many Dachshunds develop and show you some preventative measures. I then discuss the health needs of older dogs.

Chapter 16

Healthy Dachshund 101

. . . .

In This Chapter

▶ The elements of good puppy health
▶ The importance of exercise
▶ The right vet

. . . .

*Y*our Dachshund is the very picture of health. You find it difficult to imagine that your bouncing bundle of energy could ever get sick or injured. However, it's precisely when animals (and people) are at their healthiest that preventive measures are most effective. To keep your Dachshund puppy or dog in glowing health from the tip of his nose all the way to the tip of his tail (and that's quite a distance, as dogs go), read this chapter and follow a few basic preventive health measures.

Also, always remember that the people who know your Dachshund best are you, your family, and your vet. Always remain vigilant for signs that something isn't right. Changes in behavior, appetite, sleeping habits, water consumption, or movement may all be signs of a health problem. Bumps, lumps, dry patches, bare patches, and other irregularities you may detect during your daily grooming examination may also signal a problem. Never hesitate to ask your vet about your Dachshund's condition. The sooner you catch a problem, the easier it will be to resolve.

Keeping Your Puppy Healthy

Puppies are vulnerable. They look it when first born, but once they fill out a little and commandeer your entire household, bending each helpless human to their will, they may not seem so vulnerable.

Regardless of how sturdy they look, Dachshund puppies can easily fall prey to a number of serious, even life-threatening, diseases. While nursing, they receive a bevy of immunities from their mothers, but after weaning, this immune protection drops off quickly. Until they develop their own immune systems, they are particularly susceptible to the most serious contagious diseases.

Puppies can also develop nasty parasite problems, they can suffer from a lack of good grooming, and the discs in their back can rupture (although disc problems are more common a few years down the road). How do you keep your puppy healthy? A few simple measures.

Vaccinations

A debate is going on about vaccinations. Many people claim that pets are overvaccinated and that vaccines from the first year last a lifetime. Could be. However, that first year's vaccination schedule is *crucial*. Protect your puppy from canine parvovirus, distemper, hepatitis, leptospirosis, and rabies (as well as other diseases that may be more prevalent in your area, such as coronavirus and Lyme disease) by getting your puppy vaccinated first at 5 to 6 weeks of age (if you buy your Dachshund from a breeder, he or she should have had these vaccinations done already) and then according to a regular schedule suggested by your veterinarian.

Canine parvovirus is a highly contagious viral disease that comes in a diarrheal form and a cardiac form. If not treated, it's usually fatal — especially for puppies. *Distemper* is another highly contagious and often fatal viral disease that causes severe neurological damage in its advanced stages. *Hepatitis* is a highly contagious virus that begins with a fever and can end in coma and death. *Leptospirosis* is a bacterial disease that can cause death or severe kidney, liver, and digestive tract damage. It can be transmitted to humans. *Rabies* can also be transmitted to humans. It's another viral disease that can cause paralysis or severe aggression in advanced stages. Infected animals rarely survive. *Coronavirus* is rarely fatal but can cause depression, vomiting, and diarrhea. *Lyme disease* is transmitted by deer ticks and can cause severe arthritic symptoms, lameness, and loss of appetite.

The one vaccine required by law is the rabies vaccine, so even if you're an anti-vaccine person, you're required to have proof of this one. You must show this proof to license your dog, to board your dog in a kennel, and sometimes even to get veterinary care. Nobody wants to risk rabies, so be diligent about the rabies vaccine.

In rare cases, animals react adversely to a vaccination. Vaccines can make some dogs very ill and can even be fatal. The chances your Dachshund will react this way are extremely slim. But always watch your Dachshund carefully for a week or so after any vaccines. Reactions range from mild discomfort and loss of appetite to shock and death. If your Dachshund changes his behavior or seems out of it or ill in any way following a vaccination, call your vet immediately.

Some people suggest that puppies should never be around other dogs until all vaccinations are complete. But what about puppy obedience classes? If you bring your puppy to obedience classes at 3 or 4 months, be sure to choose one that requires all puppy owners to show proof of vaccination. You should be okay. Better to have a well-trained puppy and take the very small risk that something might get passed around. Not training or socializing your puppy is a bigger risk because you'll be more likely to give your Dachshund away when she gets to be too much trouble.

Sterilization

Do you want to become a Dachshund breeder? Are you ready to devote most of your waking hours to the intense and often heartbreaking efforts of breeding, whelping, raising, and studying to improve the health and temperament of Dachshunds? Are you ready to barely break even when you sell the puppies, to take any puppy back for any reason, to remain committed to every dog out of litter after litter, to watch puppies fail to thrive and die in your arms?

If not, please, *please* sterilize your Dachshund. We are in the midst of a crisis in this country. Pet overpopulation is out of control, and the number of animals euthanized each year is staggering and saddening.

The fact is, Dachshunds like to run, dig, and escape. Even under the best of conditions, your Dachshund could get out. If she does, she could easily come home pregnant. If he does, he could easily impregnate the neighbor's champion Shih Tzu. At best, you'll have a litter of puppies on your hands. At worst, your neighbor could take you to court.

Sterilization doesn't cost much. (Many local humane societies offer vouchers to make the procedure even cheaper; give them a call.) It's very safe for dogs. There is a slight risk to any dog that undergoes general anaesthetic, but almost all dogs come out of it just fine. Sterilization can even improve the behavior of dogs, and there are health benefits to early sterilization, such as a reduced incidence of mammary tumors and fewer prostate problems. Imagine being driven by an overwhelming urge to procreate. Since you aren't going to allow procreation for your Dachshund, why subject him or her to the urge?

Some staggering statistics

According to the Animal Welfare League of Alexandria, Virginia, more than 2,000 dogs are born every *hour* in the United States. In that same hour, an average of only 415 humans are born. Yearly, more than 17 million dogs are born, adding to the current dog population of 54 million. (The numbers are even bigger for cats.)

I can't think of any reason why you wouldn't want to sterilize your Dachshund, unless you specifically bought a specimen to serve as the foundation of your breeding program and have made the full-fledged commitment to be the best breeder you can be. But that is the subject of another book.

Pest control

No matter where you live, no matter how often you keep your Dachshund inside, you'll probably have some contact with some kind of pest. Fleas are everywhere, and in the southern states and parts of California, fleas have established a comfortable and prolific year-round existence, where flea season is 365 days per year.

Ticks are everywhere, too, in the wooded areas of most states. Lyme disease, a serious and sometimes fatal disease spread by the deer tick, has been detected in 47 of 50 states. Many puppies, no matter how well bred, are born with worms, and Dachshunds can easily pick up worms at any time during their lives. Mites that infect the ears or the skin abound. Heartworms can kill your Dachshund by taking up residence in his heart after transmission from a single mosquito bite.

In other words, pest control is something every pet owner must deal with. Pests come in many forms, and none of them are any fun. But each of them can, fortunately, be dealt with easily as long as you practice a little prevention and address any pest problem as soon as it is detected:

- ✔ **Fleas.** Fleas are uncomfortable for your Dachshund and can cause complications ranging from severe allergic reactions to tapeworms. You probably aren't too fond of fleas jumping on and off your arms and legs, either, and if your Dachshund isn't handy, the fleas will be happy to bite you. In rare cases, fleas can even infect humans with bubonic plague. Yikes!

  Flea solutions? Apply a spot-on adulticide flea treatment (ask your vet for a recommendation) every month during flea season. A few drops between your dog's shoulder blades will kill fleas that land on your Dachshund, even before they have a chance to bite (see Figure 16-1). As an added precaution, treat your dog with an oral insect-growth-regulator treatment once a month all year round. Any flea that does bite your dog won't be able to hatch any eggs, and the flea reproduction cycle will be halted before it can start. Again, ask your vet for her favorite brand.

- ✔ **Ticks.** Ticks can pass on severe diseases, too. The notorious Lyme disease is just one of many. Ticks are always a possibility when you walk with your Dachshund in wooded areas. They range in size, but sometimes the very smallest, barely visible ticks are the most dangerous.

Figure 16-1:
A few drops
of flea
treatment
here should
keep fleas
away.

Tick solutions? Some spot-on flea products also kill ticks. These products probably aren't necessary if you aren't outside with your Dachshund a lot. Wooded areas are the most tick-ridden. If your Dachshund does get a tick, pull it straight out with tweezers or with your fingers (wear rubber gloves or use a tissue). If your Dachshund shows signs of listlessness, fatigue, and loss of appetite, Lyme disease could be the culprit. See your vet.

Always use rubber gloves or a tissue when removing a tick from your Dachshund. If the tick is very full (of blood), it could burst when you pull it out. Bacteria from a burst tick could infect you through your skin.

✔ **Worms.** Roundworms, tapeworms, hookworms, and whipworms can cause a variety of symptoms ranging from uncomfortable to fatal. If you aren't thinking "Yuck!" at the very thought of worms, read on: Roundworms look like thin spaghetti, curled in your dog's feces. Tapeworms look like long flat ribbons, and dead ones look like translucent grains of rice in your dog's feces. Hookworms penetrate your Dachshund's skin, and the eggs can be detected under a microscope in your Dachshund's feces. Whipworms are too small to see but cause watery diarrhea and weakness.

Worm solutions? Have every new puppy dewormed, usually a few times. Always keep your yard free of dog feces. Many worms are transmitted when your Dachshund eats, or even sniffs, the feces of another dog (including your own dogs). A fence will help to keep stray dogs and their remains out of your yard. Then, once or twice a year, have your vet do a fecal examination to check for the ongoing presence or arrival of more worms.

✔ **Mites.** Mites cause severe itching and a variety of unpleasant and unattractive skin conditions, sometimes referred to collectively as *mange*. Some mites infect your Dachshund's ears; others live in his skin. Suspect ear mites if your Dachshund shakes his head a lot and scratches at his ears. Dark earwax is another sign. *Scabies* is a skin condition caused by a mite, and humans can get it too. Scabies itches and often results in hair loss. Another type of mite can also cause hair loss. It lives in the hair follicles and infects them. *Chiggers* live in wooded areas and also burrow under your dog's skin, causing itching and redness. Another type of mite causes puppy dandruff and mild itching.

Mite solutions? See your vet for various types of creams, drops, dips, or shampoos, depending on the type of mite. And don't wait. Your Dachshund won't enjoy being bald.

✔ **Heartworms.** Heartworms are transmitted from mosquitoes and, if left untreated, will kill your Dachshund. They travel to your dog's heart and mature there, reaching lengths of up to 12 inches. A dog with heartworms can be treated (the treatment isn't cheap), but if the heartworm is too advanced, it may be too late.

Heartworm solutions? Keep your Dachshund out of mosquito-infested areas. Also, give your Dachshund a heartworm pill on schedule every single month all year round. If your Dachshund never goes outside, chances are he won't be infected, but if you are an extra careful person, you may want to give him heartworm pills anyway.

Heartworm pills are great for preventing heartworms, but if your Dachshund already has heartworms, a heartworm pill could be fatal. Always have your Dachshund tested for heartworms *before* beginning heartworm pills.

Good grooming

Keeping your Dachshund well groomed is an important part of maintaining her overall health:

✔ A healthy, mat-free coat makes examination of the skin easier and doesn't harbor pests, dirt, or bacteria.

✔ Tartar-free and plaque-free teeth help prevent gum disease as well as more serious conditions like heart disease, which can result from bacteria in your dog's mouth traveling to his heart.

- Short, clipped nails keep your Dachshund's feet healthy and correctly positioned on the ground.

- Clean ears are less likely to harbor mites and develop infections, and regular ear examinations help you detect the presence of such conditions if they occur.

- Emptied anal sacs don't become impacted or infected.

What? Anal sacs? Yes, anal sacs. They're something I don't particularly like to talk about, but here goes. All dogs have anal sacs on either side of their anus, and these sacs are probably responsible for scent identification between dogs. They are possibly involved in courtship and/or in marking territory. The anal sacs fill up with a thick, extremely smelly liquid that is usually drained when dogs excrete feces.

However, some lucky breeds, including many of the small breeds and our beloved Dachshunds, tend to develop impacted anal sacs. Have you seen your Dachshund dragging his rear around on your carpet? That's your first clue.

Your vet can drain these sacs, and so can your groomer (if you ask really nicely). Depending on how often your Dachshund's sacs get impacted, this procedure should be done every six to eight weeks. Having someone else do it can get expensive if you're on a tight budget, so you can do it yourself — although I don't recommend it if you're squeamish.

Some Dachshunds aren't too happy to have you poking around back there, but some don't mind at all — especially if you know what you're doing. Look at your Dachshund's rear end and imagine a clock face with your dog's anus as the center. The anal sacs are at 4:00 and 8:00. Take a couple layers of paper towels and place them over your dog's anus; then squeeze on either side of the anus with your fingers — in, downward, then upward — until all the fluid is expelled.

If you can't get it, ask your vet or groomer to show you how. If you still can't get it, just pay somebody to do it, for heaven's sake. Cut back on groceries or whatever it takes to budget for it. It's really a dirty job. Well, truthfully, once you get used to it, it's not so bad. But you may be of the opinion that it isn't something you feel like getting used to.

Getting Regular Exercise: Move It or Lose It

Every living thing with muscles needs to exercise. Exercise helps keep your Dachshund young, strong, and slim. Couch potato Dachshunds may be more prone to disc problems, less able to fight off disease, and generally less healthy than their more athletic counterparts.

If your Dachshund is overweight, don't begin a rigorous exercise program right away. That extra weight puts a strain on your Dachshund's back, as well as on all her muscles. She needs to build up strength before she can do too much. Exercise is crucial for overweight Dachshunds, but start with slow, short walks and watch for signs of excessive fatigue, such as heavy panting or sitting down and refusing to move. (Leave it to a Dachshund to make her wishes clear.)

How much should your Dachshund weigh? That depends on her size, muscle mass, and other factors. In general, however, you can tell whether your Dachshund is too fat by checking periodically (your daily grooming session is the perfect opportunity) for the following signs:

- Look at your Dachshund from the side. Do you see a nice tuck where his tummy is, or does his tummy hang down? If it hangs down, he is too fat. He could also have worms, so check with your vet before putting him on a diet.

- Look at your Dachshund from the top (see Figure 16-2). She should look more like a squash than a sausage. Her body should get narrower between the bottom of the rib cage and the hips. A too sharp narrowing could signal that your Dachshund is underweight.

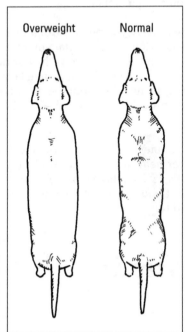

Overweight   Normal

Figure 16-2:
The signs
of an
overweight
Dachshund.

✔ Feel your Dachshund's ribs. Can you feel the individual ribs under a thin but slightly padded layer of skin? Just right. If you can't find any sign of ribs, your Dachshund is too fat. If the ribs are very visible without even touching them, your Dachshund may be too thin.

If you suspect that your Dachshund is over- or underweight, check with your vet and formulate a plan of action. A new diet, new feeding habits, or simply a decrease in treats and table scraps will probably be the prescription. Certainly, the second part of the prescription, especially if your Dachshund is overweight, will be an increase in the level of exercise.

But what if you have trouble getting up off that couch yourself? How are you supposed to get your Dachshund to exercise? Following are a few tips:

✔ A daily walk is good for you and your Dachshund. It doesn't have to be fast. Remember, your Dachshund's legs are a lot shorter than yours, so she gets far more steps per block than you do. It doesn't have to be long, either. A spin around the block in the morning and, ideally, in the evening is all it takes.

✔ Going on an errand? Walking down to the neighbor's house to borrow a cup of sugar or a power saw? Taking the kids to the park? Take your Dachshund along (see Figure 16-3). The more opportunities he gets to move, even for short periods at a time, the better.

Figure 16-3:
Your Dachshund would love a trip to the park.

Photo courtesy of Nancy Waud.

✔ If you have a fenced backyard, let your Dachshund spend time out there each day romping around. Go out with him and throw balls, play chase, and work on tricks. If you just let him out, he probably won't get enough exercise on his own (unless you have other dogs he can play with). If you don't have a fenced yard, look into installing a fence. Dachshunds adore being outside without a leash, but it just isn't safe without a fence. And remember, Dachshunds dig, so bury that fence a foot or so into the ground, if possible. If not, stay out there with your Dachshund or keep an eye on him.

✔ Training is hard, physical work for your Dachshund. Two or three daily training sessions, without fail, serve as an excellent form of exercise. Just one more reason not to skip that training session.

Choosing a Vet

This books talks a lot about the importance of a good vet, but how do you know you've got a good one? The most highly qualified vet in the world isn't a good vet if he or she doesn't seem to care for animals or gets angry or impatient with the clientele. If you feel rushed or are made to feel that your questions are silly or a waste of time, you have the right to look elsewhere. In fact, before you settle on a vet, it doesn't hurt to do a little shopping around.

The good-vet checklist

Take the following good-vet checklist with you, to make your choice easier. Make several copies and fill out one for each vet you visit:

✔ Was it easy to make an appointment?

✔ Was the person on the phone friendly and accommodating?

✔ Does the reception area look and smell clean? (A doggy smell is natural, but you shouldn't smell anything unpleasant.)

✔ Is the office staff friendly and polite when you visit?

✔ Does your Dachshund seem interested when you visit, or does he seem nervous? (This isn't always a good indicator. Some dogs are often nervous in new places, and your Dachshund may remember a previous vet's office where he received a vaccination.)

✔ Do you have a good feeling about the vet? Is she friendly, open, and easy to talk to?

✔ Does the vet seem to have a genuine interest and love for animals?

✔ Does the vet seem to bond with you and your dog?

✔ Is the vet ready and willing to answer all your questions?

✔ Does the vet make you feel like he has plenty of time for you?

✔ Is the vet willing to give you references?

✔ Is the vet open and forthcoming about her training?

✔ Does the vet have any particular experience with Dachshunds?

✔ Do you have a good feeling about the whole experience after you leave?

Make some notes so that you remember things about this individual vet. It's easy to forget when you've visited several.

Holistic health care

When searching for the perfect vet, chances are that you've encountered or at least heard about one or more holistic veterinarians in your area. The movement toward more holistic and natural health care is big right now — and nowhere more so than in the veterinary world.

Holistic vets may practice any or all of a number of different holistic healing techniques (most specialize in one or two), including homeopathy, herbalism, acupuncture, acupressure, pet massage of all types, kinesiology, chiropractic treatment, and flower essences, to name some of the more common methods.

Homeopathy works on the principle of *like treats like* — treating symptoms using very diluted substances that normally cause those symptoms, to put the system back into balance. *Herbalism* is the use of herbs as medicine to balance the system. *Acupuncture* is the application of needles to certain energy centers of the body to release blockages, and *acupressure* is the application of pressure to those energy centers. *Pet massage* helps loosen tight muscles and connective tissue. *Kinesiology* is the use of muscle testing to detect imbalances or strengths in the system. *Chiropractic treatment* aligns the spinal column to free blocked energy. *Flower essences* treat the emotional energies.

Should you use a holistic veterinarian for your Dachshund? Some Dachshund owners swear by holistic vets and would never take their pets to a regular vet again. Others wouldn't consider a holistic healer for their Dachshunds. The decision is up to you and should be based on your own personal inclinations and feelings about the matter. If you use a holistic health practitioner yourself and you think the methods make sense, your pet may benefit similarly. If you don't like the idea for yourself, you won't feel comfortable about taking your Dachshund to someone who works in a more holistic mode.

Some of the strongest proponents and strongest detractors of holistic health are among those whose Dachshunds have fallen prey to canine intervertebral disc disease. Testimonials abound about Dachshunds who regain the use of their legs through holistic techniques, after full paralysis. Others argue that only mainstream medicine should handle such a severe, acute medical event as a ruptured or herniated disc. Again, the choice is up to you. Go with your gut feeling and do what feels right.

The approach I recommend generally is a combination of the two approaches, often called complementary health care. Holistic healing is great for preventive medicine, to keep the system healthy and balanced. It can also be, in my experience, highly effective for chronic conditions, such as arthritis, for which mainstream medicine has no cure. I know people who swear by pet acupuncture or herbalism, for example, and sincerely believe it provided pain relief and a return of function for pets that the mainstream medical establishment said couldn't be helped.

I especially like the holistic methods people can practice on their own. Pet massage is a great way to bond with your pet, and Dachshunds love it. A massage every day before the daily grooming session may help your Dachshund relax, and you'll enjoy it, too. Gently massage your Dachshund's head; stroke her ears and face; gently massage her neck, ribs, back, and hips; stroke her tail; work your hands down each leg with gentle squeezes; and massage each toe and paw pad.

For acute conditions, serious injuries, and dangerous illnesses, however, I would choose the *allopathic,* or mainstream, vet every time. Mainstream medicine in this country is best in emergency situations and for curing life-threatening conditions through surgery and other procedures requiring extensive skill and training.

Chapter 17

Dachshund Discs

This books talks a lot about the fallible Dachshund back. Maybe you have a Dachshund who is already suffering from disc disease, or maybe you don't know who your Dachshund's parents are and you're a little nervous that he could fall prey to back trouble. You are right to worry a little, if worrying will encourage you to take some precautionary measures.

Any dog — or any human, for that matter — could theoretically experience disc disease, but because of the way Dachshunds are built and because of the nature of their backbones, Dachshunds are particularly susceptible to canine intervertebral disc disease, or CIDD. In fact, approximately one in four Dachshunds experiences a disc problem — most between the ages of 3 and 7, with age 4 being the most common age of onset.

Will your Dachshund develop CIDD? I sincerely hope not, but no one can tell you for sure. You can do some things that may help to prevent a ruptured disc. If your Dachshund does develop a problem, how you handle it can have a dramatic effect on whether your Dachshund will become paralyzed for life or return to normal. This chapter tells you what you can do.

Why Good Backs Go Bad

The title of this section is a bit of a misnomer because many Dachshunds don't have good backs to start with. Dachshunds are a *chondrodystrophic* breed (and so are Beagles, Pekingese, Miniature Poodles, Cocker Spaniels, Pomeranians, and Basset Hounds). That means Dachshunds have a skeletal structure that is disproportionate. They are unusually short and unusually long, so their backs take on an unusual strain. In addition, their spinal discs are thinner, more brittle, and more prone to rupture and degeneration than nonchondrodystrophic breeds. And the weakest part of the discs is typically the side nearest the spinal cord. One sudden move, one sharp turn around a corner, one leap off a bed, or even something less dramatic is sometimes all it takes to cause a disc to rupture and leak or, in severe cases, burst out of its covering, putting pressure on and injuring the delicate spinal cord.

Canine intervertebral disc disease, or *CIDD* (sometimes called intervertebral disc disease, or IVD), is a serious problem in Dachshunds and other chondro-dystrophic dogs whose thin, brittle spinal discs are more likely to rupture and compress the spinal cord, causing temporary or permanent pain and/or paralysis. Pain medication, crate rest, and, in severe cases, surgery are the recommended treatments for CIDD.

Understanding your chondrodystrophic canine

Your Dachshund's spinal column (and your own) is made up of small bones called *vertebrae* that surround and protect the spinal cord (see Figure 17-1). Spinal columns consist of four primary sections: the cervical spine, or neck area; the thoracic spine, or chest area; the lumbar spine, or lower back area; and the sacral spine, or pelvic area.

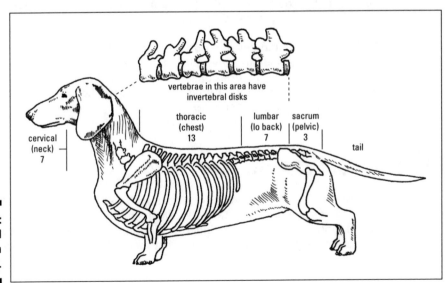

Figure 17-1: The spinal column of a Dachshund.

The spinal cord is the information highway of the body, sending messages from the body to the brain about what's going on in the environment and sending messages from the brain back to the body telling the body what to do in response to the environment.

The spinal cord is, in other words, the link between what you think and what you do. Without it, you can hear a car coming but can't jump out of the way. You can burn your hand but can't remove it from the heat source. You can see something you want but can't go get it.

Fortunately, spinal columns are very good protectors most of the time. In addition to the hard, bony vertebrae, fibrous, fluid-filled cushions in between each vertebrae protect the spinal cord. These cushions are called *discs*, and they help the spine move more easily. They also reduce shock to the spine and spinal cord by absorbing the various jolts, jerks, twists, and turns all living beings must occasionally experience.

In some instances, however, a jolt gets through to the spinal cord and injures it, or it causes a vertebrae or disc to break or rupture, injuring the spinal cord. The ruptured disc is what happens in CIDD, and as soon as it happens, every second counts.

Spinal cords can't take much pressure. A ruptured disc that presses on the cord can quickly cause lasting damage. If the spinal cord can't receive blood, oxygen, and glucose, it will eventually die. If the spinal cord dies, information can't move from the brain to the body or back again. Compare it to a road-block: Things are happening on either side, but the communication is gone. The area below the injury can't communicate with the brain, and the brain can't communicate back.

In Dachshunds, the lower spine, or lumbar region, is the most susceptible to back injury. In fact, five single discs are responsible for 99 percent of ruptures in Dachshunds.

If a disc does *herniate*, or bulge out from between the vertebrae, the severity is classified into Type I and Type II herniations. In a Type I herniation, the disc tears and the inner matter, called the *nucleus*, leaks out. This type of her-niation is most common in chondrodystrophic breeds such as Dachshunds, and it is a medical emergency. The leaking nuclear material can put damaging pressure on the spinal cord, and if the damage is too severe, your Dachshund may well be permanently paralyzed. Emergency surgery, preferably within the first 12 hours after the injury (and up to 24 hours after), is often success-ful in restoring function, although it isn't a guarantee.

Type II herniation is less severe. The disc develops small tears that allow small amounts of nuclear material to escape, causing the disc to bulge and press on the spinal cord. This type of disc event can develop gradually and may be less obvious until it becomes severe. It is common in degenerating discs and can lead to gradual paralysis. It can also be treated surgically, but some people prefer to treat this type of problem by keeping their pets confined so the disc can heal itself. Type II ruptures typically manifest as back pain that responds well to medical therapy and cage rest, but they eventually recur.

Type II herniations can be dangerous for several reasons. Too much bulging can cut off nutrients to the spinal column, causing it to die a slow but just as permanent death. Also, the body could interpret leaking nuclear material as a foreign invader. In some dogs, the immune system will attack, causing further damage to the spinal cord. Once spinal nerve tissue liquefies, it is irreparable.

Preventing disc injury

Can you prevent CIDD in your Dachshund? Maybe. Some dogs will probably get it no matter what. Others may have a tendency to get it but won't. Other dogs may have no tendency at all, so the first and best method of prevention is to find a Dachshund that isn't prone to CIDD.

The problem is, no one can tell for sure which Dachshunds are prone to developing CIDD and which ones will stay clear. Scientists do know that CIDD is genetic, however, so a great way to increase your chances of escaping CIDD is to purchase a Dachshund with no CIDD in her family history. Ask the breeder about the occurrence of CIDD in his or her lines. Of course, a breeder could tell you his lines are free of disc problems even when they aren't, but if you have done your homework and picked a breeder you like and trust with a good reputation, you're probably getting the true story.

Any good breeder knows not to breed a Dachshund with CIDD, but because the disease usually shows up at around 4 years of age, a Dachshund could have been bred several times before the disease manifests. The puppies of that dog, of course, shouldn't be bred.

Comparing Dachsie and human anatomy

In humans, the spinal cord ends at midback, before the end of the spinal column. Lower back trauma hurts but usually doesn't damage the spinal cord and so doesn't cause paralysis. Dogs aren't so well built, however, when it comes to the spinal column. Their spinal cords extend all the way into the lower back, so lower back injuries (the most common kind in Dachshunds) are much more likely to result in paralysis. Because dogs, and especially Dachshunds, are closer to the ground, with horizontal spines, a vertical jump down from a high place puts a much greater shock on the spine than it does in a human who lands on his or her feet and has long legs and a vertical spine.

Some breeders have virtually eliminated CIDD from their lines, and these are the ones to look for. Your worst bets? A breeder who won't show you the parents (maybe one or both are paralyzed), a pet store (because many of these dogs are bred with no thought to eliminating conditions like CIDD, and you don't get to see the parents), or a shelter or humane society (because you can't possibly know the Dachshund's background). That's not to say you should never adopt a needy Dachshund from a shelter or humane society. You should, however, be aware that the dog's risk of developing CIDD may be higher than average.

The next thing you can do is choose a Dachshund who isn't so dramatically short and long. The longer the back, the more strained it will be by any movement. European breeders are being encouraged by an international humane organization called the Council of Europe to breed for taller dogs with shorter backs. The Germans recently revised their standard accordingly, and many breeders in the United States are following suit — breeding for less extreme dimensions in order to ensure healthier, stronger backs.

The third thing you can do is keep your Dachshund at a healthy weight. Obesity puts a huge strain on your Dachshund's back.

The fourth thing you can do is keep your Dachshund from engaging in any sharp twisting movements, jumping from high places, or running around sharp turns. Avoid tricks that teach your Dachshund to beg on his hind legs or do anything else that puts his spine in a vertical position. Walks are great and exercise is great, but try to keep your Dachshund's back relatively straight when your Dachshund is in motion (easier said than done).

Treating Disc Disease

Sometimes, despite all the preventive measures in the world, a Dachshund suffers a disc herniation. If yours does, you must know what to do, and you must do it fast. Of course, you can't do anything if you don't know that your Dachshund is having a problem.

The warning signs

Dogs have differing pain thresholds and also have an instinct not to reveal when they are in pain. After all, in the wild, the obviously injured animal is the one who gets picked off by the predators.

Don't wait for treatment

Darryl E. McDonald, DVM, a veterinary neurosurgeon at the Dallas Veterinary Surgical Center in Dallas, Texas, has performed hundreds of disc surgeries on Dachshunds and likes to describe the urgency of surgery with the following analogy: "When a disc ruptures and damages the spinal cord, it is analogous to a houseplant that has not been watered for three weeks. It loses half its leaves. So what do you do? You water it! If you don't, it will die. Similarly, surgery is needed to remove the spinal cord pressure. The longer you wait, the more 'leaves' are lost and the less likely your Dachshund will recover."

But if you pay attention, you can tell whether your Dachshund is in pain. Look for the following signs:

- Shivering, especially when combined with unusual inactivity
- Refusal to get up and play, even for food
- A yelp when you pet your Dachshund or try to pick him up
- A pulled-in head or arched back or any other strange position
- A refusal to bend down to the food or water dish to eat or drink
- Limping of any kind
- A "drunken" rear end, which moves but looks as if it isn't completely under control
- Dragging of the back legs

If your Dachshund shows any of these signs, call your vet. If your Dachshund drags his back legs or shows any other sign of paralysis or severe pain, go immediately to the vet or nearest pet emergency facility. Don't wait.

Keep your Dachshund on the horizontal whenever possible, even when picking him up. Place one hand under his chest and the other under his abdomen or back legs. Lift him up carefully, keeping him level, and hold him in your arms with his spine parallel to the floor. Never hold your Dachshund vertically or let his back end swing from your arms. Teach children in the household how to lift and hold your Dachshund, too.

Emergency measures

I've talked to people whose Dachshunds showed signs of trouble on a Friday, but they decided to wait until Monday to act because the vet's office was closed. Several of them now have paralyzed pets. Waiting the weekend can mean the difference between permanent damage and fully restored function.

Immediate surgery, on the other hand, has a better success rate than back surgeries on humans. For Dachshunds still feeling pain (a good sign that the spinal cord is still functioning), the success rate for restoring function is 95 percent. The success rate is 50 percent for Dachshunds experiencing total paralysis, as long as the dog was feeling pain within the last 24 hours. But waiting longer than 24 hours after a disc injury causes the success rate to plummet to a meager 5 percent. If that's not reason enough to rush your injured Dachsie to the vet, nothing is.

Crate-and-wait

"Waaait a minute," you may be thinking. "Just how much is this surgery going to cost me?" That depends on where you live and where you take your Dachshund, but the all-inclusive charges could range from $800 to $2,000 (most are probably close to $1,500). For many Dachshund owners, surgery is an unaffordable option. Is surgery your only choice when your Dachshund's discs go bad?

No, although for severe episodes, it has the highest success rate. The other option is the one used more frequently for Type II herniations. In Dachshund circles, it's known as *crate-and-wait,* or crate rest.

Crate rest means confining your Dachshund to her den for an extended period of time — usually between two and four weeks. Three or four times per day, you take your Dachshund out to relieve herself and then immediately return her to her den. At first, doing so is easy. Your Dachshund is in pain, and she probably doesn't want to move.

But by the second or third day, especially if your vet has prescribed steroids or pain medication, your Dachshund is feeling a whole lot better and is getting mighty tired of that den. She wants to get out. She'll probably whine, cry, scratch, dig at the sides, and do anything she can think of to convince you to let her out.

Keeping her confined isn't going to be easy, but it is *essential.* I repeat: *essential.* A medicated Dachshund is still extremely vulnerable to spinal cord injury. That disc is still soft, still ruptured, and perhaps still oozing nuclear material. Movement could cause permanent damage, and if she isn't feeling the pain due to medication, she'll be much more likely to move in ways she shouldn't. If you don't allow her spinal discs adequate healing time, she could easily wind up losing the use of her back legs. If you keep her in there, no matter how much she begs (remember, *you* are in charge), she has a far better chance of a full and glorious recovery. *Don't let your lack of willpower stand in the way of your Dachshund's chance to walk again.*

Physical therapy is great for Dachshunds recovering from surgery and for post-crate-rest Dachshunds working to restore lost function. Commonly prescribed activities include swimming in the bathtub (never leave your Dachshund unsupervised because if her legs don't work correctly when she needs them, she could drown); towel walking, in which you hold up your dog's rear end with a towel sling draped under your Dachshund's abdomen; bicycling your Dachshund's limbs to exercise her full range of motion; and massaging the affected areas.

The surgery route

Some Dachshund people are anti-surgery, but most vets agree that it's the quickest and safest route to recovery in the case of a Type I disc herniation. It's pricey, sure. But many, many Dachshund owners have paid that price and would do it all again if they had to. (And a few *have* done it all again when their Dachshunds had more than one disc herniation.)

The downsides to surgery, other than the high price tag, are the risk to your Dachshund of enduring a general anesthetic (a small but real risk) and the risk that the surgery won't be successful (a very small risk when the surgery is performed by an experienced, board-certified veterinary surgeon within 24 hours after the injury). If surgery is unsuccessful, your Dachshund may be paralyzed anyway or may continue to suffer severe pain.

If your Dachshund needs back surgery, you can't just take her to your vet's office. The surgery is complicated and requires the experienced hand of a veterinary neurosurgeon. If you don't have a veterinary hospital in your area that specializes in this type of surgery, or at least one that has a surgeon with a lot of relevant experience, check out your nearest school of veterinary medicine. Chances are, the school will have someone who is experienced at back surgery in dogs. The better the surgeon, the better your Dachshund's chances at recovery.

But surgery is often, *very* often, successful — once again, if done within 12 to 24 hours. Surgery has a much quicker recovery time than crate rest. Because the pressure is immediately relieved on the spinal cord, the real danger is over. Your vet may still provide a shorter period of post-surgery crate rest, which you should observe. After that, however, your Dachshund will probably be, for the most part, back to normal.

Don't be too quick to take your Dachshund running again, though. Don't ignore follow-up visits or the prescribed physical therapy. Your vet or veterinary surgeon can show you what to do with your Dachshund to help him regain his strength and the use of his legs. These exercises are extremely important to help your Dachshund recover.

Preventive surgery: The debate

In some Dachshunds, back injury looks imminent. X-rays can reveal calcifications to the spine that may indicate impending disc trouble. For others, with one or more parents who suffered, disc disease is a real possibility. And what about the Dachshund who has already suffered one episode? Do you want her to endure surgery a second time?

More and more often, veterinary neurosurgeons are performing a preventive surgery called *fenestration*. This procedure essentially drains the spinal discs of fluid to prevent any possible future herniation or rupture. The surgery isn't without risks. A surgery gone wrong could injure a healthy spinal cord (although a new, experimental technique called laser disc fenestration shows great promise as a safer alternative). Your dog could suffer from a reaction to the anaesthetic, or the area could become infected. Your Dachshund could suffer from arthritis later in life because the discs aren't working to ease the friction between vertebrae.

But many vets agree that preventive fenestration can not only prevent a first or second disc episode from occurring, but it can also dramatically relieve the pain and discomfort of degenerating discs as your Dachshund ages.

Preventive fenestration is often standard procedure during surgery to repair a disc herniation and is most often performed on the discs surrounding the herniated disc. If a Dachshund is known to be at risk, it may even be performed before a rupture ever occurs.

In general, a normal, healthy Dachshund would have no cause to undergo preventive fenestration. It is definitely something to consider, however, if your Dachshund is already undergoing surgery to prevent a second incident.

Five specific discs account for about 99 percent of disc ruptures, so these five are commonly fenestrated during surgery for a ruptured disc. Fenestration is much more rare in dogs that haven't yet experienced a disc rupture, but if X-rays reveal severe calcifications, or if a mylegram or an MRI confirms severe disc compression, fenestration may be warranted.

A *mylegram* is a procedure in which the spinal cord is treated with dye before an X-ray so the pinched portion can be observed. An *MRI* is a computer-generated image that shows all structures, including bone and soft tissues.

Technological advances: The future is here

As disc fenestration gains popularity as an option to help prevent future disc ruptures, the techniques are continually being refined and improved. Laser fenestration is among the latest developments in the field and shows great promise. But it is still being used experimentally and is most useful for prevention in dogs showing signs of imminent disc disease. It can't be performed on dogs already showing symptoms of a rupture because it could cause the disc to rupture or rupture further.

Holistic health practitioners have several alternative methods for dealing with disc disease, including acupuncture and high doses of Vitamin C. If your Dachshund is having back problems but isn't in need of emergency care, you may want to consider exploring this option. Be sure you work with a reputable and experienced holistic veterinarian, however. Don't try to treat your Dachshund yourself without professional guidance.

Living with Paralysis: What Is Quality of Life?

For some Dachshunds, no matter what preventive measures have been taken, paralysis becomes an unfortunate reality. You love your pet dearly. Does paralysis necessitate euthanasia?

This is a question many Dachshund owners struggle with, and strong opinions exist on both sides of the question. A paraplegic Dachshund can still get around, with some help, but also requires more care than a fully functional Dachshund. Are you up for it?

You may think you can't put your Dachshund through it: the surgery, the pain, the crate rest, the suffering, etc. This is (arguably) the least viable reason for having your Dachshund put down. Dogs don't have all the complicated emotional associations we do when it comes to pain and paralysis. If they can recover and live free of pain, even if paralyzed, they may be perfectly happy, as long as they can be with you.

Many, many people have chosen to live with their paralyzed Dachsies and wouldn't have it any other way. These dogs are still capable of great love, affection, and good health apart from their paralysis. Their owners say they have learned much about life and love from their paralyzed pets. Some even recover full or partial use of their legs long after their owners had abandoned all hope that they would ever walk again. Many other people have chosen euthanasia for their pets, for one reason or another.

The choice, obviously, is up to you and your family. A paralyzed Dachshund and his people must endure certain challenges, even after the pain is gone.

For example, he won't have bladder or bowel control and can be more susceptible to bladder infections, urine scalding (getting burned by the acid urine), and pressure sores from sitting in one place for a long time. These challenges may or may not be things you're willing to deal with.

But I encourage you not to assume automatically that your Dachshund doesn't have quality of life just because she is paralyzed. To her, quality of life means a good meal, a pat on the head, and you by her side. She doesn't know to be embarrassed by lack of bladder control (although she will know something is very wrong if *you* are constantly upset or even irritated by her lack of bladder control or other associated conditions). She doesn't care if she can't walk across the room to get her favorite ball. She'll be perfectly happy to have you do the fetching!

Can you bear to look at that poor, pitiful dog with her legs dragging behind her? Carts are available for paralyzed dogs, and these wheeled contraptions allow paraplegic Dachshunds to get around quite nicely. Your Dachshund doesn't know the meaning of the word *pitiful*. She'll adapt, learning to pull herself with her front feet. Some tasks are more difficult, but what Dachshund isn't up for a challenge?

Of course, if your Dachshund continues to be in pain, euthanasia may be the only humane option. But if the pain resolves, your Dachshund, with your help, can find a way to have a perfectly satisfactory — even rewarding — life. One Dachshund owner I know said it best: If that Dachshund spirit returns, your dog is telling you he has quality of life. Period. If you are struggling with the euthanasia decision, let your Dachshund tell you what to do and don't listen to anyone else. Sometimes humans have awfully funny ideas about things.

If you do decide to stick it out, keep in mind that life with a paralyzed Dachsie is challenging but rewarding, sometimes heartbreaking, sometimes filled with joy, but always an adventure. May you and your special Dachshund have many more happy years together.

Chapter 18

Your Aging Dachshund

. . . .

In This Chapter

▶ Taking care of an older Dachsie

▶ Watching for illness

▶ Coping with loss

. . . .

*W*hether your Dachsie has been your best friend for years or you have adopted an older Dachshund, life with a senior Dachsie isn't exactly like life with a puppy. On the other hand, it isn't as different as you might imagine if you haven't yet traversed with your Dachshund into the canine golden years.

Aging Dachshunds have many of the same challenges as other aging breeds — and a few unique challenges as well. You want your friend to enjoy maximum longevity, of course. Knowing what's to come and taking a few simple precautionary measures now and later will help your Dachshund enjoy a long, healthy, happy life. This chapter is here to help.

Golden Dachsies

Just what is old for a Dachshund? As you may know, dog longevity is largely based on size. Small dogs often live 14 to 16 years or longer, but the giant breeds often live only half that long. Because Dachshunds are small, their longevity tends toward the high side (lucky for us), and as long as they are healthy, many enjoy life to the fullest up until the very end.

But your Dachshund will begin to show signs of aging well before his final day on Earth, and Dachshund owners are wise to pay special attention to their pets' health, behavior, and appetite starting somewhere around the seventh or eighth year. This is the age when your Dachshund has fully matured and is heading into the second half of his life. You may not have to do anything different, but do pay attention. Your Dachshund's chances of getting age-related diseases are now increasing.

What happens at the vet

During a typical geriatric veterinary visit, your vet tests your Dachshund's kidney and liver function, blood sugar level, hematacrit, and protein level. Your Dachshund may receive an electrocardiogram, and the vet generally checks for changes in weight, looks for lumps, bumps, and skin problems, and asks you about your Dachshund's appetite and behavior. Diseases like diabetes and liver and kidney disease are, in the early stages, often detectable only through a blood test. When your Dachshund starts showing symptoms, these diseases may be advanced and far less treatable.

The five most common diseases of aging in dogs are kidney disease, liver disease, diabetes, cancer, and heart disease — all diseases common to humans.

Evolving Care Needs

The good news is, once she has passed her seventh year of life, your Dachshund's chance of developing canine intervertebral disc disease decreases. The bad news is, her chances of developing kidney disease, liver disease, diabetes, cancer, heart disease, arthritis, cataracts, progressive retinal atrophy, and dementia increase. Fortunately, many of these conditions are treatable if caught in time.

Cataracts refer to the lens of the eye gradually becoming opaque. Cataracts cause a gradual loss of vision and are sometimes associated with diabetes. *Progressive retinal atrophy (PRA)* is a genetic disease in which the retina gradually degenerates, eventually resulting in blindness.

The trick is to practice a few basic precautionary measures:

- Take your Dachshund to the vet for a checkup every six months — or at least every year — once she turns 8 years old. Technically, you should take your pet to the vet once a year anyway, but many people don't bother if their pets seem healthy. During the golden years, however, this visit is particularly critical for dogs, to detect the diseases of aging that may not be readily apparent except through blood, urine, and heart tests. Be sure to report to your vet any changes in appetite, water consumption, bathroom habits, and behavior, all of which could signal health problems.

- Be prepared for behavioral changes and keep your Dachshund's routine as regular as possible. Older dogs tend to become less flexible and more resentful about changes in routine because these changes can be confusing. Feed, walk, and take your Dachshund out at the same time each day. If your Dachshund's vision or hearing declines, be sure to keep furniture and your Dachshund's food and water bowls in the same place so he doesn't get disoriented.

If you have a longhair or wirehair, keep grooming efforts to a minimum. Too much poking and pulling can irritate an older dog. Don't forego grooming altogether, however. Your older pet needs to stay clean and well groomed and will be comforted by your familiar touch. Frequent touching will also keep your pet prepared for more frequent veterinary visits.

✔ If your Dachshund shows no signs of slowing down, don't curb her exercise. If, on the other hand, she tires more easily or seems to be in pain with exercise, check with your vet and cut back on the length of your daily walks. But don't cut them out altogether unless your vet advises you to do so. Older dogs need exercise to stay healthy and vital.

✔ If you aren't already doing so, begin a Dachshund diary where you record all daily information about your Dachshund's habits and behavior: what he ate, how much he drank, how much he exercised, what medications you gave him, and how he behaved. What was his mood? Later, when your vet asks you when certain changes first occurred, you'll be able to answer with authority.

Although not necessarily an age-related disease, bloat is a disease that can occur in Dachshunds. Also called *acute gastric dilation-torsion,* bloat is a condition most common in large, deep-chested dogs. Dachshunds aren't large, but they are deep chested and are therefore at risk. Bloat is a serious, often fatal condition in which the stomach fills with gas or fluid, swells, and then twists. Immediate emergency medical care is essential to save the dog's life.

Looking at the senior diet

Browse the dog food aisles of your local pet store or supermarket, and you'll probably notice dog foods targeted for senior dogs. Does your aging Dachshund need a change in diet?

As long as her health is fine, your Dachshund can continue on her regular diet for her entire life. In fact, switching your Dachshund's diet away from a food she thrives on can actually be detrimental. Some senior formulas are low in protein, which older dogs need. Only dogs with kidney problems need to limit their protein intake. Protein won't cause kidney problems, so it shouldn't be limited in your Dachshund's diet just because she has reached her seventh or eighth year. If your vet tells you to limit your Dachshund's protein intake due to a specific health problem and recommends a senior diet, fine. Otherwise, forget it.

Senior diets are also lower in calories and fat, which makes sense because older dogs are often less active than younger dogs and because Dachshunds in particular are prone to obesity. An obese, aging dog has a greater chance of developing certain problems. But you don't need to switch to a senior diet to decrease your Dachshund's caloric intake if she has decreased her level of exercise. Simply feed her a little less or cut down on the treats.

Treats are commonly a real problem for older dogs. A treat may be only 30 calories, but if she gets ten a day, that's 300 extra calories a day.

The bottom line when it comes to diet is that your senior Dachsie is no different from the 4-year-old Dachsie down the street. Keep all things about your aging Dachshund's life the same unless a vet instructs you to do otherwise.

Remembering that old shouldn't equal lazy

An aging Dachshund may not be able to get around quite as quickly or spryly as he once did. But that doesn't mean he won't, or shouldn't, try. Old dogs need to keep moving. If they don't, they experience diminished muscle tone. Moderate exercise helps keep arthritis in check and also helps your Dachsie keep his weight down (see Figure 18-1).

Figure 18-1:
Adult Dachsies need exercise to avoid problems as they get older.

Photo courtesy of Gail Painter.

Note that your Dachshund may not show a single sign of slowing down. Age is not a disease. If your 10-year-old Dachsie races from room to room when you say "Walk?" or still scuttles eagerly through the park sniffing for squirrels, let him go for it! Dogs have a pretty good sense, in general, of how much movement they need and how much they can handle. Unless they have become lazy (because you haven't kept them on a regular exercise schedule), you can usually trust their instincts. When it comes to exercise, age alone should have no bearing on how much your Dachshund can do.

Arthritis is common in older dogs, and if your Dachshund has experienced fenestration of his spinal column during disc surgery (see Chapter 17), he may, upon aging, suffer some arthritis in his spine. See your vet if your Dachshund appears to be in pain, and although exercise shouldn't be so vigorous that it causes your Dachshund discomfort, exercise is essential to keep arthritis symptoms at bay. In advanced stages, your Dachshund may need to cease strenuous activity. However, always follow your vet's guidance.

Making allowances for ill health

If movement, or too much movement, is painful for your Dachsie, don't force the issue. Let him try to do what he wants to do (except for jumping off of high places and racing up and down the stairs, of course). If he balks, however, respect his instinct to listen to his body.

If your usually enthusiastic pet suddenly displays a lack of interest in exercise, it may be a sign of a developing illness or condition. Check it out. If you discover that your Dachshund is suffering from a health problem, temporary or permanent, keep up his exercise routine if the vet says it's okay. But don't push it. Let your pet take the lead. If he isn't up to a walk, the two of you can stay in and spend some time together on the couch.

Don't be alarmed if your Dachshund starts to sprout gray hair around his seventh or eighth year. It's perfectly normal — it happens to the best of us — and is no indication of ill health.

When It Isn't Just Old Age

It's easy to assume that slowing down, becoming confused, and even occasionally yelping in pain are simply due to old age. Aging, however, is not a disease and doesn't have any symptoms. If your Dachshund displays any of the following signs or symptoms, contact your vet.

Is your Dachshund depressed?

Some people say animals get depressed just like humans. Others say that what looks like depression in an animal is a symptom of some physical problem. My guess is that the answer falls somewhere in the middle.

Just as in humans, depression in dogs can often result from feeling rotten. If your Dachshund is sick, injured, or in pain for any reason, it's only natural that she's acting depressed.

But anyone who knows a dog well can vouch that dogs do have emotional lives as well. If a cherished companion (human, canine, feline, etc.) suddenly disappears from your Dachshund's life, or if her routine changes drastically (a move into a new house, a new baby, whatever), your Dachshund will certainly be confused and perplexed — perhaps even sad. I won't pretend to have the knowledge necessary to define the nature of sadness for a Dachshund, but it does *look* like sadness when a Dachshund mopes around, loses interest in his normal activities, and even cries for no reason.

Veterinarians have medication for depression-like symptoms in animals, although a good vet will look for an underlying cause first. If you can't cheer up your Dachshund, do see your vet and be sure that your dog undergoes a thorough medical checkup to determine whether the depression is a symptom of a serious medical problem.

Many holistic remedies exist as well. Herbal, homeopathic, and flower essence remedies are among the most popular and, according to testimonial evidence, among the most successful for depression that isn't apparently caused by a physical problem. (Aromatherapy essential oils for depression include basil, chamomile, orange, and sandalwood. The flower essence borage is thought to be helpful, as are the herbs chamomile, ginkgo, and St. John's wort.)

Whether your Dachshund is depressed as you understand the word may not really matter. What matters is helping your friend find a way to reclaim that Dachshund spirit, whether that means uncovering an underlying illness or simply increasing his daily amount of quality time with you.

It isn't just old age if your pet

- ✔ **Acts confused.** This could be a sign of dementia — something dogs can develop just like people. Canine dementia is treatable.

- ✔ **Yelps in pain.** This could be a sign of arthritis, disc disease, an injury, or any number of other maladies.

- ✔ **Loses his appetite or drastically increases his appetite for more than a day or two.** Appetite changes could signal hypothyroidism, liver disease, kidney disease, depression (itself a symptom of possible illness), or something else.

  Hypothyroidism is a disease in which the thyroid gland is underactive, causing the body to lower its *metabolic rate,* the rate at which it burns energy. Dogs may gain weight, have low energy levels, and become easily chilled.

✔ **Suddenly increases her intake of water.** Diabetes or kidney disease could be the culprit, as could any number of other problems. Trouble urinating or excessive urination is a related warning sign.

✔ **Quickly gains or loses weight.** Weight gain or loss, especially if it can't be traced directly to food intake, is a warning sign. Hypo- or hyperthyroidism could be culprits, but weight changes could signal many other problems, too. (Hyperthyroidism is relatively rare in dogs and much more common in cats, and is due to an overactive thyroid.)

✔ **Is excessively irritable.** If your once-placid Dachshund is suddenly growling, nipping, biting, snarling, or bearing her teeth, she could be suffering from pain, confusion, dementia, or a combination of these things. This and other personality changes are certainly things to report to your vet.

When You Lose Your Friend

No one with a beloved pet likes to think about it, but unfortunately, dogs live much shorter lives than humans. Most of the time, you'll outlive your Dachshund, and that means having to lose your friend.

Losing a pet is a hard passage, especially for those of us in a society where pets have become increasingly meaningful in our lives. We go to such lengths to make our pets happy and healthy. When we lose them, it's heartbreaking.

Amos and Archie — the Dachshunds that belonged to painter and pop culture icon Andy Warhol — both outlived him. When Warhol died, a friend took the Dachshunds and cared for them until they died at the ripe old ages of 19 and 20.

Making the euthanasia decision

Perhaps the most difficult part of losing a pet is making the decision to euthanize. If your Dachshund is in severe pain and can't be treated, or is otherwise suffering, your vet may recommend euthanasia. The decision is a tough one, and unfortunately, it's all yours. Your vet can make a recommendation, but only you can decide. That puts an awful lot of power in your hands, and sometimes the only way to make the decision is to listen to your Dachshund — and to your heart.

If you do decide euthanasia is the best, or only, option, don't feel guilty. Sure, you'll feel a little guilty. Who wouldn't? This is a big decision. Your Dachshund trusts you to do what is best for her, and sometimes that's not easy. Your Dachshund can't tell you in words when she is ready to go. To some extent, you have to guess, with the help of your vet. Then all you can do is act in what you, in good faith, believe to be your Dachshund's best interest. Sometimes you have to love them more to let them go.

If you do decide on euthanasia, remember that typically it involves a gross overdose of a barbiturate, which is a drug commonly used as an anesthetic. The dog is simply over-anesthetized, and the process is completely pain-free.

Some people struggle with the euthanasia decision more than others. If you really aren't sure, wait a little longer until you are sure. If your Dachshund's suffering becomes truly evident and unbearable, and you're only keeping him alive for selfish reasons, that is the time for action.

If your Dachshund requires an extensive, costly medical treatment that you simply can't afford, and you think your only option is euthanasia, consider contacting a local or national Dachshund rescue group (see Chapter 5 for contact information). Another person or even the rescue organization itself may be willing to adopt your Dachshund, pay for the surgery, and then place the Dachshund into a good home. Surely a better option than euthanasia. (You can't, however, expect a rescue organization to pay for medical treatment and then return your Dachshund.)

Grieving for your Dachsie

If you have ever known, loved, and lost a dog, you know how heartbreaking it can be. People don't like to admit that they're grieving over a pet, but why not? Dogs are true companions to humans, and our society has evolved in such a way that many of us consider our dogs to be members of our families. Of course we're grief-stricken when a member of our family passes away. It would be unnatural *not* to be saddened by such a loss.

Still, people feel silly. Who wants to admit to sobbing alone in a room because that warm body is no longer at your side? Yet people do it every day. Fortunately, more and more people are opening up about the grieving process as it applies to pets. You can even purchase sympathy cards aimed toward people who have lost pets. Such a gesture is usually appreciated far beyond the thank you that you may receive if you send one.

Send a free electronic pet-sympathy card via e-mail by going to the following Web site: http://members.tripod.com/~Sandtracker/postcards.html.

If you are the grieving one, you can do some things to help yourself get through the process. Knowing a little about the stages of the grieving process may help. You'll go through the same stages that anyone who's lost a loved one goes through:

- ✔ **Denial.** At first, you won't quite be able to believe or accept that your pet is gone. You may forget he is gone and call for him or look for him — even prepare his food. This is a protective mechanism. Your mind is giving you a chance to adjust to the notion before experiencing the full weight of grief. You may also experience this stage if your pet is very ill and you don't want to admit to yourself that he probably won't pull through.

- ✔ **Bargaining.** This stage is more common in the human grieving process, but it can still happen with pets. You may make deals with yourself or with a higher power: "If she lives, I promise never to let her escape from the backyard again." "If she pulls through the surgery, I'll never yell at her again."

- ✔ **Anger.** This stage may surprise you. You aren't angry at your pet. Yet you feel abandoned. Sometimes anger manifests as guilt: "If only I hadn't. . . ." Fill in the blank. Or you may blame someone else — a vet or another family member. Try not to let yourself get caught up in the guilt-and-blame cycle. It doesn't help, and it will just make you feel worse.

- ✔ **Grief.** Once you've let go of your anger, the real grief sets in, as an over-whelming sadness. This is the time when you need support and some-one to talk to. If you don't have an understanding and sympathetic friend or family member, call a pet support hotline. Knowing you aren't the only one who has ever felt this badly about the loss of a pet will help, and even just talking about your pet will make you feel better. This is a tough stage, but you can make it through.

- ✔ **Resolution.** Once your grief begins to fade (it may never go away entirely), you'll finally come to a resolution about the loss. Ending the grieving process doesn't mean you've forgotten your beloved friend. It simply means that you'll remember the good times more than the bad and that you'll find a sense of peace and joy in the memory of your Dachshund. You'll recognize that your Dachshund has left you more, in the way of memories and unconditional love, than he took with him. You were lucky to share your life with such a wonderful creature, and at last, when you reach this final stage, you feel lucky once again.

Having some kind of a memorial service can be of tremendous help. Formal or informal, a memorial service allows all who knew and loved your pet to come together and remember. Tears and laughter are common at such events, and the final feeling is often one of healing.

Many have derived comfort from the following anonymous poem, called "The Rainbow Bridge," revised here by me to be about Dachshunds.

Just this side of heaven is a place called Rainbow Bridge. Pets who were especially close to the people who loved them go to the Rainbow Bridge after they leave the earth, and here, they wait. The land around the Rainbow Bridge is all meadows and hills where animals run and play together. Food, water, sunshine, fresh grass, tall trees, and ponds for splashing are abundant. All the pets are warm, comfortable, and happy. Those who had been ill, grown old, or hurt are made whole again and restored to full health, just as we remember them when we dream of our lives together. All the animals are happy and content except for one thing. They miss someone special to them, someone who had to be left behind.

One day, a little Dachshund suddenly stops romping and looks up from his play, alert, eager. His bright eyes stare intently into the distance. His body wiggles eagerly. Suddenly, he breaks from the group and flies over the green grass, his short little legs carrying him faster than they've ever carried him before. He has seen you and that something he was missing has finally returned. He leaps into your arms and covers you in Dachshund kisses. You cuddle him, stroke that familiar head, those long lovely ears, that silly, beloved Dachshund body. You hug him, and know you will never be parted again. You look once more into those trusting eyes, so long gone from your life but never absent from your heart.

And then you cross the Rainbow Bridge together.

Using pet loss resources

Many, many excellent books and Web sites are available on the subject of pet loss and bereavement. Here are a few good ones:

- The Association for Pet Loss and Bereavement is a nonprofit association of concerned people who are experienced and knowledgeable in the tender subject of pet death. Members are professional counselors as well as pet-loving people from all other walks of life who are concerned with helping pet lovers cope with this intimate kind of loss. Anyone who is genuinely interested in this subject is invited to join them. Write, call, or check out the Web site for chat groups and extensive resources: P.O. Box 106, Brooklyn, NY 11230, 718-382-0690; www.aplb.org (Web site); aplb@aplb.org (e-mail).

- *The Loss of a Pet*, New Revised and Expanded Edition, by Wallace Sife, founder of the Association for Pet Loss and Bereavement (published by Howell Books, 1998).

- ✔ The Pet Loss Web site, at www.findinfo.com/petloss.htm, offers articles about pet loss, online memorials, hotlines, counselors, discussion groups, pet memorial products, stories, and poetry.

- ✔ "In Memory of Pets is an Internet pet loss cemetery at www.in-memory-of-pets.com/index.html.

- ✔ The Iowa State University Pet Loss Support Hotline was established at the Iowa State University College of Veterinary Medicine to provide a source of emotional support for those who have lost an animal friend or are anticipating the loss of their pet. It is a free service to those in need. Call the hotline toll-free at 1-888-ISU-PLSH between 6 p.m. and 9 p.m. Monday through Friday, central standard time. Or leave a message any time, and your call will be returned. Or check out the Web site at www.vetmed.iastate.edu/support/home.html.

Most of all, remember that it's okay to grieve for your lost pet. Millions of people understand and have been exactly where you are. You loved your Dachshund. Your Dachshund understood you. You are lonely without your pet. Your grief is a sign of your love, and even if you feel you made mistakes as a caretaker and Dachshund companion (we all do), remember that your love made your Dachshund's life better.

Part V
The Part of Tens

The 5th Wave   By Rich Tennant

Shoot, that ain't nothin', watch this—
Roll over, Rusty.
C'mon, roll over!
Roll over!

In this part . . .

Every *For Dummies* book ends with top-ten lists, and I'm not going to break with tradition. I give you ten great Dachsie books and Web sites, and I introduce you to ten Dachshund-related organizations.

Chapter 19

Ten Books and Ten Web Sites

● ●

In This Chapter
▶ Books on Dachshunds
▶ Web sites on Dachshunds

● ●

*L*ooking for more Dachsie info? This is the place! Read on for a list of my favorite Dachshund books and Wiener Web sites.

Ten Choices for Your Dachsie Bookshelf

Millions of dog books, so little time! These are a few worth reading:

The Complete Dachshund, by Dee and Bruce Hutchinson, Howell Book House, 1997.

The Dachshund: A Dog for Town and Country, by Ann Gordon, Howell Book House, 2000

The Dachshund: An Owner's Guide to a Happy Healthy Pet, by Ann Carey, Howell Book House, 1995.

The Encyclopedia of Natural Pet Care, by C.J. Puotinen, Keats Publishing, Inc., 1998.

Dr. Pitcairn's Complete Guide to Natural Health for Dogs and Cats, by Richard H. Pitcairn, DVM, Ph.D., and Susan Hubble Pitcairn, Rodale Press, Inc., 1995.

Earl Mindell's Nutrition & Health for Dogs, by Earl Mindell, R.Ph., Ph.D., and Elizabeth Renaghan, Prima Publishing, 1998.

Culture Clash, by Jean Donaldson, James & Kenneth Publishers, 1996.

Don't Shoot the Dog! The New Art of Teaching and Training, by Karen Pryor, Bantam Books, 1984.

Wiener Dog Art: A Far Side Collection, by Gary Larson, Andrews and McMeel, 1990 (hilarious Dachshund-inspired art "reproductions").

The American Kennel Club's The Complete Dog Book, latest edition.

Ten Wiener Web Sites

The American Kennel Club has quite a few sites of interest to Dachshund lovers. Start from www.akc.org/index.html and have a good look around. You can find the Dachshund breed standard, information on rescue groups, information on Dachshund activities, and lots of general dog information and news.

Wiener Dog pages, created by Bob Brennert, at www.dachshund.bc.ca/mainpage.html. This page has an ask-a-breeder section, where you can e-mail experienced Dachshund breeders with your question, a listing of Dachshund breeders in Canada, a list of celebrity Dachshund owners, and lots of other fun links.

For the Love of Dachsies has great information and links: www.dachsie.org.

Winston's Ultimate Dachshund Links: http://members.aol.com/kevinS1092/winston/links.htm.

Dachshund Web Ring is a giant loop of links from Dachshund homepage to Dachshund homepage. Lots of fun and lots of pictures! Start at www.geocities.com/Colosseum/Loge/9606/dachshundring.html.

Dachshund Rescue Web Ring leads you to lots of rescue sites. For information or to enter the Web ring, surf to www.geocities.com/Colosseum/Loge/9606/dachrescue.html.

The Association of Pet Dog Trainers: www.apdt.com.

Perfect Paws Dog and Cat Behavior and Training Center: www.perfectpaws.com.

Karen Pryor's Clicker Training Page: www.dontshootthedog.com.

Clicker Train: Good explanation of why clicker training works, and all about operant conditioning: www.clickertrain.com.

Chapter 20

Ten Dachshund Clubs and Organizations

- -

- -

*W*ant to network with other Dachshund owners? Maybe share training advice and exchange doggie-treat recipes? You're bound to find Dachsie friends within the organizations listed in this chapter.

Dachshund Clubs

Many local and regional as well as international clubs exist to support Dachshunds, dogs in general, or particular dog sports like obedience or agility. This chapter has just ten to get you started. Many of the Web pages for the following clubs are full of links to additional resources.

The American Kennel Club (AKC). The AKC has information about almost everything related to the care, breeding, and showing of purebred dogs. Write, call, fax, e-mail, or check out their comprehensive Web site. Registrations and related information can be mailed to The American Kennel Club, 5580 Centerview Drive, Raleigh, NC 27606. For questions on the registration of purebred Dachshunds, call 919-233-9767 or fax: 919-233-3627; e-mail address: info@akc.org; Web site at www.akc.org. You can also call their public relations office at their New York City location at 212-696-8254 for current Dachshund Club of America breeder referral contacts, or call the main number at 212-696-8200 for other questions.

The Dachshund Club of America. Check out their Web site page that lists breeder referral contacts by state at www.dachshund-dca.org/ referral%20folder/state_ref.html, or call the American Kennel Club (see above) for updated contact information on the Dachshund Club of America's breeder referral coordinator or rescue coordinator. Also check out www.dachshund-dca.org/clubs.html for a list of local branches of the national club.

The United Kennel Club. This is the second-oldest and second-largest kennel club in the United States. Dachshunds can be registered with the UKC. Check out their Web site at www.ukcdogs.com, or contact them at United Kennel Club, Inc., 100 East Kilgore Rd., Kalamazoo, MI 49002-5584; 616-343-9020, fax is 616-343-7037.

Dachshund Friendship Club. The Dachshund Friendship Club is a non-competitive club. Its purpose is to introduce dogs and their owners to each other and encourage a friendly interaction as well as responsible pet ownership. The Club sponsors two major events each year: The Dachshund Octoberfest in early October and the Dachshund Spring Fiesta in late April in NYC. The club puts out a fun and fact-filled quarterly newsletter devoted to the world of Dachsies. Articles on collecting Dachshund memorabilia, behavior and health advice, news stories, history, poems, book reviews, and much more. Dues are $15 per year payable to Adrian Milton, 245 East 11th Street, #2C, New York City, NY 10003.

National Miniature Dachshund Club, Inc. This club is entirely devoted to the improvement and advancement of miniature Dachshunds as a separate variety. They publish a digest that is free to members, highlighting breeders and shows, and discussing subjects related to improvement of the breed. Membership dues are $20 per year. Contact Ada McCord, NMDC, 266 W Rd. 600N, Winchester, IN 47394; 765-584-5623.

Canadian Dachshund Clubs. For updated contact information and a list of Dachshund clubs in Canada, check out the club page on Bob Brennert's Wiener Dogs Web site at www.geocities.com/Heartland/Acres/8282/clubs.html, including the Dachshund and Terrier Association and the Miniature Dachshund Club of Canada.

Looking for more clubs? Check out Dachshund Breed Clubs Online, which lists Dachshund breed clubs in the United States and all over the world. Find it at www.sunsong.swinternet.co.uk/brdclubs.htm.

Other Organizations Relevant to Your Dachshund

The Association of Pet Dog Trainers supports positive training methods and humane treatment of animals, as well as promoting better training through education. Contact them at Association of Pet Dog Trainers, P.O. Box 385, Davis, CA 95617; 1-800-PET-DOGS; e-mail at APDTBOD@aol.com; Web site at www.apdt.com.

The United States Dog Agility Association. This organization promotes agility and sponsors trials. Contact them at United States Dog Agility Association, P.O. Box 850955, Richardson, Texas 75085-0955; 972-231-9700, fax 214-503-0161, or check out their Web site at www.usdaa.com.

The North American Dog Agility Council. This organization sanctions agility trials and was established in 1993. For more information, write to the North American Dog Agility Council, Inc. HCR 2 Box 277, St Maries, ID 83861, or check out their Web site at www.nadac.com.

The Association for Pet Loss and Bereavement. This non-profit association of concerned people who are experienced and knowledgeable in the tender subject of pet death. Members are professional counselors as well as pet-loving people from all other walks of life concerned with helping pet lovers cope with this intimate kind of loss. Anyone who is genuinely interested in this subject is invited to join them. Write, call, or check out their Web site for chat groups and extensive resources: Association for Pet Loss and Bereavement, P.O. Box 106, Brooklyn, NY 11230; 718-382-0690; Web site at www.aplb.org; e-mail aplb@aplb.org.

Appendix A

Dachshund Dainties: Recipes for Healthy Treats

• •

Dachshunds love treats, and we love to hand them out when our Dachsies have been particularly well behaved. If you like to cook, try the following recipes, for a fun change of pace. Your Dachshund will be delighted.

By the way, members of Cybercom and the DoxClub e-mail lists contributed these recipes.

Bow Wow Bon Bons

¾ cup wheat germ
 ¾ cup nonfat dry milk
1 egg
6 ounces lamb baby food
¼ tsp. garlic powder

Mix all ingredients together and drop by teaspoonfuls onto a lightly greased cookie sheet. Bake at 350 degrees F for 15 minutes or until browned. Keep stored in your refrigerator, or freeze them in you need to keep them for longer than two weeks.

Liver Treats

1 lb. chicken or beef liver
1 cup flour
¾ cup corn meal
1 tsp. garlic powder

Mix all ingredients in blender or food processor with ¼ cup water. Spread the entire mess evenly on lightly greased cookie sheet. Bake at 350 degrees F for about 20 to 30 minutes or until done. Cut into desired sized pieces while still warm. Keep stored in a refrigerator or in the freezer for longer periods of time. This recipe makes dozens of small treats.

Frosty Paws

In blender or food processor, mix 1 ripe banana, 2 to 3 oz. of plain yogurt (non-fat is best), and 2 oz. water. Process until smooth and pour into small ice cube trays. Freeze and serve. Great for hot days!

Grape Treats

Freeze seedless green grapes and hand out a few for treats. Very popular, and great for hot days. (For mini Dachshunds, cut grapes in half or even quarters first and then freeze.)

Favorite Liver Treats

Make up a batch of Jiffy cornbread according to package directions, add a pound of raw pureed liver (you can do it in either a food processor or your blender), pour in a greased, floured cake pan, and bake. Cool and cut into Dachshund-bite-sized pieces.

Appendix B
Dachshund Diary

● ●

*K*eeping a Dachshund diary is a great way to keep track of your Dachshund's health, behavior, and even the funny things your Dachshund does. Any blank or lined book or notebook will do. Or make copies of the following templates.

The first section, Dachshund Memories, is a little like a baby book, a record of how your Dachshund came into your life and a profile of his personality, habits, favorites, challenges, and antics.

The second section, Dachshund Days, is made to copy and fill out each day. Make it a habit, after the daily grooming session or before you go to bed each night.

The third section, Dachshund Vitals, is for keeping track of your Dachshund's veterinary visits, medications, and other health-related maintenance.

Dachshund Memories

My Dachshund's Full Name: _____

What I call my Dachshund:

_____

And then there are all those nicknames:

_____

A picture of my dear Dachshund:

My Dachshund's color is: _____

My Dachshund's coat type is: _____

My Dachshund's size is: _____

As an adult, my Dachshund weighs:_____

My Dachshund is this tall: _____

I found my Dachshund at: _____

I knew my Dachshund was destined to be mine when:

_____

When I first brought my Dachshund home:

_____

My Dachshund's first night went like this:

_____

This is how my Dachshund handled housetraining:

_____

My Dachshund's very first favorite toy was. . .

_____

My Dachshund sure loves to chew. . .

_____

My Dachshund has a unique personality, best described as. . .

_____

My Dachshund makes me laugh! Here are some of my Dachshund's funniest moments:

_____

I'll never forget the time my Dachshund. . .

_____

Here's what my Dachshund thinks of my family/relatives/friends:

_____

My Dachshund's favorite treat is. . .

_____

When it comes to training, my Dachshund. . .

_____

When it comes to grooming, my Dachshund. . .

_____

When it comes to mealtime, my Dachshund. . .

_____

Sometimes I wish my Dachshund wouldn't. . .

_____

These are the things I love the most about my Dachshund:

_____

Dachshund Days

Date:_____

Breakfast:

Food served:_____ Amount:_____

How was my Dachshund's appetite? _____

Lunch:

Food served:_____ Amount:_____

How was my Dachshund's appetite? _____

Dinner:

Food served:_____ Amount:_____

How was my Dachshund's appetite?

_____

List all treats (including training treats) and any extra "people food" for the day:

_____

How much water did my Dachshund drink (estimate):

_____

Medications administered:

_____

Pest control products administered:

_____

Anything unusual in today's grooming session?

_____

Anything unusual in today's training sessions?

_____

Any unusual behavior today?

_____

Activities we did together today:

_____

Funny things my Dachshund did today:

_____

Dachshund Vitals

Vaccination record

Date and vaccination administered:

_____

_____

_____

_____

_____

_____

_____

_____

_____

Pest control record

Date and product administered:

_____

_____

_____

_____

_____

_____

_____

_____

Vet visits

Date:_____

Reason for Visit:_____

Diagnosis:_____

Prescription:_____

Date: _____

Reason for Visit _____

Diagnosis:_____

Prescription: _____

Date: _____

Reason for Visit: _____

Diagnosis:_____

Prescription: _____

Date: _____

Reason for Visit: _____

Diagnosis:_____

Prescription: _____

Date: _____

Reason for Visit: _____

Diagnosis:_____

Prescription: _____

Index

lure, dog not following, 175
lure-and-reward training, 146
  come command, 170–171
  down command, 169–170
  following lure, dog not, 175
  sit command, 166–168
  stand command, 168–169
lyme disease, 196

• **M** •

mange, 200
manipulation techniques, 10, 136
massage, 205–206
Master Earthdog (ME), 190
mature dogs, 219
  acute gastric dilation-torsion, 221
  aging, signs/symptoms not associated
    with, 224–225
  arthritis, 223
  behavioral changes, 220
  bloat, 221
  care of, 220
  cataracts, 220
  checkups, 220
  diary used to record changes in, 221
  diet, 221–222
  diseases common in, 220
  exercise, 221–223
  grooming, 221
  ill health, signs of, 223
  obesity, 222
  progressive retinal atrophy, 220
  treats, 222
McDonald, Darryl E., 212
memorial service, 227
Metal Dachshund (profile), 87
Mindell, Earl, 233
Miniature Dachshund, 19
  children and, 82
  jumping, 78
  personality of, 37–38
  quiz to determine compatibility with,
    34–36
mites, 200
mouthing, 151–154

MRI, 215
muzzle, 24
mylegram, 215

• **N** •

nail clippers, 93
names, 165–166
naps, 107, 108
National Animal Poison Control Center
    (NAPCC), 77
National Council for Pet Population Study
    and Policy, 145
National Miniature Dachshund
    Club, Inc., 236
nature versus nurture, 126–127
neck, 25
neck (breed standard), 27
new dog, first night with. *See* first night
    with new dog
nicknames, 165–166
North American Dog Agility Council, 237
Nylabones, 153

• **O** •

obedience classes, 145–146, 164
  advanced obedience classes, 180
  homework, 164
  positive training techniques, 164
  puppy kindergarten, 164
  training sessions, 164
obedience competitions, 185
  American Kennel Club, 186
  qualifications for, 186
  titles, 186
obesity, 10
  canine intervertebral disc disease
    and, 211
  mature dog, 222
  signs of, 202–203
obsessive barking, 155, 157
obstacle course, 188–189
open tunnel (obstacle), 188
open wire kennels, 91

FREE

RECITE
"for the"
"Perfect"
DACHSHUND

Kong Dog Toys are used and recommended by veterinarians and dog trainers worldwide. To see how Kong can be utilized to achieve good behavior in your Dachshund, send a self-addressed stamped envelope to Kong Company for a "Recipe for the Perfect Dog" brochure or simply log on to our website and click on **"How to Use Kong"**.

SAVE $1

KONG company 16191-D Table Mountain Parkway, Golden, CO 80403-1641 • Phone: (303) 216-2626 • Fax: (303) 216-2627
E-mail: kong@kongcompany.com • Website: www.kongcompany.com   ©**KONG**CO, 2000

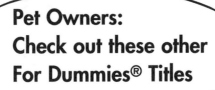

Pet Owners: Check out these other For Dummies® Titles

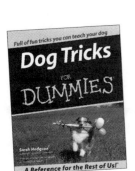

Aquariums For Dummies®	ISBN 0-7645-5156-6	$19.99
Birds For Dummies®	ISBN 0-7645-5139-6	$19.99
Boxers For Dummies®	ISBN 0-7645-5285-6	$15.99
Cats For Dummies®, 2nd Edition	ISBN 0-7645-5275-9	$19.99
Chihuahuas For Dummies®	ISBN 0-7645-5284-8	$15.99
Dog Training For Dummies®	ISBN 0-7645-5286-4	$19.99
Dog Tricks For Dummies®	ISBN 0-7645-5287-2	$15.99
Dogs For Dummies®, 2nd Edition	ISBN 0-7645-5274-0	$19.99
Ferrets For Dummies®	ISBN 0-7645-5259-7	$19.99
German Shepherds For Dummies®	ISBN 0-7645-5280-5	$15.99
Golden Retrievers For Dummies®	ISBN 0-7645-5267-8	$15.99
Horses For Dummies®	ISBN 0-7645-5138-8	$19.99
Iguanas For Dummies®	ISBN 0-7645-5260-0	$19.99
Jack Russell Terriers For Dummies®	ISBN 0-7645-5268-6	$15.99
Labrador Retrievers For Dummies®	ISBN 0-7645-5281-3	$15.99
Puppies For Dummies®	ISBN 0-7645-5255-4	$19.99
Retired Racing Greyhounds For Dummies®	ISBN 0-7645-5276-7	$15.99
Rottweilers For Dummies®	ISBN 0-7645-5271-6	$15.99
Siberian Huskies For Dummies®	ISBN 0-7645-5279-1	$15.99

Look for these titles in early 2001:

Australian Shepherds For Dummies®	ISBN 0-7645-5301-X	$15.99
Pit Bulls For Dummies®	ISBN 0-7645-5291-0	$15.99
Poodles For Dummies®	ISBN 0-7645-5290-2	$15.99
Turtles and Tortoises For Dummies®	ISBN 0-7645-5313-5	$19.99

From the Pet Experts at Howell Book House, Titles of Interest to Dog Lovers:

BOOKS ON SIBERIAN HUSKIES

The Siberian Husky: Able Athlete, Able Friend
By Michael Jennings
ISBN: 1-58245-046-3 • $24.95

TRAINING GUIDES

Dog Behavior: An Owner's Guide to a Happy,
Healthy Pet
By Ian Dunbar
ISBN 0-87605-236-7 • $12.95

Dog-Friendly Dog Training
By Andrea Arden
ISBN 1-58245-009-9 • $17.95

DogPerfect: The User-Friendly Guide to a
Well-Behaved Dog
By Sarah Hodgson
ISBN 0-87605-534-X • $12.95

Dog Training in 10 Minutes
By Carol Lea Benjamin
ISBN 0-87605-471-8 • $14.95

ACTIVITIES/GENERAL

All About Agility
By Jacqueline O'Neil
ISBN 1-58245-123-0 • $12.95

Canine Good Citizen: Every Dog Can Be One
By Jack and Wendy Volhard
ISBN 0-87605-452-1 • $12.95

The Complete Dog Book, 19th Edition, Revised
By The American Kennel Club
ISBN 0-87605-047-X • $32.95

The Dog Owner's Home Veterinary Handbook,
3rd Ed.
By James Giffin, M.D.
and Lisa Carlson, D.V.M.
ISBN 0-876605-201-4 • $27.95

Flyball Racing: The Dog Sport for Everyone
By Lonnie Olson
ISBN 0-87605-630-3 • $14.95

Holistic Guide for a Healthy Dog, 2nd Edition
By Wendy Volhard and Kerry Brown, D.V.M.
ISBN 1-58245-153-2 • $16.95

YOUR ONLINE RESOURCE

WWW.DUMMIES.COM

Discover Dummies Online!

The Dummies Web Site is your fun and friendly online resource for the latest information about *For Dummies* books and your favorite topics. The Web site is the place to communicate with us, exchange ideas with other *For Dummies* readers, chat with authors, and have fun!

Ten Fun and Useful Things You Can Do at www.dummies.com

1. Win free *For Dummies* books and more!
2. Register your book and be entered in a prize drawing.
3. Meet your favorite authors through the IDG Books Worldwide Author Chat Series.
4. Exchange helpful information with other *For Dummies* readers.
5. Discover other great *For Dummies* books you must have!
6. Purchase Dummieswear® exclusively from our Web site.
7. Buy *For Dummies* books online.
8. Talk to us. Make comments, ask questions, get answers!
9. Download free software.
10. Find additional useful resources from authors.

WWW.DUMMIES.COM

SURF THE NET

Link directly to these ten fun and useful things at **http://www.dummies.com/10useful**

For other technology titles from IDG Books Worldwide, go to
www.idgbooks.com

Not on the Web yet? It's easy to get started with *Dummies 101*®: *The Internet For Windows*® *98* or *The Internet For Dummies*® at local retailers everywhere.

IDG BOOKS WORLDWIDE

Find other *For Dummies* books on these topics:
Business • Career • Databases • Food & Beverage • Games • Gardening • Graphics • Hardware
Health & Fitness • Internet and the World Wide Web • Networking • Office Suites
Operating Systems • Personal Finance • Pets • Programming • Recreation • Sports
Spreadsheets • Teacher Resources • Test Prep • Word Processing

IDG BOOKS WORLDWIDE BOOK REGISTRATION

We want to hear from you!

Visit **http://my2cents.dummies.com** to register this book and tell us how you liked it!

- ✔ Get entered in our monthly prize giveaway.

- ✔ Give us feedback about this book — tell us what you like best, what you like least, or maybe what you'd like to ask the author and us to change!

- ✔ Let us know any other *For Dummies®* topics that interest you.

Your feedback helps us determine what books to publish, tells us what coverage to add as we revise our books, and lets us know whether we're meeting your needs as a *For Dummies* reader. You're our most valuable resource, and what you have to say is important to us!

Not on the Web yet? It's easy to get started with *Dummies 101®: The Internet For Windows® 98* or *The Internet For Dummies®* at local retailers everywhere.

Or let us know what you think by sending us a letter at the following address:

For Dummies Book Registration
Dummies Press
10475 Crosspoint Blvd.
Indianapolis, IN 46256

BESTSELLING
BOOK SERIES